Gender and Politics series

Series editors: **Johanna Kantola**, University of Helsinki, Finland and **Judith Squires**, University of Bristol, UK

This timely new series publishes leading monographs and edited collections from scholars working in the disciplinary areas of politics, international relations and public policy with specific reference to questions of gender. The series showcases cutting-edge research in Gender and Politics, publishing topical and innovative approaches to gender politics. It will include exciting work from new authors and well-known academics and will also publish high-impact writings by practitioners working in issues relating to gender and politics.

The series covers politics, international relations and public policy, including gendered engagement with mainstream political science issues, such as political systems and policymaking, representation and participation, citizenship and identity, equality, and women's movements; gender and international relations, including feminist approaches to international institutions, political economy and global politics; and interdisciplinary and emergent areas of study, such as masculinities studies, gender and multiculturalism, and intersectionality.

Potential contributors are encouraged to contact the series editors: Johanna Kantola (johanna.kantola@helsinki.fi) and Judith Squires (judith.squires@bristol.ac.uk)

Series Advisory Board:

Louise Chappell, University of New South Wales, Australia
Joni Lovenduksi, Birkbeck College, University of London, UK
Amy Mazur, Washington State University, USA
Jacqui True, Monash University, Australia
Mieke Verloo, Radboud University Nijmegen, the Netherlands
Laurel Weldon, Purdue University, USA

Titles include:

Gabriele Abels and Joyce Marie Mushaben (*editors*)
GENDERING THE EUROPEAN UNION
New Approaches to Old Democratic Deficits

Phillip Ayoub and David Paternotte
LGBT ACTIVISM AND THE MAKING OF EUROPE
A Rainbow Europe?

Elin Bjarnegård
GENDER, INFORMAL INSTITUTIONS AND POLITICAL RECRUITMENT
Explaining Male Dominance in Parliamentary Representation

Elgin Brunner
FOREIGN SECURITY POLICY, GENDER, AND US MILITARY IDENTITY

Andrea Chandler
DEMOCRACY, GENDER, AND SOCIAL POLICY IN RUSSIA
A Wayward Society

Sarah Childs and Paul Webb
SEX, GENDER AND THE CONSERVATIVE PARTY
From Iron Lady to Kitten Heels

Jonathan Dean
RETHINKING CONTEMPORARY FEMINIST POLITICS

Meryl Kenny
GENDER AND POLITICAL RECRUITMENT
Theorising Institutional change

Andrea Krizsan, Hege Skjeie and Judith Squires (*editors*)
INSTITUTIONALIZING INTERSECTIONALITY
The Changing Nature of European Equality Regimes

Mona Lena Krook and Fiona Mackay (*editors*)
GENDER, POLITICS AND INSTITUTIONS
Towards a Feminist Institutionalism

Emanuela Lombardo and Maxime Forest (*editors*)
THE EUROPEANIZATION OF GENDER EQUALITY POLICIES
A Discursive-Sociological Approach

Birte Siim and Monika Mokre (*editors*)
NEGOTIATING GENDER AND DIVERSITY IN AN EMERGENT EUROPEAN
PUBLIC SPHERE

Anna van der Vleuten, Anouka van Eerdewijk and Conny Roggeband (*editors*)
GENDER EQUALITY NORMS IN REGIONAL GOVERNANCE
Transnational Dynamics in Europe, South America and Southern Africa

Polly Wilding
NEGOTIATING BOUNDARIES
Gender, Violence and Transformation in Brazil

Gender and Politics Series
Series Standing Order ISBNs 978–0–230–23917–3 (hardback)
978–0–230–23918–0 (paperback)

You can receive future titles in this series as they are published by placing a standing order. Please contact your bookseller or, in case of difficulty, write to us at the address below with your name and address, the title of the series and one of the ISBNs quoted above.

Customer Services Department, Macmillan Distribution Ltd, Houndmills, Basingstoke, Hampshire RG21 6XS, England

LGBT Activism and the Making of Europe

A Rainbow Europe?

Edited by

Phillip M. Ayoub
Assistant Professor of Political Science, Department of Political Science, Drexel University, USA

and

David Paternotte
Assistant Professor of Sociology, Department of Sociology, Université libre de Bruxelles, Belgium

Selection and Editorial Matter © Phillip M. Ayoub and David Paternotte 2014
All Remaining Chapters © Their Respective Authors 2014
Softcover reprint of the hardcover 1st edition 2014 978-1-137-39175-9

All rights reserved. No reproduction, copy or transmission of this
publication may be made without written permission.

No portion of this publication may be reproduced, copied or transmitted
save with written permission or in accordance with the provisions of the
Copyright, Designs and Patents Act 1988, or under the terms of any licence
permitting limited copying issued by the Copyright Licensing Agency,
Saffron House, 6–10 Kirby Street, London EC1N 8TS.

Any person who does any unauthorized act in relation to this publication
may be liable to criminal prosecution and civil claims for damages.

The authors have asserted their rights to be identified as the authors of this work
in accordance with the Copyright, Designs and Patents Act 1988.

First published 2014 by
PALGRAVE MACMILLAN

Palgrave Macmillan in the UK is an imprint of Macmillan Publishers Limited,
registered in England, company number 785998, of Houndmills, Basingstoke,
Hampshire RG21 6XS.

Palgrave Macmillan in the US is a division of St Martin's Press LLC,
175 Fifth Avenue, New York, NY 10010.

Palgrave Macmillan is the global academic imprint of the above companies
and has companies and representatives throughout the world.

Palgrave® and Macmillan® are registered trademarks in the United States,
the United Kingdom, Europe and other countries.

ISBN 978-1-349-48309-9   ISBN 978-1-137-39176-6 (eBook)
DOI 10.1057/9781137391766

This book is printed on paper suitable for recycling and made from fully
managed and sustained forest sources. Logging, pulping and manufacturing
processes are expected to conform to the environmental regulations of the
country of origin.

A catalogue record for this book is available from the British Library.

Library of Congress Cataloging-in-Publication Data

    LGBT activism and the making of Europe : a rainbow Europe? / [edited by]
Phillip Ayoub, Assistant Professor of Political Science, Department of Political
Science, Drexel University, USA, David Paternotte, Assistant Professor of
Sociology, Department of Political Science, Université libre de Bruxelles.
    pages cm
    Includes bibliographical references and index.
    ISBN 978-1-349-48309-9
    1. Gay liberation movement – Europe. 2. Sexual minorities – Political
activity – Europe. 3. Homosexuality – Europe. I. Ayoub, Phillip, 1983–
II. Paternotte, David.

HQ76.8.E85L46 2014
306.76'6094—dc23   2014025706

Contents

Part III Becoming European

List of Illustrations

Figures

Tables

Acknowledgments

This project began with a conversation while standing in line at the dessert buffet of the 2010 ILGA-Europe annual conference in The Hague. We were both visiting the conference for our individual research projects on LGBT rights in Europe, and as so many activists have also come to experience before us, these conferences have a way of brokering fruitful collaborations. Out of that conversation grew a friendship that led to a series of conference panels and dinners with the collaborators who have contributed to this volume.

We first wrote a short "ideas paper" for the journal *Perspectives on Europe*, published by the Council for European Studies, which set the stage for a panel at the 2012 Crossing Boundaries workshop on sexuality at the American Sociological Association meeting in Denver, Colorado. The following year we met for a second panel at the European Conference on Gender and Politics, organized in Barcelona by the European Consortium for Political Research's standing group on Gender and Politics, to flush out new versions of the chapters that formed the ultimate lineup and outline for this book.

There are far too many people to thank who have inspired and encouraged us along the way, but a few must not go unmentioned. Our greatest intellectual debt goes to the authors who are part of this volume. They not only approached our theoretical framework with much creativity and inspiration, but they also patiently and thoughtfully addressed our many requests for revisions and improvements to make this book hold together so well. It was a delightful collaboration with many fruitful discussions on the idea of Europe and LGBT rights, from the numerous angles and often-differing perspectives of our various fields. All chapters went through multiple revisions, which also benefited from the generous comments we received from participants at the aforementioned conferences.

We warmly thank Nancy Naples and Alison Woodward, who kindly agreed to chair and discuss the conference panels. Along with Nancy, Jennifer Bickham Mendez offered constructive comments on an earlier chapter related to this project written for their edited volume, *Borders Politics: Social Movements, Collective Identities, and Globalization*. Mieke Verloo, associated with our collaboration with Palgrave Macmillan, enthusiastically offered her advice in looking for a publisher. Judith

Squires and Johanna Kantola, the editors of the Gender and Politics series, supported this project in its infancy, and Andrew Baird patiently advised us across the finish line with his editorial assistance. At the EUI, Donatella della Porta and Ludivine Broch graciously offered their encouragement and Alyson Price aided us with copy-editing two of the chapters. Finally, we wish to thank Gérard Edsme (gerard.edsme.over-blog.com), the artist who designed the poster for a 1992 ILGA conference held in Brussels, which provided us with a meaningful image for this book's cover.

Notes on Contributors

Phillip M. Ayoub is Assistant Professor of Political Science at Drexel University. His research bridges insights from international relations and comparative politics, engaging theories on transnational politics, gender and politics, norm diffusion, and the study of social movements. His academic publications are forthcoming or have appeared in the *European Journal of International Relations,* the *European Political Science Review,* the *Journal of Human Rights, Mobilization, Perspectives on Europe,* and *Trans-Atlantic Perspectives.* Currently, he is revising his book manuscript, *When States Come Out: Europe's Sexual Minorities and the Politics of Visibility.* Further details are available at www.phillipmayoub.com.

Carsten Balzer (aka Carla LaGata) holds a PhD and a master's in Cultural Anthropology from the Free University of Berlin. S_he wrote hir PhD thesis on gender-variant/trans communities in Brazil, Germany and the United States, and has taught cultural anthropology and Latin American Studies at the Free University of Berlin. Hir work has been published in numerous journals and edited volumes in the US, Brazil, Germany, Spain, Turkey and the UK. Currently, she works as TGEU's Senior Researcher and as lead researcher of the "Transrespect versus Transphobia Worldwide" research project, which she initiated in 2009.

Jon Binnie is Reader in Human Geography in the Division of Geography and Environmental Management in the School of Science and Environment at Manchester Metropolitan University in the UK. He is an urban, social, cultural and political geographer whose research interests concern the urban and transnational geographies of sexualities. His work focuses on the geographies of LGBTQ political claims and their connection to issues of social and economic justice. He is the author of *The Globalization of Sexuality* (2004) and co-author of *The Sexual Citizen: Queer Politics and Beyond* (2000), *Pleasure Zones: Bodies, Cities, Spaces* (2001) and *Sexual Politics Beyond Borders: Transnational Activist Networks and LGBTQ Politics in Europe* (forthcoming). He is also co-editor of *Cosmopolitan Urbanism* (2006).

Gianmaria Colpani is a PhD student at the University of Verona, Italy, and Utrecht University, the Netherlands. He obtained his bachelor's in Philosophy at the University of Turin, Italy, and master's in Gender and

Ethnicity at Utrecht University. His fields of research are postcolonial and queer theories. His main interests concern the intersections of sexuality, race and citizenship in contemporary Europe. More specifically, he works on the current negotiations of the idea of Europe taking place at the (Southern) borders of the continent in relation to sexual politics.

Konstantinos Eleftheriadis is a researcher in the Department of Social and Political Sciences at European University Institute (EUI) in Florence, Italy. His work is supervised by Professors Donatella della Porta (EUI) and Didier Eribon (University of Amiens). He has been a guest lecturer in European Studies in the Department of Politics at Maastricht University. His other works are published or forthcoming in international journals (*L'Homme et la société, Lamda Nordica, ACME*). At the EUI, he is a member of the Gender, Race, and Sexuality Working Group (GRASE) and the Consortium on Social Movement Studies (COSMOS).

Adriano José Habed obtained his bachelor's in Philosophy at the University of Turin, Italy, and master's in Philosophical Anthropology at Radboud University Nijmegen, the Netherlands. He is primarily interested in the relationship between psychoanalysis, feminism and postcolonial theory. His current research explores the possibilities offered by a psychoanalytical approach, while looking at the configurations of the nation-state in contemporary Europe and the inclusions/exclusions those configurations produce along sexual and racial lines.

Jan Simon Hutta is Lecturer at the University of Bayreuth, working in the Cultural Geography Research Group. He has conducted research in Brazil and Germany on sexual and transgender politics, urban governmentality, and relations of affect, subjectivity and space. He is currently working on a monograph on affective enactments of citizenship in Brazil. Between 2010 and 2012, he worked for the international research project *Transrespect versus Transphobia Worldwide* of the NGO Transgender Europe. He is founding editor of the German-language open access journal on critical urban research, *s u b \ u r b a n.Zeitschrift für kritische Stadtforschung.*

Christian Klesse is Senior Lecturer in the Department of Sociology at Manchester Metropolitan University, UK. His research interests include sexual politics, social movements, non-monogamies and body modification. His most recent publications include work on transnational LGBTQ activism (e.g. "The Politics of Age and Intergenerationality in Transnational Lesbian, Gay, Bisexual, Transgender and Queer Activist Networks", *Sociology* 47(3): 580–595 and "Solidarities and Tensions: Feminism and Transnational LGBTQ Rights Politics in Poland" *European*

Journal of Women's Studies 19(4): 444–459 (both with Jon Binnie)). A co-edited special issue on "Gender, Sexuality and Political Economy" is forthcoming in the *International Journal of Politics, Culture and Society*.

Kelly Kollman is Senior Lecturer in Politics at the University of Glasgow where she has taught since 2005. Her research focuses on the influence that transnational networks and soft law norms have on policy outcomes in the established democracies of Western Europe and North America. She is the author of *The Same-sex Unions Revolution in Western Democracies: International Norms and Domestic Policy Change* (2013), which examines the role that international social learning has played in the widespread adoption of same-sex union policies since 1989. Kelly also has published numerous peer-reviewed articles in journals such as *World Politics, International Studies Quarterly, Social Politics* and *International Studies Review*.

Kevin Moss is the Jean Thomson Fulton Professor of Modern Languages and Literature at Middlebury College. He holds a joint position in the Russian Department and the program in Gender, Sexuality, and Feminist Studies. He has written on Russian and East European film, on Olga Freidenberg, and on Mikhail Bulgakov's *Master and Margarita*. Since 1990 he has studied gay and lesbian culture in Russia and Eastern Europe, and in 1997 he edited the first anthology of gay writing from Russia, *Out of the Blue: Russia's Hidden Gay Literature*. Recently he has published on films with gay protagonists from ex-Yugoslavia.

David Paternotte is Assistant Professor of Sociology at the Université libre de Bruxelles, and the coconvener of the Atelier Genre(s) and Sexualité(s). His work has been published in several academic journals including the *Canadian Journal of Political Science, Social Politics, Perspectives on Europe,* and *Politique et sociétés*. He is the author of *Revendiquer le "mariage gay"* (2011) and the coeditor of *Au-delà et en deçà de l'État* (2010), *The Lesbian and Gay Movement and the State* (2011) and *Imaginer la Citoyenneté* (2013). He is currently preparing the *Ashgate Research Companion to Lesbian and Gay Activism* with Manon Tremblay.

Leila J. Rupp is Professor of Feminist Studies and Associate Dean of the Division of Social Sciences at the University of California, Santa Barbara. Her most recent books are *Sapphistries: A Global History of Love between Women* (2009), *Drag Queens at the 801 Cabaret* (2003), with Verta Taylor, *A Desired Past: A Short History of Same-Sex Love in America* (1999) and *Worlds of Women: The Making of an International Women's Movement* (1997). Her current research is on new queer intimacies and sexual identities among women college students.

Anna van der Vleuten is Associate Professor of European Integration at the Institute for Management Research, Radboud University Nijmegen, the Netherlands, and Associate Fellow of the Potsdam Centrum für Politik und Management, Germany. Her research focuses on comparative regionalism, gender equality policies, LGBTI rights and the political role of supranational courts. She is the author of *The Price of Gender Equality: Member States and Governance in the European Union* (2007) and the co-editor of *Gender Equality Norms in Regional Governance: Transnational Dynamics in Europe, South America and Southern Africa* (2014). She has published in *Comparative European Politics, Journal of Common Market Studies* and *West-European Politics*, among others.

Cai Wilkinson is Lecturer in International Relations at Deakin University, Australia. Her research interests include Critical Security Studies, fieldwork-based securitization studies, and genders and sexualities in International Relations. Her geographic focus is on the former Soviet Union, and she is currently working on projects about LGBT rights and human rights norms in Kyrgyzstan and Russia. She has published articles in *Security Dialogue, Central Asian Survey* and *Europe-Asia Studies* and recently co-edited a special issue of the *Journal of Human Rights* on resistance to LGBT rights. Further details can be found at http://www.deakin. edu.au/arts-ed/shss/staff-directory2.php?username=caiw.

List of Abbreviations

AIDS	Acquired Immunodeficiency Syndrome
CDA	Christian Democratic Appeal [Christen Democratisch Appèl]
CEE	Central and Eastern Europe
CHE	Campaign for Homosexual Equality
CLAGS	Center for Gay and Lesbian Studies at the Graduate Center, City University New York
COC	Cultuur- en Ontspanningscentrum [Center for Culture and Leisure]
CoE	Council of Europe
CSCE	Council for Security and Cooperation in Europe
CEEWG	Central and Eastern European Working Group
ECHR	European Convention on Human Rights
ECJ	European Court of Justice
ECtHR	European Court of Human Rights
EEAS	European External Action Service
EEC	European Economic Community
EU	European Union
HDZ	Hrvatska demokratska zajednica [Croatian Democratic Union]
HIV	Human Immunodeficiency Virus
ICD	International Classification of Diseases
ICSE	International Committee for Sexual Equality
IGA	International Gay Association
IHWO	International Homophile World Organization
ILGA	International Lesbian, Gay, Bisexual, Trans and Intersex Association
LGBT	lesbian, gay, bisexual, trans
LGBTIQ	lesbian, gay, bisexual, trans, intersex and queer
LGBTQ	LGBT and queer
LGBTQA	lesbian, gay, bisexual, trans, queer and allies
LORI	Lesbian Organization Rijeka
LSVD	Lesben- und Schwulenverband in Deutschland [Lesbian and Gay Federation in Germany]
MEP	Member of the European Parliament
MP	Member of Parliament
NATO	North Atlantic Treaty Organization

NGO	non-governmental organization
OAS	Organization of American States
OHCHR	Office of the United Nations High Commissioner for Human Rights
OSCE	Organization for Security and Cooperation in Europe
PvdA	Partij van de Arbeid [Labour Party (Netherlands)]
RP	Registered Partnership
SC	steering committee
ŠKUC LL	Student Cultural-Art Center – Lesbian Lilith
SPD	Sozialdemokratische Partei Deutschlands [Social Democratic Party]
SSU	same-sex union
SVD	Schwulen Verband Deutschland [Gay Federation in Germany]
TGEU	Transgender Europe
TIG	Transgender Initiative Group
TvT	Transrespect versus Transphobia Worldwide
UK	United Kingdom
UN	United Nations
UNESCO	United Nations Educational, Scientific and Cultural Organization
US	United States
WHO	World Health Organization
WWII	Second World War

1
Introduction

Phillip M. Ayoub and David Paternotte

> Of course, this means the expansion of the sphere of the so-called gay culture, which has now turned into the official policy of the EU.
>
> *Alexei Pushkov, Chairman of the Russian Parliament's*
> *Foreign Affairs Committee, December 2013*[1]

Alexei Pushkov's remarks were made in the winter of 2013, in the context of escalating tensions between Russia and the European Union (EU), when thousands of Ukrainians lined the streets of Kiev to protest against their government's intensifying relationship with Russia, which threatened Ukraine's deeper relations with the EU. As both Ukrainian society and state authorities weighed the tradeoffs of orienting themselves to "the East" or to "the West," Pushkov's warning to Ukrainians reflects the prominent role that lesbian, gay, bisexual and trans (LGBT) rights have come to play in geopolitical struggles across the region. His cautionary remarks harp on the idea that an alignment with Europe not only would result in forgoing decisive Russian economic support for Ukraine, but would also affect Ukrainian identity: national values and morals were at stake in the face of a rainbow-tinged European threat.

Connecting LGBT rights to the idea of Europe has become a recurring theme in international politics; such rights become a contentious element of belonging to Europe and a rhetorical vehicle used by those offering an alternative cultural paradigm to the EU. The global relevance of this association by those who oppose LGBT rights, and the various reactions provoked by its policies, only strengthens the bonds that tie this association and reinforce its perceived reality. Indeed, current debates in Russia and Ukraine, as well as worldwide reactions to the anti-gay propaganda law of Vladimir Putin's Russia, demonstrate that

1

LGBT rights increasingly belong at the core of European values in the imagination of many actors.

Putin's position is, for example, partly inspired by a nationalistic project that aims to return Russia to the world stage. As he outlined in his 2013 State of the Federation speech, Russia is prepared to be the leader of a new political and cultural model that offers an alternative to both the EU and "the West."[2] One of the model's defining features is the promotion of traditional values and the defense of "authentic" national cultures, through the rejection of democratic standards imposed from abroad:

> We know that there are more and more people in the world who support our position on defending traditional values that have made up the spiritual and moral foundation of civilization in every nation for thousands of years: the values of traditional families, real human life, including religious life, not just material existence but also spirituality, the values of humanism and global diversity. (Putin 2013)

As Putin outlines his alternative project, LGBT rights become a powerful symbol of the Europe he seeks to oppose.

At the same time, the reactions of institutional and civil society to Putin's policies, both in Russia and in Ukraine, have contributed to a further isolation of Russia from Europe, and subsequently also to an increasingly strengthened value association between Europe and LGBT rights. This was clearly illustrated by the European Parliament's resolution on the joint EU–Russia Summit, adopted in February 2013, which voiced serious concerns over the status of LGBT rights in Russia.[3] Such reactions often confirm the imagined "Europeanness" of LGBT rights, which have been used in geopolitical contests at the margins of the continent.

These comments made by Pushkov and Putin refer to a "special relationship" between LGBT rights and a certain idea of Europe, in which "Europe" as a concept extends beyond strict institutional categories. Indeed, such an association between Europe and LGBT rights is not new in the scholarly literature (e.g. Kollman 2009; Stychin 2001; Kuhar 2011; Paternotte 2011; Paternotte and Kollman 2013; Ayoub 2013b; Wilson 2013), tracking occurrences of this association in countries as geographically and politically varied as Romania (Carstocea 2006), Poland (Chetaille 2011), and Hungary (Rédai 2012). Furthermore, this phenomenon is not restricted to Europe. As exemplified by recent scholarship on debates surrounding LGBT rights in Africa (e.g. Currier 2012), the relationship is also used as a rhetorical tool in other parts of the world, where Europe is often conflated with the United States (US) or "the West." With actors at both ends of the ideological and political spectrum increasingly repeating this mantra, the idea that Europe and LGBT rights are linked has taken on a role of its own, with important implications for the political sociology of the region.

This book is an attempt to understand better the emergence and the historical development of the "special relationship" that unites issues of sexuality and Europe. By looking at its various dimensions, we hope to critically examine how this relationship has been constructed and how it has become, especially in rhetoric and the imagination, a reality. We aim to explain the origins and the development of this relationship, addressing the paradox that, while being marginal within EU policies, LGBT rights have become a powerful symbol of Europe, featuring centrally in debates ranging from foreign relations to economic trade. We thus hope to shed light on the reasons why contemporary discourses, such as those surrounding the crisis in Ukraine, can refer to LGBT rights as a meaningful symbol with which to oppose the idea of Europe.

In doing so, this book explores the alleged uniqueness of the European experience, and investigates its ties to a relatively long and established history of LGBT and queer (LGBTQ) movements in the region. As we demonstrate, the earliest notions of the idea that Europe has a special relationship to LGBT rights first appeared in activists' discourses, long before it was adopted and championed by European and national institutions. We argue that LGBT movements were inspired by specific ideas about Europe – democratic values and a responsibility toward human rights – and sought to realize them on the ground through activism, often crossing borders to foster a wider movement. While LGBT issues are linked to Europe's normative structures from above, by using "Europe" as an argument for demanding LGBT recognition from their states and societies, the activists on the ground subsequently, and indirectly, recreate the idea that Europe is united around the LGBT issue. In turn, the link between being European and accepting LGBT people becomes established, and the understanding of LGBT rights as a European value is further cemented, paradoxically also allowing others to use it as a strategic argument against the idea of a united Europe itself.

In the Introduction to this volume, we first discuss the idea of Europe and highlight how it relates to LGBT rights. Second, we give a brief overview of the history of LGBT movements in the region. Third, we introduce the historical role of European institutions in adopting policies on the issue. Fourth, we explore the problematic construction of European "others" – those at the disciplined margins – who are left out of the process as Europe starts to wave its rainbow colors. Finally, we close the chapter by outlining the content of this book according to the three thematic areas we address: (1) *meaning-making*, how LGBT activists define "Europe" in the LGBT movement; (2) *practice*, how LGBTQ movements deploy the "idea of Europe" on the ground; and (3) *identity*, the ways in which this activism strengthens the European identification of regional LGBT movements.

LGBT rights and the making of Europe

The European project

Questions of what it means to be European have perplexed observers – whether scholars or not – for centuries. The broad sweep of a concept that has no clear boundaries in terms of geography and culture has left open the questions of "what is Europe" and "who is European." While these questions have gone unanswered, there has always been a plurality of interpretations of the ideas that bind Europe together. From a revolution in France, to the formation of the European Coal and Steel Community, to discussions of "East" and "West," "Europe" as a multi-faceted idea is always present. It helps shape the political understandings of a plethora of issues and the values that become associated with being "European." In this volume, we do not attempt to answer these questions, but we do note an association with the "idea of Europe" and LGBT rights in contemporary politics, an association we wish to chart and explain.

While the "idea of Europe" has been deployed "by anarchists, nationalists, and romantic poets as a motto for everything from socialism to pan-Slavism" (Case 2009: 116), Deutsch's (1969) theories considered the project of European identity building to be pronounced among groups that had sustained positive interactions and solidarity that functioned across borders. If a European identity were to emerge, then such groups would need "to come to a positive sense of solidarity based on the idea that they were all members of an overarching group" (Fligstein 2009: 136). This is true of European LGBT politics, where the idea of Europe re-forms and re-presents itself in multiple dimensions, and in the reverse process in which LGBT politics have become associated with European politics. When the organizers of LGBT marches wave EU flags and use

European slogans to define their claims (Ayoub 2013a: 299–300), they establish this relationship, giving "Europe" symbolic meaning, beyond the common institutional understanding of what Europe is.

Checkel and Katzenstein carefully distinguish between Europe as a *political project*, driven by purposeful political elites and their choices, and as a *socio-political process*, driven by "social mediation and exchange" (2009: 3). This latter process is a far more fluid conception of Europe, beyond institutions and elites in Brussels and Strasbourg (Hooghe 2005), which relies on deliberation, social networking, and political bargaining at subnational, national, supranational, and transnational levels. Thinking of both top-down and bottom-up approaches to Europe more reasonably captures the processes of European identity- and value-making that shape the spaces in which minority groups can pursue their specific European identity projects. These spaces are important for minority claims making, because supranational institutions do indeed allow for similar issues to become politicized in multiple countries in the European public sphere (Risse 2010). While the idea of Europe is appropriated in different ways across national contexts, 50 years of European integration have led both to an emotional attachment to Europe, as well as to a secondary identity, which Europeans attach to the broader European idea (ibid.).[4]

Beyond the institutions and economics commonly theorized in contemporary studies on politics and markets, Europe holds normative content – and some argue "soft power" – in terms of the ideational and symbolic impact it exercises over its own international identity (Manners 2002: 238). According to this understanding, the idea of Europe has an "ability to shape conceptions of 'normal' in international relations" through a set of values (239), covering a broad range of core issues from environmentalism to inalienable human rights. Scholars have criticized a Habermassian understanding of core European values (Castiglione 2009: 45), encompassing a rich sense of Europeanness and overestimated value convergence, but most agree that Europe has been made and remade over the centuries in the image of different values. While there is no mass consensus around a European value-based identity (Checkel and Katzenstein 2009), we do recognize such a link between LGBT rights and European values in international politics.

The idea of Europe and LGBT rights

In his abdication speech in July 2013, Albert II, former king of Belgium, discussed the unique contributions that the European project offers. Drawing on the memory of the Second World War (WWII), he emphasized that Europe's importance and relevance depended on it protecting its fundamental values:

> In our world, the European project is more necessary than ever. In numerous domains, challenges can only be met at European level and it is at this level that some values can be best defended. I think of the wealth of diversity, democratic pluralism, tolerance, solidarity and the protection of those that are weak.[5]

The same values are put forward when talking about the European contribution to LGBT rights. For instance, in March 2013, the Belgian, French, and Italian ministers of equal opportunities, Joëlle Milquet, Najat Vallaud-Belkacem and Elsa Fornero respectively, published a statement in leading European newspapers to announce a European LGBT strategy. The ministers related Europe to specific values and claimed that these values provide the moral grounding for EU action on LGBT rights:

> EU member states put the respect of fundamental rights at the top of their values. We want to foster these values, the defense of freedoms and the rejection of discrimination. We want to see these values in the external policy of the European Union ... We want to adopt new European legislation against homophobia ... We want to live in a European space in which individual freedoms are effectively protected, regardless of one's sexual orientation or gender identity ... We, Europeans, must be united ... These are the conditions to develop the project of a full recognition of the right of all citizens in the world to have their identity respected.[6] (Vallaud-Belkacem, Milquet, Fornero 2013)

As the ministers' statement and the former Belgian king's speech exemplify, Europe's normative resonance is rooted in a set of values that LGBT activism has latched onto. This is not to say that there is consensus around these values (Hooghe and Marks 2009). There are multiple "ideas of Europe" in Europe, but one of these core ideas in contemporary European politics is that the European project is associated with the same values that are at the foundation of LGBT rights. Both those who attack and those who support LGBT rights as a value acknowledge that the association exists, which is exemplified in the politics we chart in this book.

Social movements contribute to these processes of establishing new "ideas of Europe" from below, which scholars have demonstrated in the rising use of European targets, frames, and transnational networks that have responded to Europe's multilevel governance structures (Della Porta and Caiani 2007; Imig and Tarrow 2001). An idea of Europe is shaped differently, according to the local and national goals of movement actors, blurring boundaries of a national and supranational conception of European identity (Case 2009: 111, 131). For LGBT movements, this sense of "Europe" – appearing both as a set of values and normative commitments, and as a strategic means by which to gain rights in various domestic realms – is present.

The movement is embedded in multiple institutions and connected through a series of transnational ties across the region, as a geographical, political and (sometimes) cultural entity. However one defines "Europe," LGBT activists have contributed to transcending its traditional borders by symbolically associating the continent with LGBT rights. Europe is a normative framework that constitutes LGBT actors' interests and strategies, and in turn these actors (re)create European structures and institutions by linking them to LGBT rights. Thus, activists are not simply extending a liberal European notion of rights to an unrecognized group; they are helping define what the definition of "rights" encompasses. For these activists, LGBT people have always belonged to the project of a united Europe.

We thus look at domestic and regional forms of activism and the imagined community that has come to span the European continent. While campaigns still often target states, both the grievance and vision driving this activism contribute to contemporary ideas of Europe. Adopting a constructivist approach to European identity, which recognizes that agents and structures interact and are mutually constituted (Katzenstein 1996), we explore how transnational LGBT activists represent Europe and what kind of Europe they build through their strategies and actions. In our story, LGBT civil society actors are nested in institutional and normative European structures. This environment, within which these actors function, is not only material but also imagined and socially constructed (Anderson 1983). By discussing the contours of Europe that social actors imagine (Anderson 1983; Diez-Medrano 2009; Favell and Guiraudon 2011; Kauppi 2013), we show that these ideas – and more importantly the various ways in which they are embodied – further contribute to the making of Europe, an insight that is crucial for the study of European integration. The idea of a rainbow Europe is shaped by, and shapes, LGBT activism.

LGBTQ activism in Europe

LGBTQ activism in Europe provides a particularly useful vantage point from which to study the contribution of contemporary social movements to the construction of Europe. In particular, it highlights the multitude of levels on which contemporary politics take place (local, domestic and supranational), and the dense networks that are formed across state borders.

Europe is indeed the birthplace of homosexual activism. According to Foucault's (1978) analysis, doctors and psychiatrists invented the concept of "the homosexual" in the 1800s, as they transformed morally condemned sexual practices and applied them to a derided social personage and a scientifically established species. It was also during this period that homosexual identity was politicized, leading to early forms of activism in the late 1800s (Hekma forthcoming). The word "homosexuell" itself (it was first written in German) was coined in 1864, when the Hungarian journalist Karoly Maria Kertbeny used it in a letter to Karl Heinrich Ulrichs (Takács 2004). Ulrichs, a homosexual German lawyer, is often considered to be the first homosexual activist; he mobilized against the extension of Prussian Paragraph 175 – which criminalized same-sex intercourse – to Catholic southern Germany, where same-sex intercourse had been decriminalized prior to the German unification of 1871. Just over three decades later, in 1897, Magnus Hirschfeld established the first homosexual organization, the *Wissenschaftlich-humanitäre Komitee* (Scientific Humanitarian Committee) in Berlin, which campaigned for the decriminalization of same-sex relations in Germany. Interestingly, such groups born before WWII mostly emerged in countries in which the idea of a pathology of homosexuality was reinforced by legal discrimination, including Germany, the Netherlands (after 1911), and the United Kingdom.

The persecution of European homosexuals under the Third Reich put an end to these early organizational experiments, leaving neutral Switzerland the only place where organized forms of homosexual activism survived the War (Delessert 2012). A new wave of activism – called homophile activism – began after 1945, and groups were established in the Netherlands, Scandinavia, the United Kingdom, Germany, Belgium and France (Chapter 2, this volume). The sexual liberation of the 1960s and 1970s brought with it new forms of activism, as gay liberation groups contested the aims of earlier homophile movements. This was the time of the first gay pride marches and the invention of the rainbow flag, when gay movements regarded gay identity as revolutionary and encouraged coming out of the private sphere for both personal and political fulfillment (Weeks forthcoming). With gay liberation, new groups emerged in most Western European countries, and national movements were formed in Italy and Francoist Spain. Lesbians, who had often been absent from earlier forms of organizing, mobilized in increasing numbers, together with men, as well as within women's groups (Podmore and Tremblay forthcoming). In the 1980s, gay and lesbian organizations also emerged in Central and Eastern Europe (CEE) (Greif 2005), but the movement there developed far more extensively after the fall of the Berlin Wall (Chetaille 2011). Finally, trans rights groups began to appear in the 1990s in most European countries, blossoming at the turn of the century.

For many of these groups, Europe has been a propitious region for transnational activism. Notwithstanding linguistic diversity, short geographic distances and efficient transport networks have given an incentive to activist collaborations across borders. LGBTQ movements were no exception, and the first displays of transnational exchange can be traced back to the early twentieth century. The roots of transnational activism are tied to the aforementioned Magnus Hirschfeld, who later established the *Weltliga für Sexualreform* (World League for Sexual Reform) in 1928 (Kollman and Waites 2009: 3). Further attempts to build structured networks of LGBT groups across Europe occurred in the 1950s, when the Dutch COC (Cultuur- en Ontspanningscentrum) set up the International Committee for Sexual Equality (ICSE). This transnational organization met annually and included most of the homophile groups of the time (Chapter 2 this volume; Jackson 2009). In the 1970s, radical movements, such as the Italian FUORI! and the French FHAR, also attempted to establish transnational structures (Hellinck 2004: 22; Prearo 2012; Guaiana 2010).

The first enduring transnational LGBT organization, however, only appeared in 1978, when the International Lesbian, Gay, Bisexual, Trans and Intersex Association (ILGA), called International Gay Association until 1986, was created in Coventry, United Kingdom (Paternotte 2012). This organization later played a central part in the globalization of LGBT activism (Binnie 2004; Paternotte and Seckinelgin forthcoming). Despite its global vocation, ILGA has been predominantly European. As suggested in Figure 1.1, the organization has always considered Europe a high priority, which mirrors its almost exclusively European membership for the first decade after its inception. From the start, ILGA was also inspired by a specific idea of Europe and, crucially, of its usefulness for the progress of LGBT rights (Ayoub and Paternotte 2014). Founding activists believed that European values held meaning for LGBT people and thought that European institutions (the EU and CoE), along with the United Nations, could be used to gain rights by increasing pressure on reluctant states.[7] This European orientation was further confirmed in 1996, when a specific European umbrella, ILGA-Europe, was established as the regional branch of ILGA-World (Beger 2004; Paternotte 2013). ILGA-Europe was the result of a regionalization process related to the globalization of LGBT activism, and a will to improve network structures in order to take advantage of emerging European opportunities. This trend toward the increasing Europeanization of LGBT activism has been confirmed in recent years, as exemplified by a diversification of European umbrella organizations, which include groups such as European Pride Organizers Association, the Network European LGBT Families Associations, the European Forum of LGBT Christian Groups or RainbowRose, the European network of socialist parties' LGBT caucuses.

ILGA and ILGA-Europe have been instrumental in organizing LGBT groups on a European scale and in articulating a stronger voice across the continent. However, as the authors of this volume demonstrate, they were neither the first nor the only groups to be motivated by an idea of Europe. Despite the fact that they do not always agree about what they mean by Europe and its usefulness for LGBT rights, numerous movements across the region were, and continue to be, inspired by "Europe," an inspiration they have tried to realize through activism. Their activism, which so often posits Europe as an imagined community, has also displaced regional borders, expanding Europe and reinforcing its definition as a set of values and a socio-political community linked to universal human rights, as illustrated by our opening remarks on Ukraine.

In brief, the history of European LGBT activism offers a rare opportunity to study the self-reflexivity of a social movement through time and to understand how it is shaped by a complex relationship between normative commitment, institutional support, and strategic aims. Especially for research on social movements, which was traditionally confined within the borders of nation states, LGBTQ activism in Europe provides a rich source of information from which we can broaden our understanding. Beyond a study of transnational and regional networks, this volume looks at the process of building a movement both from above and from below. It examines the various ways in which LGBTQ activists engage with regional politics and does not confine the study to the hallways of Brussels.

Figure 1.1 Poster for ILGA's 14th European Conference, held in Brussels in 1992
Source: © Gérard Edsme, gerard.edsme.over-blog.com.

Europe and LGBT rights

The idea that Europe enshrines fundamental values crucial to LGBT rights has not only been imagined by LGBT activists across the continent, but has also been increasingly endorsed by national and European institutions. In a global comparison, Europe is the region where LGBT rights are the most "advanced." LGBT people enjoy comparatively high levels of tolerance and a vibrant LGBTQ community life characterizes many parts of the continent. On a legal basis, same-sex intercourse has been decriminalized throughout the region, most European countries offer generous antidiscrimination provisions, and many recognize, in some form, same-sex partnerships. Nine of the fourteen countries that recognize same-sex marriage at the federal level are European (Paternotte and Kollman 2013). Over the years, Europe, in its various forms, has emerged as a distinct space for sexual citizenship.

While legal changes have happened at a national level, European institutions have increasingly endorsed LGBT claims, confirming the latter are related to Europe's normative commitments. Without attempting to give an exhaustive summary of achievements at the European level (Beger 2004; Bonini-Baraldi and Paradis 2009), it is important to bear in mind that the Council of Europe was the first international institution to consider LGBT issues, partly because of its human rights mandate (unlike the former European Economic Communities).[8] In 1981, in the Dudgeon case, the European Court of Human Rights (ECtHR) obliged the United Kingdom, one of its member states, to decriminalize same-sex intercourse in Northern Ireland. This first ECtHR ruling in favor of LGBT rights was later confirmed by court cases both within (Ireland, Cyprus) and beyond European borders. The decision opened a key venue for the contestation of LGBT rights in Europe, and the ECtHR has been instrumental on issues such as freedom of assembly, expression and association (in particular, pride marches), age of consent, partnership benefits and family life, access to the military or gender reassignment. In the same year, 1981, the parliamentary assembly of the Council of Europe adopted the report and recommendation on the discrimination against homosexuals, calling for the decriminalization of homosexuality, an equal age of consent, and for equality in employment and in custody rights. The political institutions of the Council (the parliamentary assembly and the Committee of Ministers) have regularly endorsed the defense of LGBT rights in the region, and the Human Rights Commissioner Thomas Hammarberg more recently (in 2009 and 2011) cemented his broader support for the cause by conducting an extensive report on the discrimination of LGBT people in Europe.

The European Community, which became the European Union in 1992, took on a social mandate later, despite the fact that ILGA's foresight had made this organization a target of their activism since 1979. Beginning with the adoption of the Squarcialupi Report in 1984, the Parliament became the movement's core ally within the European institutions, adopting numerous resolutions, including the crucial 1994 Roth Report. In 1997, the Parliament's Intergroup on LGBT Rights was established, rapidly becoming the driving force for LGBT rights inside the institution.

Other EU institutions have increasingly supported LGBT activists. The first contacts with the European Commission date back to 1990, when ILGA representatives met Vaso Papandreou, the European Commissioner for Social Affairs, who agreed to fund a study on "the rights of lesbians and gay men in the legal order of the European Commission" (Waaldijk and Clapham 1993). At the end of 1995, ILGA activists had their first meetings with representatives of the president of the Commission.

However, official collaboration only flourished after the adoption of the Treaty of Amsterdam by the Council in 1997; it officially included protection against discrimination on the grounds of sexual orientation as part of the European project. As a result, a directive forbidding discrimination based on sexual orientation in the workplace was adopted in 2000 (Waaldijk and Bonini-Baraldi 2006; Mos 2014). During the same period, ILGA-Europe was recognized as the official partner of the European Commission on LGBT issues (which includes its significant core funding) and started to play a central role in EU policymaking (Swiebel 2009). The European Court of Justice, which played a minor role until recently (Chapter 6 this volume), as well as the Fundamental Rights Agency (established in 2007) created new venues for LGBT activists.

These institutional achievements are largely the result of activism, both at the national and transnational levels, but they have also had an impact on social movements. At a transnational level, increasing recognition and support from European institutions has allowed ILGA-Europe to become a professional non-governmental organization (NGO) and an influential lobby for the defense of LGBT rights (Paternotte 2013). A similar process occurred with domestic organizations in several Western European countries. However, the impact is not comparable with what happened in CEE, particularly during the enlargement period. Indeed, within and alongside Europe's material resources, LGBT activists were often able to use the "idea of Europe" to frame the LGBT issue as a European norm. As European institutions adopted a normative structure that advanced the visibility of the LGBT issues – by introducing the issue into the legal framework of member states (Kollman 2007, 2009; Ayoub 2013b, 2015(forthcoming)) – activists involved in the CEE developed innovative and appealing frames to deliver a coherent message on LGBT recognition. European frames offered an opportunity to link the issue to modernity and the responsibilities associated with being European (Kuhar 2011; Holzhacker 2012). For EU and Council of Europe members, these frames legitimized the LGBT issue through the constitutive effect of shared membership in a European community. European frames have also been used as a rationale for the mobilization of other Europeans in various domestic realms that are not their own. Foreign visitors are common participants at LGBT marches across the region, and they justify their involvement in such domestic affairs by highlighting that *Europeans* were protesting for shared *democratic values* (Ayoub 2013a). In doing so, they link their activism to shared values, solidarity and responsibilities as Europeans, especially in the face of state repression and societal resistance that so often cite national values as threatened by movements which challenge social mores (Ayoub 2014, 2010; Langlois and Wilkinson 2014). The idea of LGBT rights as European, and thus indirectly also Polish, Latvian, Hungarian, Slovenian, Romanian, and so on – because they are members of this shared community – is evident (Ayoub 2013a).

Constructing European others

When discussing the contours of what it means to be European, Risse (2004: 257) reminds us that "social identities not only describe the content and the substance of what it means to be a member of a group. They also describe the boundaries of the group, that is, who is 'in' and who is 'out'." In other words, this Europeanization process of internal identity construction will also fortify certain existing boundaries, as well as erect new ones at the periphery (Della Porta and Caiani 2007: 10).

Therefore, we are careful to not only enumerate the successes of social movements, but also think critically about the potential dynamics of exclusion in the process within which LGBT rights became conceptually linked to "Europe." The hegemony of a new European LGBT discourse has overshadowed some claims and modes of organizing, created new hierarchies among activists, targeted both states and peoples as non-European, and paradoxically reinforced a distinction between the "modern West" and the "homophobic East" – all side effects that still characterize European LGBT politics. These issues raise crucial questions related to the way LGBT movements contribute to defining who and what is considered European, where Europe is, and who has been left out in this process at three analytical levels: claims and modes of organizing, peoples and states.

First, successes of movement seem to be closely linked to a reorganization of both claims and forms of activism. Scholars have debated issues of normalization, both in LGBT people's everyday lives and in activism (e.g. Warner 1999; Duggan 2003; Hekma and Duyvendak 2011), a debate that we do not intend to reopen here. Yet, it is apparent that, as LGBT rights made progress in the region, some issues and some forms of organizing were deliberately left out, suggesting that an idea of rainbow Europe excludes certain forms of activism. This is true of a set of issues – ones that had inspired LGBT activism in the past and continue to do so in other parts of the world – that are increasingly more absent. HIV/AIDS and sexual and reproductive rights are rarely engaged, despite the central role they play at the UN level. The formulation of claims related to sexual expression has also changed. Sexual orientation has been turned into an abstract, legal and sometimes naturalized category (Waites 2005), as both movement claims and institutional discourses become focused on the three "Rs" articulated by the 2007 European Year for Equal opportunities: Recognition, Respect and Rights.

This process is closely intertwined with specific forms of activism, through which movements – often transformed into NGOs – have become more institutionalized and more professionalized (Lang 2013; Paternotte 2013). This was a striking feature of the expansion of LGBT activism to CEE, and of the process of selective endorsement of local groups by Western NGOs. As we have highlighted elsewhere (Ayoub and Paternotte 2014), beyond empowering LGBT groups and endowing them with financial resources and new mobilization frames, this process often creates hierarchies among LGBT organizations, namely between those who can and are willing to work transnationally and those whose work is locally focused. The transnationalization of the issue often privileges young activists who have spent time abroad and have language skills, particularly English, as well as those whose claims and repertoires resonate more harmoniously with the frames of Western European LGBT organizations and potential funders.

Second, through this process, a certain idea of who qualifies as European has been constructed. Connecting to the values defended by the former Belgian king and the three ministers discussed earlier, the notion of Europeanness intersects with an idea of civilization, positing some individuals and some peoples as less civilized than others. This not only creates cultural borders at the edges of what is considered

Europe but also reinforces internal boundaries (Jenson 2007). Within Europe, "homophobes" qualify not only on an individual basis, but also because of group membership. Critical scholars have indeed recently emphasized that members of some social groups are labeled "barbarians" because of their very belonging to this group, constructing them as "absolute others" and eliminating any opportunities for intersectional identities. This is especially the case for Muslim minorities in Western Europe (Mepschen, Duyvendak and Tonkens 2010; El Tayeb 2011; Fassin 2010; Petzen 2012), and can also apply to other peoples or nations, illustrated, for example, by debates surrounding homophobia among Poles around the time of EU accession (Chetaille 2013), or among the French following the mobilization of an opposition movement to same-sex marriage in 2012 and 2013.

As Carl Stychin (1998) has argued, "national" identities are often also constructed against an "other," and, over time, we have seen the emergence of LGBT-Europe's "sexual others." Internally, Muslim and migrant communities have been at the fore of an "othering" process that has portrayed them as more homophobic, and thus less European. Externally, LGBT rights are used as part of European identity construction against countries at the questioned borders, such as Russia or Turkey. Scholars have also emphasized the distinct European path on LGBT rights in relation to the United States, noting that differences in welfare systems explain varied LGBT policies across the Atlantic (Wilson 2013), or, as illustrated by recurrent debates in France, that some countries have attempted to build a way toward LGBT emancipation that does not mimic American examples (Fassin 2009).

Therefore, while activists have seen the idea of Europe – and the deconstruction of traditional borders that is associated with that imagination – as having great potential for LGBT rights, activists and scholars alike must pay close attention to the cases where borders still exist and where new borders arise. Although European identity construction is often presented as a way to transcend violent European state nationalisms, activists and institutions have sometimes tried to foster a common sense of belonging, using strategies akin to those used by nation states in the past. In an attempt to aid the building of a common European identity, they have promoted the values of the LGBT activists that they would endorse, connecting to recent debates on "homonationalism" (Puar 2007; Jaunait, Le Renard and Marteu 2013). However, the study of sexual nationalism should not be restricted to nation states. Chapters 4 (Colpani and Habed) and 10 (Moss) in this book demonstrate this by exploring the emergence of a European form of sexual nationalism.

While reaching somewhat divergent conclusions, they analyze the various ways in which European sexual nationalism is deployed on the ground, establishing new forms of exclusion and privilege.

This brings us to our third and final point, which is that the "idea of rainbow Europe" has contributed to defining Europe's geographic positioning. Indeed, the various processes of exclusion at work here not only target peoples on the basis of their alleged hostility, but also locate Europe in a specific space. It generates problematic questions: Are Ukraine or Turkey really in Europe and on what basis? Furthermore, are some parts of Europe more European than others? Indeed, as several scholars working on LGBT politics in the CEE have emphasized, EU enlargement and the expansion of LGBT rights further East has paradoxically reenacted the binary juxtaposition of "East" versus "West" (Chetaille 2013; Kulpa and Mizielińska 2011). Indeed, the values promoted by the EU and the wealthier LGBT organizations in Europe expand an understanding of LGBT rights that was consolidated in the Western experience, and LGBT activists, including in CEE countries, often present their claims in terms of "catching up" with this ideal. This is problematic, in the sense that a European LGBT frame inadvertently "others" some states as a deviation from the European norm. Additionally, discourses tend to aggregate many diverse CEE or Southern European countries into one, as if the situations of LGBT peoples were uniform across regions.[9] This relates to old debates on the European core and its peripheries, which are engaged with in several chapters in this volume.

Meanings, practices and European identities

The volume addresses the themes of the idea of Europe and LGBT rights by focusing on the status of Europe in various forms of LGBTQ mobilization across time and space, covering the critical moments and types of movements in various geographic subregions. The chapters investigate European movements – homophile, lesbian and gay, queer, and trans – dating back to the 1950s, and in their different forms of radical and institutional activism. Geographically, we explore how movements employ the "idea of rainbow Europe" in Western, Southern, Central and Eastern Europe, as well as in the European neighborhood of Central Asia. Reflecting the kaleidoscopic nature of Europe itself and the diversity of its use in LGBT activism, we deliberately leave the definition of Europe open. This allows for a more complete inventory of what Europe means to LGBT activists and how they use it.

The book is divided into three parts, each tackling different themes. Part I tries to understand questions of meaning-making by exploring how LGBT activists have defined Europe in different forms of mobilization. Part II examines how actors both use and practice the "idea of Europe" in their work. Finally, Part III examines the various ways in which this activism reinforces the European identity of LGBT movements in the region. An intriguing aspect of European politics, explored in all the chapters, is that most forms of contemporary LGBTQ activism have deployed some notion of Europe, in some cases long before European integration had a social mandate.

Part I: Meanings of Europe

An underlying theme of all the chapters in this first part on meaning-making is that LGBT movements developed visionary understandings of the concept of "Europe" long before regional integration had social dimensions, and outside of the traditional geographic boundaries of the continent. These chapters illustrate the strong normative value of "Europe" for LGBT groups in the region, across time and place, which the authors execute in three different ways.

Leila Rupp's chapter (Chapter 2) looks at the movement over time, tracing back the history of transnational activism to the postwar period's homophile movement. By going back to the roots, she illustrates the formative role of "Europe" in shaping what we have come to understand by "Western" LGBT activism. Both transnational activism and sexual identity are entangled – often problematically – with a specific time and place that is anchored in "Europe."

Cai Wilkinson (Chapter 3) shifts our focus to space by exploring the relationship between "Europe" and LGBT activism in Central Asia. Using the case of Kyrgyzstan, she provides an intriguing insight into the broad spatial reach of "Europe" – in this context, understood mainly as the EU – and how LGBT rights take on a meaning associated with European values. Though limited in many respects, Europe's influence extends beyond its political role as a promoter of democracy to a wide range of informal roles – from bilateral relationships with NGO donors to the dissemination of know-how – that brand "European values" as a reference point for socio-political reform outside of its borders.

Finally, Gianmaria Colpani and Adriano José Habed (Chapter 4) investigate the meaning Europe takes for those at the European core, in relation to the consequences such a meaning holds for those at the Southern European periphery. Using the case of Italy, which is paradoxically situated both within and without the "European map of liberal sexual politics," they grapple with the political workings of European homonationalism, understood as distinct from national variations of sexual nationalism, and what it suggests for how we think of who fits within the core of contemporary Europe, and who is pushed to its disciplined margins. In all of these cases, the idea of Europe takes on a specific meaning in the vision and imagination of LGBT activism.

Part II: Practicing Europe in LGBTQ Activism

The second part of the book examines how actors both use and practice the "idea of Europe" in their activism. By practice, we mean that social movement actors do not only imagine Europe, but that they put the concept in motion on the ground. This motion occurs in multiple forms in activism; just as the opening anecdote on the use of LGBT rights in political debates related to Russia and the Ukraine demonstrates, "Europe" and "LGBT rights" have become connected in contemporary political discourses as two halves of the same coin.

In Kelly Kollman's chapter (Chapter 5), activists use Europe as a discursive instrument to push for rights in distinct national arenas. By comparing the debate surrounding same-sex unions in Germany, the Netherlands and the United Kingdom, she shows how "Europe" is discursively practiced in relation to the different national settings. Rather than build a transnational community, these activists bring important concepts of "Europe" from outside into the domestic contexts.

Next, Anna van der Vleuten (Chapter 6) investigates the use of "Europe" at the critical point where legal activism and European supranational courts meet. She highlights how the idea of Europe enables and constrains both activism and court rulings, and how it is constructed and implemented by the courts. She compares the European Court of Human Rights and the European Court of Justice, highlighting the different uses and successes of such references. She also shows, in both cases, that the centrality of the idea that Europe relies on specific values, which must be enforced by the courts.

In other movements, as Konstantinos Eleftheriadis explains in his chapter (Chapter 7) on queer festivals, actors practice Europe without discussing the content of the idea of Europe. They embody Europe and produce it through their activities – by traveling to meet across borders, overcoming linguistic barriers, and building a transnational community of European activists – rather than imagining it or developing a discourse about Europe. In sum, the authors of this part explore the dynamic of practicing Europe on the ground and from above, from inside and outside institutional settings and in both reformist and radical forms of organizing.

Part III: Becoming European (identities)

The third part examines the various ways in which this activism reinforces the European identity of LGBT movements in the region. It looks at the consequences of such activism in terms of constructing new rights and identities that come to be associated with the meanings and practices of Europe. All three of these chapters in this section explore how the "idea of Europe," defined by a set of values and as an imagined alternative to the nation state, shapes the identity outcomes associated with movement.

Carsten Balzer and Jan Simon Hutta (Chapter 8) look at such consequences in the professionalization of a grassroots movement, which navigates both its grassroots and NGO identities in an increasingly pan-European understanding. By examining the formation of a network of trans activists in Europe, the authors explore how European identity becomes increasingly pronounced and produces a new institutionalized dimension of the movement that propels the movement from the national to the transnational sphere. At the same time, activists have negotiated this shift by maintaining a specific European space outside of LGBT organizational frameworks to better defend their grassroots claims.

Jon Binnie and Christian Klesse (Chapter 9) then shift the focus to Poland to look at the complexities and potential contradictions of European transnational grassroots solidarities. The challenges associated with negotiating a common identification across national (and other) boundaries illuminate the complex processes behind activism's role in constructing European identity and reinforcing the European project. While there is an extensive literature on transnational actors and social movements, the deployment of transnational networks, solidarities and identities by LGBT activism is widely understudied and all three chapters further our understanding in this regard.

In another vein, Kevin Moss (Chapter 10) demonstrates how activists in Croatia established a direct link between LGBT rights and "Europe" as they introduced the issue to the public leading up to EU accession in 2013. The many references to the EU reinforce the European dimension of LGBT rights in "becoming European." He emphasizes the role played by transnational LGBT activists in imagining Europe as a political alternative to confines of national borders and subsequently how it cements LGBT rights as constitutive of European values.

Taken together, the volume addresses issues of meaning, practice and identity to highlight an understudied movement and its ties to European integration. Far from being limited to LGBT activism and to Europe, however, we hope that the insights drawn from the analyses that follow will offer us much that we can extrapolate to further our understanding of transnational social movements and regional integration in contemporary world politics.

Notes

Some passages of the text in this chapter have appeared in our earlier publications (Ayoub and Paternotte 2012, 2014).

1. Cited in "Pro-EU protesters at Kiev's Maidan cannot decide Ukrainian destiny for entire nation – Pushkov," *The Voice of Russia*, 10 December 2013.
2. Take, for example, Ugandan President Museveni's response to US President Obama's condemnation of the Ugandan Anti-homosexuality Bill in which he claims he would prefer to work with Russia. http://www.monitor.co.ug/News/ National/I-ll-work-with-Russians–Museveni-tells-Obama/-/688334/2217532/-/ w6gkn6/-/index.html (accessed 21 February 2014).
3. http://www.europarl.europa.eu/sides/getDoc.do?type=MOTION&reference= P7-RC-2014–0150&language=EN (accessed 21 February 2014).
4. The diversity of views on what Europe represents makes it a challenge to see strong shifts in individual identities, but it is no longer disputed that an increasing attachment to Europe exists (Risse, 2004).
5. Translated from the French.
6. Ibid.
7. This echoes the literature on "boomerang politics" in international relations. According to Keck and Sikkink (1998: 12): "Where channels between domestic groups and their governments are blocked, the boomerang pattern of influence characteristic of transnational networks may occur: domestic NGOs bypass their state and directly search out international allies to try to bring pressure on their states from outside."
8. ILGA activists also approached the Council for Security and Cooperation in Europe (CSCE), later the OSCE, because of its clear human rights mandate. Its accessibility to activists made it a strategically fruitful venue to lobby and it would play a role in combating homophobic violence.
9. Substantial variation in legislation and attitudes toward LGBT people exists across CEE countries (Ayoub 2013b).

References

Albert II. 2013. "Discours d'abdication." *La Libre Belgique*, 3 July, http:// www.lalibre.be/actu/belgique/le-discours-d-abdication-du-roi-albert-ii-51- d46aa135708c786994fe3d (accessed 3 March 2014).
Anderson, Benedict. 1983. *Imagined Communities: Reflections on the Origin and Speed of Nationalism*. London: Verso Books.

Ayoub, Phillip M. 2010. "Repressing Protest: Threat and Weakness in the European Context, 1975–1989." *Mobilization* 15(4): 465–488.

———. 2013a. "Cooperative Transnationalism in Contemporary Europe: Europeanization and Political Opportunities for LGBT Mobilization in the European Union." *European Political Science Review* 5(2): 279–310.

———. 2013b. "When States 'Come Out': The Politics of Visibility and the Diffusion of Sexual Minority Rights in Europe." PhD Diss. Cornell University. http://hdl.handle.net/1813/34332

———. 2014. "With Arms Wide Shut: Threat Perception, Norm Reception and Mobilized Resistance to LGBT Rights." *Journal of Human Rights* 13(3): 337–362.

———. 2015, forthcoming. "Contested Norms in New-Adopter States: International Determinants of LGBT Rights Legislation." *European Journal of International Relations*. Epub ahead of print. DOI: 10.1177/1354066114543335.

Ayoub, Phillip M. and David Paternotte. 2012. "Building Europe: The International Lesbian and Gay Association (ILGA) and LGBT Activism in Central and Eastern Europe." *Perspectives on Europe* 42(1): 50–56.

———. 2014. "Challenging Borders, Imagining Europe: Transnational LGBT Activism in a New Europe." In *Border Politics, Social Movements and Globalization*, eds. Jennifer Bickham-Mendez and Nancy Naples. New York: New York University Press.

Beger, Nico J. 2004. *Tensions in the Struggle for Sexual Minority Rights in Europe: Que(e)rying Political Practices*. New York: Manchester University Press.

Binnie, Jon. 2004. *The Globalization of Sexuality*. London: Sage.

Bonini-Baraldi, Matteo and Évelyne Paradis. 2009. "European Union." In *The Greenwood Encyclopedia of LGBT Issues Worldwide*, ed. Chuck Stewart. Westport: Greenwood, 123–145.

Carstocea, Sinziana. 2006. "Between Acceptance and Rejection – Decriminalizing Homosexuality in Romania." In *The Gay's and Lesbian's Rights in an Enlarged European Union*, eds. Anne Weyembergh and Sinziana Carstocea. Brussels: Éditions de l'Université de Bruxelles, 207–222.

Case, Holly. 2009. "Being European: East and West." In *European Identity*, eds. Jeffrey T. Checkel and Peter Katzenstein. New York: Cambridge University Press, 111–131.

Castiglione, Dario. 2009. "Being European: East and West." In *European Identity*, eds. Jeffrey T. Checkel and Peter Katzenstein. New York: Cambridge University Press, 29–51.

Checkel, Jeffrey T. and Peter J. Katzenstein, eds. 2009. *European Identity*. New York: Cambridge University Press.

Chetaille, Agnès. 2011. "Poland: Sovereignty and Sexuality in Post-Socialist Times." In *The Lesbian and Gay Movement and the State*, eds. Manon Tremblay, David Paternotte, and Carol Johnson. Farnham: Ashgate, 119–134.

———. 2013. "L'Union européenne, le nationalisme polonais et la sexualisation de la 'division Est/Ouest'." *Raisons Politiques* 49(1): 119–140.

Currier, Ashley. 2012. *Out in Africa: LGBT Organizing in Namibia and South Africa*. Minneapolis: University of Minnesota Press.

Delessert, Thierry. 2012. "Le « milieu » homosexuel suisse durant la Seconde Guerre mondiale." *Cahiers d'histoire: Revue d'histoire Critique* 119: 65–78

Della Porta, Donatella, and Manuela Caiani. 2007. "Europeanization from Below? Social Movements and Europe." *Mobilization* 12(1): 1–20.

Deutsch, Karl W. 1969. *Nationalism and Its Alternatives*. New York: Knopf.

Diez-Medrano, Juan. 2009. "The Public Sphere and the European Union's Political Identity." In *European Identity*, eds. Jeffrey T. Checkel and Peter J. Katzenstein. Cambridge: Cambridge University Press, 81–108.

Duggan, Lisa. 2003. *The Twilight of Equality? Neoliberalism, Cultural Politics, and the Attack on Democracy*. Boston: Beacon Press.

El Tayeb, Fatima. 2011. *European Others: Queering Ethnicity in Post-Racial Europe*. Minneapolis: University of Minnesota Press.

Fassin, Eric. 2009. *Le Sexe Politique: Genre et Sexualité au Miroir Transatlantique*. Paris: Editions de l'EHESS.

———. 2010. "National Identities and Transnational Intimacies: Sexual Democracy and the Politics of Immigration in Europe." *Public Culture* 22(3): 507–529.

Favell, Adrian, and Virginie Guiraudon. 2011. *Sociology of the European Union*. Basingstoke: Palgrave Macmillan.

Fligstein, Neil. 2009. "Who Are the Europeans and How Does It Matter for Politics?" In *European Identity*, eds. Jeffrey T. Checkel and Peter Katzenstein. New York: Cambridge University Press, 132–167.

Foucault, Michel. 1978. *The History of Sexuality: Volume One*. London: Allen Lane.

Greif, Tatjana. 2005. "The Social Status of Lesbian Women in Slovenia in the 1990s." In *Sexuality and Gender in Postcommunist Eastern Europe and Russia*. New York: Haworth Press, 149–169.

Guaiana, Yuri. 2010. Clasped Hands in Giarre: The Italian Media Between Homophobic and Homophile Declarations. Paper presented at the *Queer Crossing Conference*, Università degli Studi di Palermo.

Hekma, Gert. forthcoming. "Sodomy, Effeminacy, Identity: Mobilizations for Same-Sexual Loves and Practices before the Second World War." In *Ashgate Research Companion to Lesbian and Gay Activism*, eds. David Paternotte and Manon Tremblay. Farnham: Ashgate.

Hekma, Gert and Jan Willem Duyvendak. 2011. "The Netherlands: Depoliticization of Homosexuality and Homosexualization of Politics." In *The Lesbian and Gay Movement and the State: Comparative Insights into a Transformed Relationship*, eds. Manon Tremblay, David Paternotte and Carol Johnson. Farnham: Ashgate, 103–117.

Hellinck, Bart. 2004. "Le MHAR en Avait Marre." *Het Ondraaglijk Besef* 10: 19–23.

Holzhacker, Ron. 2012. "National and Transnational Strategies of LGBT Civil Society Organizations in Different Political Environments: Modes of Interaction in Western and Eastern Europe for Equality." *Comparative European Politics* 10(1): 23–47.

Hooghe, Liesbet. 2005. "Several Roads Lead to International Norms, but Few via International Socialization: A Case Study of the European Commission." *International Organization* 59(4): 861–898.

Hooghe, Liesbet, and Gary Marks. 2009. "A Postfunctionalist Theory of European Integration: From Permissive Consensus to Constraining Dissensus." *British Journal of Political Science* 39(1): 1–23.

Imig, Doug, and Sidney Tarrow, eds. 2001. *Contentious Europeans*. Lanham: Rowman & Littlefield.

Jackson, Julian. 2009. *Living in Arcadia. Homosexuality, Politics and Morality in France from the Liberation to AIDS*. Chicago: Chicago University Press.

Jaunait, Alexandra, Amélie Le Renard and Elisabeth Marteu, eds. 2013. "Nationalismes Sexuels? Reconfigurations Contemporaines des Sexualités et des Nationalismes." *Raisons Politiques* 49(1): 5–23.

Jenson, Jane. 2007. "Des frontières aux lisières de la citoyenneté." In *L'état des citoyennetés en Europe et dans les Amérique*, eds. Jane Jenson, Bérengère Marques-Pereira et Éric Remacle. Montreal: Editions de l'Université de Montréal, 23–30.

Katzenstein, Peter J. 1996. "Introduction: Alternative Perspectives on National Security." In *The Culture of National Security: Norms and Identity in World Politics*, ed. Peter Katzenstein. New York: Columbia University Press, 1–32.

Kauppi, Niilo 2013. *A Political Sociology of Transnational Europe*. Colchester: ECPR Press.

Keck, Margaret E., and Kathryn Sikkink. 1998. *Activists beyond Borders: Advocacy Networks in International Politics*. Ithaca: Cornell University Press.

Kollman, Kelly. 2007. "Same-Sex Unions: The Globalization of an Idea." *International Studies Quarterly* 51(2): 329–357.

———. 2009. "European Institutions, Transnational Networks and National Same-Sex Unions Policy: When Soft Law Hits Harder." *Contemporary Politics* 15(1): 37–53.

Kollman, Kelly, and Matthew Waites. 2009. "The Global Politics of Lesbian, Gay, Bisexual and Trans Human Rights: An Introduction." *Contemporary Politics* 15(1): 1–37.

Kuhar, Roman. 2011. "Use of the Europeanization Frame in Same Sex Partnership Issues across Europe." In *The Europeanization of Gender Equality Policies: A Discursive Sociological Approach*, eds. Emanuela Lombardo and Maxime Forest. Basingstoke: Palgrave Macmillan, 168–191.

Kulpa, Robert, and Joanna Mizielińska. 2011. *De-Centring Western Sexualities: Central and Eastern European Perspectives*. Farnham: Ashgate.

Lang, Sabine. 2013. *NGOs, Civil Society, and the Public Sphere*. Cambridge: Cambridge University Press.

Langlois, Anthony, and Cai Wilkinson. 2014. "Not Such an International Human Rights Norm? Local Resistance to LGBT Rights." *Journal of Human Rights* 13(3).

Manners, Ian. 2002. "Normative Power Europe: A Contradiction in Terms?" *Journal of Common Market Studies* 40(2): 235–258.

Mepschen, Paul, Jan Willem Duyvendak and Evelien Tonkens. 2010. "Sexual Politics, Orientalism and Multicultural Citizenship in the Netherlands." *Sociology* 44(5): 962–979.

Mos, Martijn. 2014. "Of Gay Rights and Christmas Ornaments: The Political History of Sexual Orientation Non-discrimination in the Treaty of Amsterdam." *Journal of Common Market Studies* 52(3): 632–649. .

Paternotte, David. 2011. *Revendiquer le "Mariage Gay": Belgique, France, Espagne*. Brussels: Éditions de l'Université de Bruxelles.

———. 2012. "Back into the Future: ILGA-Europe before 1996." *Destination Equality: Magazine of ILGA-Europe* 11(1): 5–8.

———. 2013. Article 13 and the NGOisation of ILGA-Europe. Paper presented at the *European Sociological Association Conference*, Turin, Italy.

Paternotte, David, and Hakan Seckinelgin. forthcoming. "'Lesbian and Gay Rights are Human Rights': Multiple Globalizations and Lesbian and Gay Activism." In *Ashgate Research Companion to Lesbian and Gay Activism*, eds. David Paternotte and Manon Tremblay. Farnham: Ashgate.

Paternotte, David, and Kelly Kollman. 2013. "Regulating Intimate Relationships in the European Polity: Same-Sex Unions and Policy Convergence." *Social Politics* 20(4): 510–533.

Petzen, Jennifer. 2012. "Contesting Europe: A Call for an Anti-Modern Sexual Politics." *European Journal of Women's Studies* 19(1): 97–114.

Podmore, Julie and Manon Tremblay. forthcoming. "Lesbians, Second-Wave Feminism and Gay Liberation." In *Ashgate Research Companion to Lesbian and Gay Activism*, eds. David Paternotte and Manon Tremblay. Farnham: Ashgate.

Prearo, Massimo. 2012. "La trajectoire révolutionnaire du militantisme homosexuel italien dans les années 1970." *Cahiers d'histoire: Revue d'histoire Critique* 119: 79–97.

Puar, Jasbir. 2007. *Terrorist Assemblages: Homonationalism in Queer Times.* Durham: Duke University Press.

Putin, Vladimir. 2013. "Presidential Address to the Federal Assembly." http://eng. kremlin.ru/news/6402 (accessed 21 February 2013).

Rédai, Dorottya. 2012. "Un/Queering the Nation? Gender, Sexuality, Nationality and Homophobia in the Media Discourse on the Violence against the 2008 Gay Pride in Budapest." *Sextures* 2(2): 47–64.

Risse, Thomas. 2004. "European Institutions and Identity Change: What Have We Learned?" In *Transnational Identities: Becoming European in the EU*, eds. Richard Herrmann, Thomas Risse, and Marilynn B. Brewer. Lanham: Rowman & Littlefield, 247–273.

———. 2010. *A Community of Europeans? Transnational Identities and Public Spheres.* Ithaca: Cornell University Press.

Stychin, Carl. 1998. *A Nation by Rights: National Cultures, Sexual Identity Politics, and the Discourse of Rights.* Philadelphia: Temple University Press.

———. 2001. "Sexual Citizenship in the European Union." *Citizenship Studies* 5(3): 285–301.

Swiebel, Joke. 2009. "Lesbian, Gay, Bisexual and Trans Human Rights: The Search for an International Strategy." *Contemporary Politics* 15(1): 19–35.

Takács, Judit. 2004. "The Double Life of Kertbeny." In *Present and Past of Radical Sexual Politics*, ed. Gert Hekma. Amsterdam: Universiteit van Amsterdam, 26–40.

Vallaud-Belkacem, Najat, Joëlle Milquet and Elsa Fornero. 2013. "Contre les discriminations homophobes." *Le Soir*, 25 March.

Waaldijk, Kees and Andrew Clapham (eds.). 1993. *Homosexuality: A European Community Issue.* Dordrecht: Martinus Nijhoff.

Waaldijk, Kees, and Matteo Bonini-Baraldi. 2006. *Sexual Orientation Discrimination in the European Union: National Laws and the Employment Equality Directive.* The Hague: T.M.C. Asser Press.

Waites, Matthew. 2005. "The Fixity of Sexual Identities in the Public Sphere: Biomedical Knowledge, Liberalism and the Heterosexual/Homosexual Binary in Late Modernity." *Sexualities* 8(5): 539–569.

Warner, Michael. 1999. *The Trouble with Normal: Sex, Politics, and the Ethics of Queer Life.* Cambridge: Harvard University Press.

Weeks, Jeffrey. forthcoming. "Gay Liberation and Its Legacies." In *Ashgate Research Companion to Lesbian and Gay Activism*, eds. David Paternotte and Manon Tremblay. Farnham: Ashgate.

Wilson, Angelia R. 2013. *Why Europe Is Lesbian and Gay Friendly (and Why America Never Will Be).* Albany: SUNY Press.

Part I
Meanings of Europe

2
The European Origins of Transnational Organizing: The International Committee for Sexual Equality

Leila J. Rupp

In 1951, at a congress convened in Amsterdam, representatives from Denmark, Germany, Great Britain, Italy, the Netherlands, and Switzerland formed a new organization, the International Committee for Sexual Equality (ICSE), which linked existing homophile groups across national borders within Europe. The new body sent a telegram to the United Nations demanding equal rights for homosexual minorities based on the principles of the UN, the "findings of modern psychological, biological and medical research," and "mankind's greater awareness of social injustice," a clear reference to the Nazi Holocaust.[1] Picking up the work of transnational organizing around sexuality first launched by Magnus Hirschfeld's World League for Sexual Reform in the 1920s, the ICSE carried the torch into the 1960s, when other groups kept the movement alive and then connected in 1978 with the founding of the International Gay (now International Lesbian, Gay, Bisexual, Trans and Intersex) Association (ILGA), the contemporary face of the global lesbian, gay, bisexual, and transgender movement. Although the International Committee for Sexual Equality fostered a theoretically universal homophile identity, in fact the membership remained predominantly male and European. That Europe played such a formative role in the creation of transnational activism around same-sex sexuality helps us to understand the contemporary dominance of Europe in the ILGA. In addition, the history of the ICSE shows how homophile activists in the immediate postwar period were already fashioning an idea of Europe that moved beyond the divided continent of wartime.

In the context of the contemporary recognition that a Western conception of what it means to be gay or lesbian is widely understood globally but in uneasy interaction with more local and national conceptions (Manalansan 1995; Povinelli and Chauncey 1999; Boellstorff 2005; Blackwood and Wieringa 2007), I point here to three fundamental ways in which transnational homophile activism in the 1950s was fundamentally European (Herzog 2009): (1) the centrality of European groups and the shift of the center of transnational activism around same-sex sexuality from Germany in the early 1900s to the Netherlands in the 1950s; (2) the fostering of a homosexual cosmopolitanism and sexually expressive culture; and (3) a sense of superiority of European modes of organizing. This history suggests the way that sexual identity and activism around sexuality is entangled with place, the way Europe shaped transnational activism in the 1950s and beyond, and the way that transnational organizing around sexual identity remains problematic, given the variety of ways in which people across the globe conceptualize what it means to have and act on same-sex desires.

The European composition of the ICSE

The ICSE traced its origins to Magnus Hirschfeld's Scientific Humanitarian Committee, founded in 1897. A Dutch version of the organization, the *Nederlandsch Wetenschappelijk Humanitair Kommittee*, emerged in 1911 in response to a penal code reform that criminalized same-sex sexual relations with men under the age of 21 (16 was the age of consent for heterosexual relations). From 1911 to 1940, the Dutch group, with connections to its German parent until the Nazis came to power, published brochures, built a library, and distributed yearly reports to doctors, jurists, and students. The German occupation of the Netherlands spelled the end of the committee's existence, but as the war came to an end, former members organized a new group, at first called the Shakespeare Club and later the *Cultuur- en Ontspannings Centrum* [Cultural and Recreational Center, known as the COC]. The COC, which had attracted some 3000 members by 1958, claimed status as the largest homosexual organization in the world in that decade.[2]

The decision to found a transnational organization emerged from the leadership of the COC (Warmerdam and Koenders 1987). The insistence on transcending national borders certainly had a great deal to do with the traditional internationalism of the Dutch and their admirable ability to speak multiple languages. As the vice-president of the ICSE put it in a 1957 interview, "it is commensurate with Dutch mentality to open the doors to all countries of the world."[3] But the commitment to transnational action also represented a nod to the Hirschfeld legacy. In 1928, Hirschfeld had founded the World League for Sexual Reform, denoting the International Conference for Sexual Reform on the Basis of Sexual Science, held in 1921 in Berlin, as the first congress of the transnational group. The new body, which held congresses in Copenhagen (1928), London (1929), Vienna (1930), and Brno (1932), brought together activists and scholars on birth control, marriage reform, eugenics, free love, sex education, and homosexuality. Congresses planned for Moscow, Paris, and the United States never took place, and the organization, which functioned only as the sponsor of the congresses, folded in 1935 (Dose 2003). It perhaps seemed natural to convene a transnational gathering following in this tradition, although the ICSE differentiated itself from the broader focus of Hirschfeld's group on sexuality since it "has its foundations in the circles of homosexuality and has been established by internal co-operation in their own ranks."[4]

In 1951, the president and vice-president of the COC, Nico Engelschman and Henri Methorst, took the initiative of convening the first International Congress by contacting existing European homophile groups.[5] A document in the files of the ICSE described the organization as continuing the work of the Scientific Humanitarian Committee "in a form suitable for our period and generation and adapted to a new mentality which is growing in man today," calling it "for us a UNO, a highest authority."[6] Engelschman, in his speech at the first congress, emphasized the importance of transnational contact. "We want to know and understand the conditions under which people [in other countries] work and love. We want, through international cooperation, to help like-minded friends in more difficult situations." He mentioned wanting to let UNESCO "hear our voices" and learn about their needs, and he ended with the hope that the congress would strengthen organizations throughout Europe and lead to a "deepening of friendship and love from person to person and peoples to peoples."[7] Italian count Bernardino del Boca de Villaregia, picking up on this theme, sent a message to the second congress expressing that "all our energy should be directed to the internationalisation of our work."[8]

At the first gathering of the nascent group, Engelschman sought to explain the reasons why "after the termination of five calamitous years of war" they wanted to form a union with "so special a character." Rather than seeing wartime hostility as an obstacle to transnational organizing, Engelschman insisted that the war "had awakened the burning desire in all peoples to bridge the borders of their own lands [and] to work together."[9] This is especially remarkable given the emphasis on establishing connections across the war's battle lines. Engelschman credited "a concentrated friendship" between the Netherlands and Germany for the launch of international activities, noting as well "a growing friendship between Germany and France."[10] As one German man writing to the organization put it, since the two countries were wartime enemies, "we should not recognize this hate, we should forget what was, we should be friends across the German border."[11] The German groups emphasized the fact that the Nazis sent homosexuals to concentration camps as a way of distancing themselves from wartime enmity and fostering solidarity based on sexual identity. In the aftermath of the war the center of homosexual activism, on both the national and transnational level, moved from Germany to the Netherlands, but retained a sense of European unity.

The national homophile organizations that joined the ICSE had different origins and took various forms. The *Forbundet af 1948* [League of 1948], the name calling attention to the importance of the 1948 UN Declaration of Human Rights, originally spanned Denmark, Norway, and Sweden. Later Denmark and Norway separated but both kept the name *Forbundet*, and Sweden formed its own organization, the *Riksförbundet för Sexuellt Liksaberättigande* [Swedish Union for Sexual Equality]. Two French groups belonged to the ICSE: *Le Verseau* [Aquarius], a small group, and, until it broke with the ICSE over control of the 1955 Paris congress, André Baudry's *Arcadie* [Arcadia], the subject of a magisterial study by Julian Jackson (2009). In Belgium, the *Centre de culture et de loisirs* [Cultural and Recreational Center] modeled itself, as the name suggests, on the Dutch COC. The group around *Der Kreis* [*The Circle*], the long-lived Swiss-based journal of male homosexual culture founded in 1932, played an active role (Kennedy 1999). The ICSE sought to unite a host of local German groups in Hamburg, Bremen, Frankfurt, and Berlin, although the leadership periodically threw up their collective hands about the unwillingness of local groups to merge into a national organization and the personal conflicts and scandals that spilled over into the international work.[12] The Homosexual Law Reform Society in Great Britain made contact with the International Committee but did not officially join, not wanting to be identified as an organization of homosexuals, although British individuals regularly attended the congresses.[13] The ICSE reached across the Atlantic to the United States, in 1953, welcoming to its ranks the two major homophile groups, the Mattachine Society, launched in Los Angeles in 1950, and ONE, Incorporated, the sponsor of an independent gay and lesbian magazine, also based in Los

Angeles. The ICSE also made contact with the Daughters of Bilitis, the US lesbian organization founded in 1955 in San Francisco.

Because the ICSE relied on affiliation from existing groups, it remained Eurocentric. Like other transnational organizations, its official languages were European (English, German, French), its conferences and meetings took place in Europe (Amsterdam, Frankfurt, Copenhagen, Paris, Brussels, Bremen), and its officers were European. This is not to suggest that national differences among European countries never reared their heads. One challenge the group faced was the use of languages, in publications and correspondence as well as at the congresses. A newsletter appeared right after the founding congress, at first mainly in English with some German and French articles and a few in other languages. It came out somewhat irregularly in changing formats over the years, always challenged by a shortage of both staff and funds. The publication had a dual purpose: not only to present "our point-of-view to a wider public," including "men of science," but also to keep contact with members in the months between congresses.[14] At a business meeting in 1954, members spoke passionately about the need to reach members who could not read English: "If the ICSE wants to accomplish something in the future, as we hope it will, it must be represented by a three- if not four-language paper with a high international level."[15] The International Committee launched a German periodical, *ICSE KURIER*, and then a German press service, *ICSE-PRESS*, in the mid-1950s in response to "the special position of Germany (i.e., small independent groups, most without periodicals, and periodicals on a commercial basis without organizations)."[16]

Languages also came into play at the congresses. At the 1955 Paris congress, stenciled German and English translations of the speeches given in French were made available, and only in 1958, at the Brussels congress, was simultaneous translation from, and to, English, French, and German provided. While some members apologized for their imperfect use of second or third languages – Holger Bramlev from Copenhagen asked forgiveness, in German, that "my German is certainly very bad" – others complained about the imperfections of others' linguistic abilities ("it was difficult enough to hear a translation into English which didn't always make sense," wrote a US member).[17] Danish member Ewald Bohm found it "really amusing, how much confusion can arise from such a small international conference, where everyone seemingly understands the others, but only seemingly [emphasis in the original]." He then went on to point out that the term *Unfähigkeit* used to describe a member not fulfilling his duties was also used in the literature to describe sexual impotence, "so that this *Unfähigkeit* of a member comes across as a bit involuntarily comical."[18] Such misunderstandings and miscommunications, whether amusing or serious, plague all transnational efforts, and the International Committee, despite Dutch linguistic abilities, was no exception.

National differences also troubled the organization, and not just because the different countries had a range of laws regulating homosexuality. The most liberal laws, in the Netherlands and the Scandinavian countries,[19] criminalized same-sex relations only if an adult had sex with a minor, defined in different ways, but sometimes as under the age of 21. In these countries, homophile activists worked to set the same age of consent for same-sex as for heterosexual sex. In 1954, the ICSE newsletter reported on proposed changes to the Norwegian penal code, which would have fined any person who conducted a meeting or other gathering for homosexual persons without proper controls to prevent those under the age of 21 from entering.[20] In Germany and England, all male same-sex sex was illegal, and the ICSE put a great deal of effort in supporting German efforts to amend Paragraph 175, the law that criminalized male homosexuality. The International Committee also took great interest in the Wolfenden Committee in England, the group that deliberated about and ultimately recommended reform of the British penal code.[21] The prospects for legal reform in England – a country Methorst considered "in a hopelessly and despairing situation" – led the International Committee to shift focus away from Germany, where it had expended a great deal of effort, but after the Wolfenden Report appeared in 1957, the Committee bought a thousand copies in German translation with the intent to send them to members of the German parliament and other major figures.[22]

Although the organization insisted that it "extends its action fundamentally to all civilized countries of the earth," the leaders had to admit that "at present the area of its activity is largely confined to Europe."[23] Because the ICSE relied on existing homophile groups to affiliate, there was little way to reach beyond the boundaries of Europe. In addition, homophile identity, as articulated in the ICSE and in national homophile organizations (Weeks 1977; D'Emilio 1983; Churchill 2008; Jackson 2009; Wolfert 2009; Pretzel 2010) assumed a common notion of what it meant to be homosexual. Some recognition of cultural differences in conceptions of same-sex sexuality emerges in the records. A document from the second congress called for "better mutual understanding between the Western and Oriental civilizations and those of the so-called under-developed countries," suggesting that the introduction of the "Western anti-sexual way of life" would do harm to civilizations from which the West might learn much.[24] At the third congress, Methorst stated that "the homo-eroticism in Arabia f.i. [for instance] or in Greece, shows an entirely different aspect from ours."[25] This suggests an awareness that a homophile identity might not have resonance in places beyond Europe and the "neo-Europes" (Crosby 1987) of the United States, Canada, and Australia.

Homosexual cosmopolitanism and sexually expressive culture

Another less obvious way that the transnational homophile movement was shaped by European culture was in the importance of a traditional elite homosexual cosmopolitanism along with the impact of a (some-times-fraught) sexual expressiveness. Homosexual cosmopolitanism in this period – by which I mean the sense of a shared homosexual culture across national borders and interest in travel to partake of it – was not uniquely European, but because of the relative ease of travel among countries west of the Iron Curtain was more at play there. Sexual expressiveness within European homophile culture was not uniform, with notable differences between countries (Herzog 2009) and a certain ambivalence about sexualized images and connections to the urban homosexual subculture within homophile organizations (Churchill 2008), but in contrast to Britain and the United States, the only other countries in which homophile groups existed, publications and events sometimes pushed the boundaries of respectability. The reigning assumption was that the Netherlands and the Scandinavian countries – although, according to a Norwegian author, Denmark more than Norway and Norway more than Sweden – were relatively tolerant, that Germany, England, and the United States were puritanical, and that the "Latin countries" were backward.[26]

The significance of cosmopolitanism can be seen in a handwritten draft of an application form in the ICSE archives, making it clear that one early vision of the organization was as a "necessary link that can bring you in contact with thousands of sympathetic fellows everywhere" through a magazine and card that would admit members to existing clubs in Denmark, Germany, the Netherlands, and Switzerland.[27] And, in fact, congresses and business meetings included cultural events that drew members to the organization. One Danish participant wrote to thank the ICSE for the third congress, where he "contacted many friends of different nationalities and found the very importance of the international co-operation."[28] An English physician commented on the "eager hands and friendly smiles" encountered in the conference hall and found the experience of hanging up his mask (the favored metaphor for being out at this time) "together with his hat and coat in the cloakroom" at the COC club in Amsterdam a "revelation."[29] One letter, thanking the Amsterdam office for "the kindness and hospitality" of the first congress, expressed "real longing" for the "nice evenings in the club in Amsterdam."[30] In this way, the ICSE utilized the desire to connect with others in a homosexual space to build the movement.

This kind of social connection across national borders was captured in the concept in this period of the "homintern," a supposed vast international conspiracy of homosexual writers and artists who controlled the world of culture as anti-Communists imagined the Komintern sought to dominate the globe. A Danish newspaper reported that "the homosexualists in a number of European countries are in very close contact with each other, and that there exists a very wide-spread network of contacts extending far beyond the frontiers of this country."[31] That this was not only an external impression – the term "homintern" itself is attributed to gay poet W.H. Auden – is suggested by a comment from the editor of an early *Periodical Newsletter* that "homosexuals...are and have always been inclined to international, more or less impersonal or transient contacts."[32]

The ICSE sought to mobilize this inclination to attract members. Along with dinners, the congresses featured dances and cabarets, connecting to the commercialized homosexual culture of the time. Member Marc Dufour, working to organize the first congress, wrote from Paris to ask if he needed to wear fancy dress to the Carnival dance, hoping that there would be "some costume available for me – Prince Charming of Queerland or a white naval uniform." He also asked for "one or two really nice boys free from conjugal ties."[33] The officers of the ICSE, expressing the ambivalence about such requests that permeated homophile organizations, responded that fancy dress was obligatory but "no travesty allowed," that they were "too terribly busy organizing all this" to be able to help with the boys, and that he would find them himself in any case.[34] The proceedings of the Frankfurt meeting in 1957, held in the rooms of the *Cherie am Hafen* – "in bilingual literality: 'My dearest on the waterfront'!" – on *Gutleutstrasse* – "The Street of Good People, literally" – commented on the "ironic circumstances and place names we 'giddy' people find ourselves in sometimes."[35] The 1958 Brussels congress featured a *Soirée de Variétés* with performances by "Mae West," "Little J.P.," "Marlène and her boys," "Lola Florès," and "La Troupe du CCL" [the Belgian homophile group].[36]

Despite such appreciation for the campiness of homosexual culture and the kind of entertainment characteristic of commercial homosexual clubs, the ICSE leadership emphasized that they were "serious people" whose aims were "of a somewhat higher standard than only dancing and purely physical pleasure."[37] ICSE editor Johannes Werres worried that "those who came to the party" at the Frankfurt congress in 1952 "outnumbered by far those who joined our congress-sessions."[38] Yet, despite such misgivings, the ICSE utilized the trappings of homosexual culture in its events. Expressing disgust with this familiar aspect of ICSE culture, a US representative from ONE complained that the yearly meeting in Bremen opened with "a cabaret performance in drag of course, to which I did not go."[39] As David Churchill (2008) has pointed out, US homophile publications celebrated the virtues of Europe as a tourist destination but warned about European sexual culture, in particular working-class bars and commercial nightlife.

That some individuals had goals that were more personal than political in contacting the ICSE is clear from the letters that poured in from individuals seeking travel advice (especially about the laws in different countries), pen pals, or potential partners, although ICSE publications, unlike many European national homophile organs, did not include personal advertisements. Some of the letters were very explicit about particular erotic desires – a German man sought a big young man, "not a feminine type," a Danish man wanted a uniformed "master" in riding boots, but not a sadist – and some were desperate – "LIFE is UNBEARABLE" from Australia, and "I NEED THIS URGENTLY, SO VERY MUCH. PLEASE!!!!!!!" from California.[40] The organizational leadership seemed somewhat torn about these requests for personal assistance. Occasionally officers did give out travel advice and even post personal advertisements for correspondents in the COC's magazine, *Vriendschap*.[41] At the same time, president Henri Methorst wrote to one US man asking if he wanted to "adhere to our international movement" or was he "seeking personal friendship or correspondence," and he lectured the Californian, who expressed interest in big strong masculine men, at length about the foolishness of looking for a companion half a world away. Even so, he published a personal ad for the man.[42] An Italian member, who lamented that his countrymen "are all only interested in the phallic love, and they will croos [sic] all Europe for see a boy, but not to speak about our problems," expressed the concern of some within the ICSE that the draw of personal connections would not attract the right kind of members.[43] That personal ads seemed especially inappropriate to US homophiles is suggested by a contributor to ONE, who criticized a German periodical for "a good-sized 'personals' column in which men of thirty advertise for 'young, blond, good-looking' youths to accompany them on a trip to southern France." He concluded that this was not the kind of publication "anyone would care to be caught with, in America at any rate" (quoted in Churchill 2008: 41).

The same kind of differentiation between Europe and the Anglo-Saxon countries can be found in debates about appropriate representations of sexuality. A British man, for example, wrote from London before the first congress objecting to recruitment materials that, to him, gave "an impression of depressing inadequacy and moral bankruptcy," adding that "you are probably unaware of the profound differences in behaviour between 'our people' here and on the Continent."[44] Likewise, Joost Adriaansen, the first editor of the newsletter, warned of the need to consider different national sensibilities: "Articles that easily could be accepted in some countries on the continent could cause a scandal in Anglo-Saxon countries."[45]

One aspect of the European cultural scene that "could cause a scandal in Anglo-Saxon countries" was the practice of publishing photographs and reproductions of works of art of boys, sometimes naked and sometimes scantily clothed. *Der Kreis*, the Swiss bi- and eventually trilingual journal (English was added to German and French in 1951), also featured photographs, illustrations, and fiction that eroticized young men, although the journal avoided any direct discussion of intergenerational relationships (Kennedy 1999; see also Evans 2013). This aesthetic, of course, hearkened back to the ancient Greek ideal of love between a man and a boy and has been, throughout time and across place, a more common conception than lack of differentiation between sexual partners (Hekma 2008). Theo Sandfort (1987), in a study of pedophilia in the COC, argues that the period from 1946 to 1958 was characterized by a lack of distinction between the categories of homosexuality and pedophilia. This began to change in succeeding years, marked by the ICSE's proposal of the theme "Pedophilia versus Homosexuality" for its 1960 congress. Despite the apparent attempt to decouple the two phenomena, the theme aroused opposition. One member wrote from Denmark that it was "not a very happy choice" and that "people in general will be induced to connect the homosexual problem with attraction toward children – a misconception which is but too widespread already."[46] Karl Meier (pseudonym Rolf), longtime editor of *Der Kreis*, agreed that the theme was detrimental to movement goals.[47] In the end, most speakers turned down invitations, and the congress, at first postponed with another theme, never took place.

Yet, as Sandfort argues, there was an association between pedophilia and homosexuality in the postwar years, within as well as outside the movement, and the greater relative sexual expressiveness of European homophile culture brought the issue into the open in ways that are unimaginable in the United States. One of the most active officers of the International Committee, editor Johannes Werres, a German national, described himself publicly as a pederast interested in "youthful-looking partners above that dangerous age from fourteen to eighteen," if one who sublimated his desires and later formed a lasting relationship with a man older than him. A Danish friend then living in New York wrote to Werres in 1956 to ask, "Why not enjoy what is available? The photograph or even the nearest boy."[48] Werres not only admitted his attraction to boys and young men and in the 1970s edited a publication titled *Boy Love News* but also identified others in the homophile movement as "boy lovers" (Werres 1990).

The tensions over sexual expressiveness and pedophilia emerged clearly in what became known as the "*Vennen* affair." *Vennen* [*Friends*], an independent publication that was originally put out by the Danish League of 1948, included photos of boys and young men in scanty clothing. In 1954, when *Vennen* applied for membership in the ICSE, fear of scandal led to objections. At a working session of the ICSE, a representative of the Danish League of 1948 objected to the level of the magazine, and a member from the Swedish homophile organization agreed, pointing to the photos and personal ads and adding, "We want no photos in a homosexual magazine of children under 18." Another Swedish colleague asked the question of whether or not the photographs were pornographic and worried that such photos would "give a false impression of our movement." In defense of *Vennen*, its representative insisted that "it is more important for us to publish a magazine that draws in a lot of homosexual readers than one that is acceptable to a few heterosexuals." That they published a thousand copies, he insisted, showed its worth.[49] *Vennen*'s editor, Axel Lundahl Madsen, made the same point in a letter to the International Committee, asserting that it was "more important that our magazine pleases <u>many</u> homophiles than that it is accepted by a few heterophiles."[50] A German member spoke up in the ICSE meeting to say that "he would be enormously rich if he could start a pornographic publication in Germany," and this remark was met with great approval.[51]

Then, in 1955, the Danish police arrested Lundahl Madsen and his partner, Eigel Eskildsen, for distributing pornography and for sexual contact with men under the age of 18, because they took some of the photos published in *Vennen* themselves (Wolfert 2009).[52] The two men also ran businesses that imported homosexual magazines and nude photographs of men. Raids on the offices of the businesses, which shared space with *Vennen*, led to the arrest of dozens of men. When the arrests of Lundahl Madsen and Eskildsen hit the newspapers, the ICSE scrambled to distance itself further from *Vennen*, emphasizing that the publication had applied for but not been admitted to the ICSE because of the "moral standard" of the periodical. The ICSE newsletter referred to the "unfortunate affair" in Copenhagen but added optimistically that "surely no one possessing normal common sense will attach too much importance to the case, as dealing in so-called pornographic material, should this in fact have taken place, certainly is no privilege to homophile circles."[53]

The *Vennen* affair shows that, despite ambivalence about erotic photographs and the International Committee's attempt to disassociate homosexuality from pedophilia, there was acceptance in at least some of the European national movements of sexually expressive representations, including of boys and young men. These representations, along with the personal ads in many of the European publications and the emphasis on a cosmopolitanism focused on socializing across national borders, distinguished European homophile organizing from its counterparts across the English Channel and the Atlantic.

The superiority of European styles of organizing

The third way in which we can see the European nature of transnational homophile organizing is in the assertion of the superiority of European ways. The first American to contact the International Committee was Henry Gerber, who had learned about homosexual activism as a soldier in Germany and launched the short-lived Chicago Society for Human Rights in 1924. Writing from the US Soldiers Home in the District of Columbia in 1951, he complained about how difficult it was to organize because "in America people are woefully ignorant of sex matters."[54] A German immigrant to the United States wrote to the ICSE after learning of the founding congress from *Der Kreis*, lamenting the "dire and very discouraging absence of anything of its type in the United States," and concluding that "for the time being, the more responsible ones among us here will have to look to Europe."[55] The president of the ICSE responded that it was the mentality of the people in the United States that stood in the way, adding that despite legal obstacles German groups had sprung up shortly after the war, "inspired no doubt by the historical example of the first sexologist Magnus Hirschfeld."[56] Returning to his original point, the émigré asserted that "I cannot help feeling, that the initial step must come from our side."[57] Defending the honor of US homophiles, Donald Webster Cory [pseudonym of Edward Sagarin], author of an influential early book about homosexuals as a minority group, wrote to the ICSE to assert that such views "fail to see the dynamics of the social changes in the United States, and only see the virtual impossibility of a movement that is patterned after the European scene."[58]

The difference between European and "Anglo-Saxon" ways became even more pronounced once US homophile groups joined in 1953. Their way of working struck the Europeans as too ambitious and optimistic. As Johannes Werres put it, reading about ONE was "like looking into a strange and sometimes curious country of a – you might excuse – fairy tale." He conceded that he admired US "courage, initiative, phantasy and hard working will, but – BUT I think (from my own European, typically German and Non-American point of view) you might as well do good or even better by doing just less." And then he added, "I forget that you are Americans, and this means more optimism than realism." William Lambert, from ONE, responded with a lecture about how the United States was settled by those who were not content to wait and how those who stayed on in Europe "produced the technological, political and cultural apathy which characterizes so much of the European scene." He commented on "what we take to be the lessons from the German homophile movement, beginning with Hirschfeld and earlier. We feel that their great error was that they believed it was possible to build slowly, 'patiently,' and through the influence of highly-placed persons." Ending on a more conciliatory note, he suggested that each side deepen its understanding of their differences – differences he saw to be stark.[59] When the president of the ICSE visited the United States in 1959, he commented in the ICSE newsletter that the trip "showed how little we know about each other really on both sides of the ocean – of all three oceans we may well say!"[60]

Distinctions between Europe and the United States also emerged in reports in ICSE publications emphasizing the dangers of homosexual life in the United States in the context of McCarthyism. A Norwegian journalist visiting Dallas in 1951 reported that there were no organizations, pubs, or private clubs and that the bars were dangerous because of the plainclothes policemen, blackmailers, and mobsters who frequented them to arrest, blackmail, rob, or beat up gay men.[61] In Los Angeles, a 1954 article reported, "the situation as regards sexuality and particularly homoeroticism … can seem nothing but fantastic" for "anyone who has spent his life in the cities of Western Europe."[62] A publication designed for the German-speaking countries reported on a visit to New York in 1957. In such a large city, the article noted, only 38 members belonged to the Mattachine Society. The anonymous author found Americans "immature," described a raid on a bathhouse as "à la Hitler," and described the United States as "this so-called democratic country."[63] In all these ways, transnational homophile organizing declared its European character, in contrast to the repressed, naïve, and dangerous nature of homosexual life in the United States.

Conclusion

The International Committee for Sexual Equality, by bringing together existing national homophile groups, carried on a legacy of organizing around sexual identity across national borders. In this sense, it was a transnational organization, yet it was also profoundly European. As we have seen, groups and individuals from Northern and Western Europe dominated the ICSE, with the Netherlands taking over from Germany as the center of transnational activism around same-sex sexuality. Although the organization had explicitly political goals, homosexual cosmopolitanism, including a desire for personal connection across national borders, and a relative openness to sexually expressive culture marked homophile activism as more European than Anglo-Saxon. And the ICSE was, as debates with US members made clear, also convinced of the superiority of European modes of organizing.

That the ICSE succeeded in uniting citizens from opposite sides of the lines of battle so soon after the end of a devastating war is a sign that the idea of Europe meant something to homophile activists. And, in fact, connections across national boundaries in Europe continued to play a role in the history of transnational gay activism. Although there is no straight line to connect the ICSE with the emergence of the ILGA, there are suggestive connections. A group known as the International Homophile World Organization (IHWO), founded by the Axgils (the joint name taken by Axel Lundahl Madsen and Eigel Eskildsen), moved across the border of Denmark to Germany in the 1960s and published a short-lived seven-language paper, *International Periodical for Friendship, Information, and Tolerance* (Wolfert 2009). Johannes Werres, in addition to Lundahl Madsen and Eskildsen, served as a link between the ICSE and the IHWO, although the two organizations never acknowledged a connection. When Lundahl Madsen was fighting for acceptance of *Vennen* in the ICSE, he had warned, "If our cooperation in the international work is not wanted, we intend to put our work on an international basis in the service of the homophile cause."[64] In 1969 and 1970, the IHWO held international meetings in Denmark and Sweden, and in 1973, the COC, which remained suspicious of the IHWO, sponsored an international seminar that the IHWO attended along with other representatives from Germany and from Denmark, England, the Netherlands, and Norway (ibid.).

By the mid-1970s, both existing homophile and emerging gay liberation groups in Europe were organizing transnational conferences. Everywhere the older organizations found themselves out of sync with and criticized by the new liberation groups, although it would be a mistake to think of some definitive end of the homophile phase and beginning of gay liberation. At a gathering claiming to be the "First International Gay Rights Congress" in Edinburgh in December 1974, Frank Kameny of the US Mattachine Society, a figure who brought militancy to the US homophile movement, spoke at what was a very feminist and liberationist event.[65] In 1975, the COC sponsored a conference on women and men in homosexual movements in the Netherlands, attended by representatives of the homophile groups in Belgium, Norway, and Great Britain.[66] The Campaign for Homosexual Equality (CHE), which represented Britain at that conference and which had had contact with the ICSE, in 1978 announced that its annual conference in Coventry would have an "international flavour" as an International Liaison Commission would be meeting at the same time, bringing together "delegates from homophile organizations" in the European Economic Commission countries, the United States, Canada, and Jamaica.[67]

It was that meeting, attended by representatives from the COC, the Danish *Forbundet af 1948*, and the Swedish *Riksforbundet for Sexuellt Likaberattigande*, all groups that had belonged to the ICSE, that gave birth to the ILGA. At the first annual conference of the new group in the Netherlands the next year, delegates from 17 countries established "a network of political cooperation and informational exchange to link gay organizations at [the] global level." Resolutions echoed the ICSE's focus on the United Nations, calling for the revocation of the World Health Organization's classification of homosexuality as a disease and calling for consultative status at the UN, although a new tone was evident in statements of support for the women's movement, attention to gay rights in the Third World, and sensitivity to transsexuals and transvestites.[68]

Interestingly, both the Edinburgh conference in 1974 and the new International Gay Association (IGA) discussed the rights of "sexual minorities," by which they meant sadists, masochists, and pedophiles, in the context of the Council of Europe's Committee on Decriminalization. Participants at an IGA workshop in England in 1979 discussed "pedophilia and its particular urgency for the gay and lesbian movement," with the Danish *Forbundet af 1948*, which had so distanced itself from the Axgils and *Vennen*, coordinating consideration of age of consent laws.[69] Ironically, this very issue lost the ILGA consultative status at the UN in 1995 when right-wing groups in the United States charged that some member groups, in particular the North American Man-Boy Love Association, promoted pedophilia, and the US Senate threatened to withhold payments to the United Nations.[70]

Although now countries from around the world have joined the ILGA, whatever might be characterized as a transnational LGBT culture is no longer marked as European, and assertions of European superiority are not part of public discourse, the continuing centrality of Europe in the technically global ILGA and the strength of ILGA-Europe, as Phillip Ayoub and David Paternotte point out in the Introduction, speak to the predominance of European influence (see also Ayoub and Paternotte 2014). In 2011, the United Nations Human Rights Council passed a resolution endorsing LGBT rights for the first time, finally meeting the demands that the ICSE made 60 years earlier.

One consequence of the long history of European leadership of transnational activism around sexuality is the identification of the rights of sexual minorities as a European value, as many chapters in this volume (particularly those by Ayoub and Paternotte (Chapter 1), Colpani and Habed (Chapter 4), and Moss (Chapter 10)) suggest. Another is the creation of a dominant "Western" notion of the contours of gay and lesbian identity. The contemporary Western notion of homosexuality as defined by sexual object choice, rather than gender inversion or sexual role, spread from European sexologists to other parts of the world, reversing the previous European conception of same-sex desire as something found in the Middle East or Asia or Africa and fostering the notion in many places that homosexuality is a Western perversion (Bleys 1995; Rupp 2009). As numerous scholars have pointed out (Blackwood and Wieringa 2007; Povinelli and Chauncey 1999; Grewal and Kaplan 2001; Manalansan 2003; Boellstorff 2005), there is a gay and lesbian identity based on Western conceptions that is understood in various places around the world, but it has not displaced indigenous identities and understandings of what it means to have same-sex desire. What I would suggest is that there is a history to that dominance of European – which is now more in sync with the US and so has become "Western" – concepts of sexual identity, and that we would do well to understand how the trajectory of transnational organizing and the struggle to forge a global gay, lesbian, bisexual, and transgender identity has been profoundly shaped by the imagined and experienced community of Europe.

Notes

Some of the text in this chapter appeared originally in Leila J. Rupp, "The Persistence of Transnational Organizing: The Case of the Homophile Movement," *American Historical Review* 116 (2011), 1014–1039.

1. "Report of the First International Congress for Sexual Equality, Whitsuntide 1951, Amsterdam," Nationaal Archief, Den Haag, Cultuur- en Ontspannings Centrum [COC], 1940–1971, 2.19.038 [hereafter NL-HaNA, COC], box 158; "Telegramm an die UNO," *Der Kreis* 7 (July 1951), 1. See also *Periodical Newsletter*, n.d. [September 1951], NL-HaNA, COC, box 159.
2. "An Instructive Interview with the Chairman of the World's Largest Homosexual Organization: The C.O.C. in the Netherlands," *ICSE Newsletter*, March 1957, International Committee for Sexual Equality files, ONE Institute and Archives, Los Angeles [hereafter ICSE, ONE, LA]; Floris van Mechelen (F.v.M.), "Short Historical Survey of the Dutch C.O.C.," *Periodical Newsletter*, July 1953, ICSE, ONE, LA.
3. "An Instructive Interview with the Chairman of the World's Largest Homosexual Organization: The C.O.C. in the Netherlands," *ICSE Newsletter*, March 1957, ICSE, ONE, LA.
4. "Letters from Readers," *Periodical Newsletter*, Bulletin No. 4, n.d. [1952], NL-HaNA, COC, box 159.
5. "Historique," n.d. [1960], German, NL-HaNA, COC, box 166; Jan de Groot to Canadian Council on Religion and the Homosexual Incorporated, 13 December 1965, NL-HaNA, COC, box 168; F.v.M., "Perspektiven der Bewegung für sexuelle Gleichberechtigung Ihre Wege und Ziele," *Der Kreis* 20 (October 1952), 7–8; F.v.M., "Short Historical Survey"; Draft of invitation, n.d. [January 1951], NL-HaNA, COC, box 161–162.
6. "A World Parliament," n.d., NL-HaNA, COC, box 158.
7. "Holland ruft auf zur internationalen Mitarbeit," *Der Kreis* 7 (July 1951), 3–6.
8. Bernardino del Boca de Villaregia to second congress of the ICSE., 12 August 1952, NL-HaNA, COC, box 158.
9. "Holland ruft auf zur internationalen Mitarbeit," *Der Kreis*, 3–6.
10. Jack Argo, "Congress Impressions," *Periodical Newsletter*, October 1952, NL-HaNA, COC, box 159.
11. Werner Schlemmer-Meyer to Lieber Freund, 21 August 1954, German, NL-HaNA, COC, box 161–162.
12. Dieter Berner to ICSE, 23 July 1954, German; Erwin Haarmann to ICSE, 5 October 1954, German, box 161–162, NL-HaNA. COC; Berner to ICSE; Haarmann to ICSE.
13. Report of the Meeting of February 5 1959, ICSE, ONE, LA.
14. "Clive Alderson to Dear Subscriber," *ICSE Newsletter*, August 1958, ICSE, ONE, LA; F.v.M. to ONE, 15 January 1955, NL-HaNA, COC, box 163; Gert Lantman to Liebe Freunde, 27 April 1957, German, NL-HaNA, COC, box 165.
15. "Protokoll der Arbeitssitzung des I.C.S.E.," Copenhagen, 23–25 October 1954, NL-HaNA, COC, box 164.

16. Norbert Weissenhagen, "ICSE-Radaktie," German, in "Witboek," 28 February 1957, NL-HaNA, COC, box 160.
17. [Holger] Bramlev to ICSE, 8 July 1954, German, NL-HaNA, COC, box 161–162; Wayne to Don [Slater], n.d. [1958], ICSE, ONE, LA.
18. Ewald Bohm to Herr Angelo, 9 November 1954, German, NL-HaNA, COC, box 161–162.
19. The same was true of laws in Belgium and France.
20. "Report from Norway on the amendments of the penal code"; Hans Weil, "Bericht aus Schweden," *ICSE Newsletter*, March–April 1954, ICSE, ONE, LA.
21. "Protokoll der Arbeitssitzung des I.C.S.E.," Copenhagen; Bob Angelo to Secretary of the Departmental Committee on Homosexual Offences and Prostitution, 14 May 1955, NL-HaNA, COC, box 161–162; *Periodical Newsletter*, Bulletin No. 5, July 1955, ICSE, ONE, LA.
22. "Witboek inzake de werkzaamheden en resultaten van het ICSE in her afgelopen jaar 1956," 28 February 1957, NL-HaNA, COC, box 160 (translation by Nanette Pawelek); Brief Minutes of the Business Session of the ICSE. at Brussels, 1958; "Protokoll der I.C.S.E.-Arbeitstagung in Bremen," 8–9 August 1959, ICSE, ONE, LA.
23. "Zur Information für die Presse," 24 June 1957, NL-HaNA, COC, box 160.
24. "Petition of the Second International Congress for Sexual Equality Assembled at Frankfort Germany," 29 August–2 September 1952, NL-HaNA, COC, box 158. See Churchill (2008) for an analysis of the ways in which transnational homophile culture mobilized non-Western cultures to argue for the naturalness of homosexuality.
25. "Report of the Third International Congress of the International Committee for Sex Equality," 12–14 September 1953, NL-HaNA, COC, box 158.
26. On the Scandinavian countries, see O.E., "Conditions in Norway," *Periodical Newsletter*, March 1953, NL-HaNA, COC, box 159.
27. Handwritten drafts, n.d. [1951], NL-HaNA, COC, box 161–162.
28. Jørgen Tews to ICSE, 20 September 1953, NL-HaNA, COC, box 161–162.
29. "From England a Physician, Participant of the Third Congress Wrote Us the Following," n.d. [1953], NL-HaNA, COC, box 159.
30. Kaj Staun to Bob Angelo, 1 June 1951, NL-HaNA, COC, box 158.
31. "International Pornography Affair Disclosed in Copenhagen," typescript, n.d.; "Declaration," n.d., NL-HaNA, COC, box 163.
32. "Letters from Readers," *Periodical Newsletter*.
33. Marc [Dufour] to Dear friends, 16 January [1951], NL-HaNA, COC, box 161–162.
34. Bob Angelo and F.v.M. to Marc Dufour, 28 January [1951], NL-HaNA, COC, box 161–162.
35. "Proceedings of the 7th Conference of the ICSE," Frankfurt, 29–30 June 1957, ICSE, ONE, LA.
36. "Programme du Congres de L'ICSE à Bruxelles," 23–26 May 1958, NL-HaNA, COC, box 1645; "Soirée de Variétés," 24 May 1948, NL-HaNA, COC, box 160.
37. ICSE to H.W. Ehrmann, 5 August 1959, NL-HaNA, COC, box 165.
38. Argo, "Congress Impressions."
39. Wayne to Don [Slater], n.d. [August 1959], ICSE, ONE, LA.

40. Werner Schlemmer-Meyer to Lieber Freund, 21 August 1954, German, NL-HaNA, COC, box 161–162; N.W. Bugge to Dear Sir, 25 August 1960, NL-HaNA, COC, box 166; H.W. Ehrmann to ICSE, March 12, 1960, NL-HaNA, COC, box 166; Frank Peterson to Director, COC, 7 March 1955, NL-HaNA, COC, box 163.
41. Handwritten drafts, n.d. [1951].
42. F.v.M. to Robert Crosby, 4 July 1954, NL-HaNA, COC, box 161–162; F.v.M. to Frank Peterson, 16 May 1955, NL-HaNA, COC, box 163.
43. Bernardino del Boca de Villaregia to F.v.M., 23 February 1952, NL-HaNA, COC, box 161–162. See also H. Bramlev to ICSE, 4 February 1959, German, NL-HaNA, COC, box 165; "Protokoll der I.C.S.E.-Arbeitstagung in Bremen," 8–9 August 1959.
44. Geoffrey A. Whitall to Mr. Angelo, 24 January 1951, NL-HaNA, COC, box 161–162.
45. Joost Adriaansen, "Editorial," *Periodical Newsletter*, no. 4, n.d. [1952], NL-HaNA, COC, box 159.
46. Dermot Mack to ICSE, 27 January 1960, NL-HaNA, COC, box 166.
47. Rolf to Liebe Kamaraden, 16 May 1960, German, NL-HaNA, COC, box 166.
48. Unsigned letter to Johannes, 25 November 1956, NL-HaNA, COC, box 159.
49. "Protokoll der Arbeitssitzung des I.C.S.E.," 23–25 October 1954, NL-HaNA, COC, box 164.
50. A.J. Lundahl Madsen to ICSE, 24 October 1954, NL-HaNA, COC, box 161–162.
51. "Protokoll der Arbeitssitzung des I.C.S.E.," 23–25 October 1954.
52. Wolfert, who had access to Lundahl Madsen and his papers, reports the charge. The only document in the ICSE files to mention this aspect of the case is the confidential Dutch "White Book," which reports that, in addition to the sale of pornographic photos, Lundahl Madsen was imprisoned for "copulation with underage boys." "Witboek inzake de werkzaamheden en resultaten van het ICSE in her afgelopen jaar 1956," 28 February 1957.
53. F.L., "The I.C.S.E. and Modern International Trends," *Periodical Newsletter*, Bulletin No. 5, July 1955, ICSE, ONE, LA.
54. Henry Gerber to ICSE, n.d. [received 26 January 1951], NL-HaNA, COC, box 161–162.
55. Henry Sergévich to Bob Angelo, 23 October 1951, NL-HaNA, COC, box 161–162.
56. F.v.M. to Henry Sergévich, 2 November 1951, NL-HaNA, COC, box 161–162,
57. Henry Sergévich to F.v.M., 15 December 1951, NL-HaNA, COC, box 160.
58. D.W. Cory to F.v.M., 3 July 1952, NL-HaNA, COC, box 161–162.
59. Jack Argo to Editors of ONE, 31 May 1957; Bill L[ambert] to Jack Argo, 27 June 1957, NL-HaNA, COC, box 165.
60. "ICSE President Floris van Mechelen visits the U.S.A.," *ICSE Newsletter*, December 1959.
61. "Homosexual Life in Dallas, Texas," *Periodical Newsletter*, November 1951.
62. Robert Freigedank, "Los Angeles 'The home of Angels," *ICSE Newsletter*, March–April 1954.
63. "Man schreibt uns: Das ist Gay New York heute!" *ICSE-KURIER*, no. 3, April 1957.

64. A.J. Lundahl-Madsen to ICSE, German, 24 October 1954, NL-HaNA, COC, box 161–162.
65. "First International Gay Rights Congress," Hall Carpenter Archives [HCA], London School of Economics, Ephemera/164. I am grateful to Justin Bengry for research assistance in London.
66. "Conference on Women – Men Cooperation in Homosixual [*sic*] Movements," May 1975, Oegstgeest, the Netherlands, HCA, Ephemera/219.
67. CHE News Release, 20 June 1978, HCA, CHE/8/19.
68. IGA Press Release, 16 April 1979, HCA, Ephemera/361.
69. IGA, Informal workshop, Brighton, England, 24–27 August 1979, HCA, Palmer/7/2/6.
70. Craig Kaczorowski, "International Lesbian and Gay Association," *GLBTQ: An Encyclopedia of Gay, Lesbian, Bisexual, Transgender, & Queer Culture*, http://www.glbtq.com/social-sciences/int_lesbian_gay.html, accessed 14 August 2009.

References

Ayoub, Phillip M. and David Paternotte. 2014. "Challenging Borders, Imagining Europe: Transnational LGBT Activism in a New Europe." In *Border Politics, Social Movements and Globalization*, eds. Nancy Naples and Jennifer Bickham-Mendez, New York: New York University Press.

Blackwood, Evelyn and Saskia E. Wieringa. 2007. "Globalization, Sexuality, and Silences: Women's Sexualities and Masculinities in an Asian Context." In *Women's Sexualities and Masculinities in a Globalizing Asia*, eds. Saskia E. Wieringa, Evelyn Blackwood, and Abha Bhaiya. New York: Palgrave Macmillan, 1–20.

Bleys, Rudi 1995. *The Geography of Perversion: Male-to-Male Sexual Behavior outside the West and the Ethnographic Imagination, 1750–1918*. New York: New York University Press.

Boellstorff, Tom. 2005. *The Gay Archipelago: Sexuality and Nation in Indonesia*. Princeton: Princeton University Press.

Churchill, David S. 2008. "Transnationalism and Homophile Political Culture in the Postwar Decades." *GLQ: A Journal of Lesbian and Gay Studies* 15(1): 31–66.

Crosby, Alfred. 1987. *Ecological Imperialism*. New York: Cambridge University Press.

D'Emilio, John. 1983. *Sexual Politics, Sexual Communities: The Making of a Homosexual Minority in the United States, 1940–1970*. Chicago: University of Chicago Press.

Dose, Ralph. 2003. "The World League for Sexual Reform: Some Possible Approaches," *Journal of the History of Sexuality* 12(1): 1–15.

Evans, Jennifer V. 2013. "Seeing Subjectivity: Erotic Photography and the Optics of Desire." *American Historical Review* 118(2): 430–462.

Grewal, Inderpal and Caren Kaplan. 2001. "Global Identities: Theorizing Transnational Studies of Sexuality." *GLQ: A Journal of Gay and Lesbian Studies* 7(4): 663–679.

Hekma, Gert. 2008. "The Drive for Sexual Equality." *Sexualities* 11(1–2): 46–50.

Herzog, Dagmar. 2009. "Syncopated Sex: Transforming European Sexual Cultures." *American Historical Review* 114(5): 1287–1308.

Jackson, Julian. 2009. *Living in Arcadia: Homosexuality, Politics, and Morality in France from the Liberation to AIDS*. Chicago: University of Chicago Press.

Kennedy, Hubert. 1999. *The Ideal Gay Man: The Story of "Der Kreis."* New York: Harrington Park Press.

Manalansan, Martin F. IV. 1995. "In the Shadows of Stonewall: Examining Gay Transnational Politics and the Diasporic Dilemma." *GLQ: A Journal of Gay and Lesbian Studies* 2(4): 425–438.

——. 2003. *Global Divas: Filipino Gay Men in the Diaspora*. Durham: Duke University Press.

Povinelli, Elizabeth A. and George Chauncey. 1999. "Thinking Sexuality Transnationally: An Introduction." *GLQ: A Journal of Gay and Lesbian Studies* 5(4): 439–450.

Pretzel, Andreas. 2010. *Homosexuellenpolitik in der Frühen Bundesrepublik*. Hamburg: Maënnerscharm.

Rupp, Leila J. 2009. *Sapphistries: A Global History of Love between Women*. New York: New York University Press.

——. 2011. "The Persistence of Transnational Organizing: The Case of the Homophile Movement." *American Historical Review* 116(4): 1014–1039.

Sandfort, Theo. 1987. "Pedophilia and the Gay Movement." *Journal of Homosexuality* 13(2): 89–110.

Warmerdam, Hans and Pieter Koenders. 1987. *Cultuur en Ontspanning: Het COC, 1946–1966*. Utrecht: Interfacultaire Werkgroep Homostudies.

Weeks, Jeffrey. 1977. *Coming Out: Homosexual Politics in Britain, from the Nineteenth Century to the Present*. London: Quartet Books.

Werres, Johannes. 1990. "Als Aktivist der ersten Stunde: Meine Begegnung mit homosexuallen Gruppen und Zeitschriften nach 1945." *Capri: Zeitschrift für schwule Geschichte* 1: 33–45.

Wolfert, Raimund. 2009. *"Gegen Einsamkeit und 'Einsiedelei'": Die Geschichte der Internationalen Homophilen Welt-Organisation*. Hamburg: Männerschwarm Verlag.

3
LGBT Activism in Kyrgyzstan: What Role for Europe?

Cai Wilkinson

Drawing on fieldwork conducted in Bishkek in February 2013,[1] this chapter examines the different ways in which "Europe" as both an idea and an actor (or actors) features in the activities and discourses of LGBT activists in Kyrgyzstan. Given this small post-Soviet Central Asian republic's location well beyond not only the borders of the EU, but also outside the scope of the Eastern Neighborhood Policy, it may seem somewhat odd to ask what role Europe plays in local LGBT activism. This is especially true considering that both international and domestic political dynamics seem to suggest that European influence in post-Soviet Central Asia is seriously constrained by competition from Russia and, increasingly, China in a "New Great Game" that is driven by the desire of all actors to gain access to resources and markets and maintain geopolitical strategic influence (Kim and Indeo 2013). However, as this chapter demonstrates, such thinking significantly underestimates Europe's "normative power" (Manners 2002), even in light of the EU being a "[l]atecomer in Central Asia's Great Game" (Delcour 2011: 91) and criticism of the EU's Central Asia Strategy for being overly focused on strategic interests at the expense of commitment to the values of human rights and democracy (Boonstra and Hale 2010: 10; Melvin 2012; Youngs 2010).

Centrally, an examination of Europe's role in the development of LGBT activism in Kyrgyzstan reveals the multiple forms that Europe's influence takes, with the idea of Europe frequently being a more salient point of reference than Europe as a political institution. For, although the EU is Europe's "official face" with the European External Action Service (EEAS) as its official representative to third countries, Europe's influence extends far beyond that of high-level formal political relationships. It manifests itself in a wide range of modalities and contexts, ranging from the bilateral donor activities of NGOs and Europe-based agencies in Kyrgyzstan, to knowledge exchange between groups and organizations based in Europe and those based in other regions, and on to "European values" serving as a point of reference for local efforts to promote socio-political reform such as recognition of LGBT rights. While some may see such diversity as problematic, obscuring the projection of a clearly defined European identity, this chapter argues that it is precisely the inherent multiplicity of Europe's identities and the variety of "means and mechanisms" through which it is represented (Manners and Whitman 1998: 236) that has facilitated Europe's role in the development of LGBT activism in Kyrgyzstan by endowing it with sufficient fluidity to remain relevant and avoid being positioned irrevocably as "other."

As this chapter explores, Europe's influence on LGBT activism in Kyrgyzstan has been principally evident in two ways.. Firstly, a considerable range of Europe-based organizations and agencies either have a presence in the republic and/or maintain relationships with local NGOs, providing various forms of support to local LGBT NGOs. Secondly, despite wide variations in EU member states' positions on LGBT rights (European Union Fundamental Rights Agency 2013), the idea of Europe provides an informal benchmark of sorts both for the protection of the human rights of LGBT people and for LGBT activism, acting as a source of inspiration and aspiration. Particularly in the latter case, the multiplicity of European identity and its ability to transcend territorial borders has meant that the idea of Europe has remained salient to local debates over identity and values, even in the face of claims that it promotes alien phenomena such as homosexuality and gender diversity, or is involved in neo-cultural imperialism via the organizations that it funds (Cherikov 2014).

In the following section a brief overview of Europe's engagement with post-Soviet Central Asia and Kyrgyzstan is provided to contextualize subsequent discussion and analysis. Particular attention is paid to debates about the EU's record in promoting human rights in the region, which has been complicated by strategic concerns and the sensitivities of local regimes. Attention is then turned to review the history of LGBT community organizing in the republic and particularly the development of rights advocacy as a function of LGBT organizations and groups in the 2000s, before discussion moves to focus on activists' views about Europe's influence on LGBT activism. Opinions were inevitably mixed about the extent and form of Europe's influence. In addition, although all interviewees thought that contact with European organizations and actors has been positive in terms of supporting LGBT activism overall, it was also noted that "European values" are seen as immoral and culturally alien by some sections of Kyrgyzstani society, making associations between LGBT rights and Europe a potentially double-edged sword. Significantly, however, despite the presence of such potentially undesirable facets of "Europe," it has been possible for activists to counter them by invoking aspects of Europe that are viewed more positively, such as supporting the observation of universal human rights and rule of law, and use these to emphasize the commonality of "European values" beyond national and geographical affiliations. In doing so, local activists capitalize on Europe's normative power in a way that would arguably not be possible in the presence of a singular and instititutionalized European identity, as is discussed in the chapter's conclusion.

Europe and human rights in Central Asia

Although formally the EU has had a presence in Central Asia since 1994 and Partnership and Cooperation Agreements with Kazakhstan, Kyrgyzstan, and Uzbekistan came into force in 1999 and with Tajikistan in 2000, it was only in 2007 that the EU made any substantive commitment to active engagement with the region. The launch of the EU's new Central Asia Strategy in June 2007 was billed as the beginning of a "new partnership between the EU and Central Asian States in a globalized world," with the EU emphasizing that "the development and consolidation of stable, just and open societies, adhering to international norms, is essential to bring the partnership between the European Union and Central Asian States to full fruition" and its ability to facilitate this process:

> Good governance, the rule of law, human rights, democratization, education and training are key areas where the EU is willing to share experience and expertise. The EU can offer experience in regional integration leading to political stability and prosperity... With their rich traditions and centuries-old exchanges, the EU and Central Asia can contribute actively to the dialogue between civilisations.[2]

The Strategy presented the EU's interests in the region as being underpinned by a "strong interest in a peaceful, democratic and economically prosperous Central Asia" and noted the centrality of the rule of law and human rights to achieving these aims, asserting that

> The EU strongly believes that strengthening the commitment of Central Asian States to international law, the rule of law, human

rights and democratic values, as well as to a market economy will promote security and stability in Central Asia, thus making the countries of the region reliable partners for the EU with shared common interests and goals.[3]

One of the five central components of the Strategy, therefore, was the establishment of "a regular, result-oriented 'Human Rights Dialogue' with each of the Central Asian States."[4] In principle, these bilateral dialogues provided the opportunity for the EU to raise concerns over particular human rights issues and violations with local government with a view to initiating projects to improve standards and practices that can be funded under the European Instrument for Democracy and Human Rights. Structured dialogues were established with Kazakhstan, Kyrgyzstan, and Tajikistan in April 2008 and the first dialogues were held in October of the same year.[5] The second Human Rights Dialogue with Kyrgyzstan was held as planned in October 2009, but the overthrow of Kurmanbek Bakiev in April 2010, which cost the lives of more than 75 people, and the interethnic violence experienced by residents of Osh in June of the same year meant that the third dialogue was not held until June 2011.[6] A primary focus of both the third and the fourth dialogues, which were held in September 2012, was the human rights situation in the south of the republic and particularly addressing violations of the rights of ethnic and religious minorities.[7]

Alongside the official Human Rights Dialogues and in accordance with EU Guidelines on Human Rights Dialogues with third countries,[8] the EU has organized civil society seminars "with the aim of opening up the official dialogues to civil society communities and independent human rights experts," either on a bilateral or regional basis.[9] The seminars are used to prepare recommendations for the official dialogues. To date, two bilateral civil society seminars have been organized with Kyrgyzstan in 2009 and 2012, and representatives of Kyrgyzstani NGOs participated in the regional EU-Central Asia Civil Society Seminar on Women's Rights that was held in Brussels in 2010.[10] In addition, the European Commission maintains contact with European and local NGOs for the purposes of information exchange and consultation on matters to be raised during the official dialogues. These processes involved closed briefings for Europe-based NGOs, but are organized on a less regular and more "ad hoc" basis in each Central Asian republic (Axyonova 2011: 2–3).

Inevitably in light of the Central Asian republics' poor human rights records,[11] concerns have been raised about the efficacy of the EU's formal dialogue-based approach. Melvin (2012: 2) is damning in his evaluation of the EU's overall Central Asia Strategy, calling it "a clear failure at reversing the deterioration in the human rights and democracy situation" and arguing that the approach has sidelined human rights by "compartmentalising these issues into projects and set piece dialogue mechanisms, to allow progress on other issues." Axyonova, meanwhile, is more temperate in her assessment and recognizes the contextual limitations faced by the EU, not least of which is a relative lack of leverage to impose conditionality. Taking a longer-term perspective, she concludes that the EU's approach offers a starting point for engagement with Central Asian governments in that the purpose of the Human Rights Dialogues is "information exchange and confidence building with the final aim of the [*sic*] human rights norm diffusion" (Axyonova 2011: 4).

A key issue, therefore, is how the EU can move beyond formal dialogues and begin to effect improvements on the ground. Here it is a question of negotiation with governments in order to agree on the scope of specific projects, as a member of the EU Delegation to the Kyrgyz Republic outlined:

> The emphasis is on human rights rather than democratization ... The government is a fan of our program – now they are convinced that is it more about human rights and is a "half social" [program], rather than being about bringing in printing machines, or financing revolution. Once they understand that we are not doing that, they are very cooperative.
>
> ...we try and find a common tone, we are not there to criticize them ... We say that we would like to do some regulations, OK, you would like to have this and this and this, OK, we are clear, but how about this as well?
>
> ... We try to mainstream human rights wherever we can.[12]

While not capable of producing systemic change, this approach has resulted in the Kyrgyzstani government becoming more willing to engage with the EU over human rights issues, especially in the wake of the political and societal upheaval the republic experienced in 2010. As my interviewee from the EU Delegation observed, there has been growing recognition among government officials that improving the human rights situation is part of wider efforts to raise standards of governance and address social issues – something that is very much in the government's interests if it wishes to avoid falling victim to popular discontent as previous regimes have. Consequently, she commented, talking about human rights is "not taboo, at least not when we discuss it, but then we are donors, we are euros."[13]

The EU's portfolio of bilaterally funded projects in Kyrgyzstan as of 2012 included eight financed under the European Instrument for Democracy and Human Rights that focused on youth and children's rights, women's rights, and the rights of the elderly, as well as touching upon ethnic minority rights and prisoners' rights.[14] However, even in the case of the "Bir Duino – One World: International Human Rights Documentary Film Festival in Kyrgyzstan," the program of which controversially included Chris Belloni's film *I'm Gay and Muslim* until it was banned (Trilling 2012), there is no explicit mention of LGBT people or LGBT human rights, and LGBT NGOs were not included in the EU-Kyrgyz Republic Civil Society Seminars on Human Rights that were held in 2009 and 2012.[15]

The logic for this, as my EU Delegation respondent explained when discussing whether there was any formal place for LGBT people as a minority group in EU projects, is that LGBT rights are part of general human rights.[16] However, given that EU projects often focus on the support of vulnerable groups "such as work with people with disabilities, work with women's groups, work with street children, prisoners and the elderly,"[17] this reasoning seems somewhat shortsighted and disconnected from local research on LGBT people, which clearly indicate that LGBT people in Kyrgyzstan are a socially vulnerable group who frequently experience discrimination, marginalization, and violations of their rights due to their sexual orientation and/or gender presentation (Human Rights Watch 2008a, 2008b, 2014; Karagapolova 2010; Soros Foundation – Kyrgyzstan 2007; van der Veur 2004).

LGBT activism in Kyrgyzstan

Kyrgyzstan is anomalous in Central Asia in that it possesses a vibrant and sizable civil society, which since the early 2000s has included several locally founded NGOs that provide a variety of services for LGBT people and undertake human rights advocacy work on their behalf. Consequently, while the situation of LGBT people in Kyrgyzstan could be described as positive only in the most relative terms (homosexuality remains criminalized in Uzbekistan and Turkmenistan, for example), the socio-political situation has meant that while local activists "could not be said to be pushing at an open closet door, they have certainly found that the door is unlocked, and have capitalized on this situation by pushing the door even more and taking tentative steps into public arenas" (Wilkinson and Kirey 2010: 486).

The result has been a growing community of LGBT activists, who have made impressive progress in promoting the rights of LGBT people in Kyrgyzstan and the wider Central Asian region. Particularly since the mid-2000s, LGBT activists have worked hard to destigmatize homosexuality and gender variance through a wide range of activities outside of the LGBT community, ensuring that LGBT people are included in discussions of human rights both nationally and internationally. Serious efforts have also been made to tackle everyday homophobia and transphobia among state employees, such as medical professionals and law enforcement agents, and among the general public. The result, as one local activist observed, has been significant progress in raising awareness of LGBT issues and helping to "normalize" discussion of previously taboo topics – a fact reflected, for example, in that over the past five years or so the media has increasingly reported on LGBT topics and the activities of LGBT NGOs as "normal news," rather than something inherently scandalous and salacious.[18]

The first group for LGBT people in Kyrgyzstan was founded in 1995 and officially registered as an NGO called Oazis in 1998 following the decriminalization of homosexuality. As its founder, Vladimir Tyupin, recounts, officially Oazis' aim was "to support young people and organize efforts to fight AIDS. We didn't draw attention to precisely which young people we were helping, but everyone knew that we were a gay organization" (Kirey 2007: 15). In addition to its official anti-HIV/AIDS work in conjunction with the Republic's Anti-AIDS clinic, Oazis also organized social events for the LGBT community in Bishkek, including holding the first ever event for gay men and lesbians in a local night club in 1999. Oazis' activities were the first public efforts at LGBT community organizing in Kyrgyzstan, and Gender Vektor, which was founded in 2002 in the town of Kara-Balta, adopted a similar approach, primarily providing opportunities for socializing and conducting anti-HIV work among gay men and men who have sex with men.

By 2004, however, there was a growing sense that the focus needed to expand to actively address the marginalization and discrimination faced by LGBT people. This view was particularly strong among lesbian and bisexual women, who felt that their needs and problems were not being addressed by existing organizations, which were primarily focused on gay men. As a result of this dissatisfaction, and spurred on by an incident in a Bishkek café, a group for lesbian and bisexual women and trans men that went by the name Labrys was founded. Significantly, among the founding members were people with experience of civil society organizations and LGBT activism in Europe and the US. While the emphasis was on being responsive to the needs of the local community, this awareness of how to "do" activism provided an important knowledge base and a source of inspiration, since despite the bleak situation it was known based on first-hand experience that change was possible. The initiative group met regularly through the summer of 2004 to discuss plans and gather material for a special issue of Oazis' in-house journal entitled "Lesbians in Kyrgyzstan: Who Are They?" that was designed to raise awareness within the LGBT community of lesbians and bisexual women (Wilkinson and Kirey 2010: 492). Late in 2004 a meeting with a representative of Dutch international women's rights fund Mama Cash led to a successful application for funds to rent an office space and publish a quarterly journal that would help connect local lesbian and bisexual women. This development marked the official beginning of Labrys' activities, with three issues of the journal published in the first six months and more than 80 lesbian and bisexual women visiting the office (Kirey 2007: 17).

The year 2006 saw Labrys officially register as an NGO and commence work on large-scale capacity-building and research projects funded by COC Nederland and Hivos, thus continuing Dutch influence on transnational LGBT activism (Rupp 2011, and Chapter 2 in this volume). These projects formed the basis of an expanding remit for Labrys, which was now working on an increasingly advocacy-orientated agenda in addition to providing support to the LBT, and later LGBT, community. Central to Labrys' advocacy work has been addressing violations of LGBT people's human rights. This work has been developed in a variety of fora, including organizing training sessions on LGBT rights for local law enforcement officers and journalists, publishing information booklets, conducting hate crime monitoring, and lobbying the government for legislative changes regarding gender markers on identity documents, and for action to address violence and discrimination against LGBT people. Much of this work has been conducted in partnership with international organizations, including the Open Society Institute, the Organization for Security and Cooperation in Europe (OSCE), and Civil Rights Defenders, the implications of which are discussed in the following section.

The other outcome of Labrys' activities has been the founding of new NGOs and initiative groups by local LGBTQA activists. The NGO Kyrgyz Indigo, which started out in 2009 as an anti-AIDS project aimed at gay and bisexual men funded by the Global Fund and Anti-AIDS Association (a local NGO) supported by Labrys,[19] registered as an NGO in 2010. To date, Kyrgyz Indigo's projects have focused on HIV prevention and personal development for LGBT people, with funding provided by amfAR, COC Nederlands, and Schorer.[20] While Kyrgyz Indigo is the most established of the latest cohort of LGBT groups and, especially in light of the support of the COC, could be viewed as a direct product of transnational homophile organizing that began in Europe in the 1950s (Rupp 2011 and Chapter 2 in this volume), two further organizations have been founded since 2009. In contrast to Kyrgyz Indigo, Bishkek Feminist Collective SQ (founded in 2009) and Pathfinder (registered in 2011) represent a further development in LGBTQA activism in Kyrgyzstan in that they explicitly seek to create solidarity between different groups in order to affect positive change for everyone, rather than focusing exclusively on LGBT people. Thus, for example, Pathfinder's mission is described as "to turn the movement for equality regardless of people's sexual orientation and gender identity into an influential social force and the building of a society without discrimination or segregation in Kyrgyzstan."[21] A central feature of Pathfinder's activities in this respect has been creating space for discussion of religion, sexual orientation, and gender identity, especially for LGBT Christians, who frequently feel marginalized within LGBT communities as well as in faith communities.[22]

Bishkek Feminist Collective SQ, meanwhile, was founded in 2009 as a queer-friendly feminist group that aims "to promote feminist values of ending all forms of oppression (sexism, homophobia, transphobia, ageism, ableism, nationalism, xenophobia, islamophobia, class and socio-economic oppression, etc.) in Bishkek."[23] The collective has the most socially radical agenda, which is concerned with emancipation and challenging existing socio-political and cultural institutions and norms via "a culture of peaceful civil disobedience, alternative activism, feminist philanthropy and solidarity for achieving our goals as well as for changing stereotypes about protests and the civil society in Kyrgyzstan." Members of SQ have participated in a wide range of activities, including staging performances of *The Vagina Monologues* in 2009, 2011, and 2013, holding a dance flash mob and recording videos as part of "One Billion Rising" in February 2013 (Wilkinson 2013), and partnering with Labrys, COC Nederlands, and the St Petersburg-based Side-by-Side film festival for the 2013 "Week Against Homophobia and Transphobia."[24] In addition, SQ has also provided space and support for groups wishing to self-organize to address issues affecting them. In 2012 this led to the establishment of a Transgender Initiative Group (TIG) by members of the local transgender community to provide peer community support and undertake advocacy on trans issues, thus taking forward the work done by Labrys and further diversifying the LGBT activist community.

Europe's influence in Kyrgyzstan: activists' views

During the course of individual semi-structured interviews, respondents were asked about the impact of support from external donors and organizations and whether they thought that international actors, including the EU and the OSCE, could influence the human rights situation for LGBT people. People's answers and the examples they gave varied considerably depending on their personal and professional experiences, and in the majority of cases "Europe" was used as a catch-all name for a wide range of European or Europe-based organizations and institutions, reflecting the multiple character of European identity discussed earlier. Three clear themes emerged in their responses: firstly, "Europe" as a source of funding for activism; secondly, "Europe" as a source of solidarity, knowledge, support, and inspiration for both LGBT activists and the wider LGBT community; and thirdly, "Europe" as an actor and promoter of specific values that has the ability to influence the government and public opinion. This section discusses each of these themes and also explores related tensions and contradictions.

"Europe" as donor

Respondents were unanimous in their recognition that funding from external actors has been a significant facilitator of the growth of LGBT activism in Kyrgyzstan. Firstly, funding means that people are able to devote time to activism – something that is far from typical in socio-economic circumstances such as Kyrgyzstan's, where the average monthly salary is approximately €174[25] and 30% of people live below the poverty line. After all, as an activist from Kyrgyz Indigo commented, "Everyone understands that it's very difficult for activists to live without money. You'll keep going, but if you have a full-time job elsewhere, then you won't have time for LGBT activism."[26] In addition, funding has been vital to sustaining activism and supporting their cause, as a member of Labrys explained:

> It's thanks to donor funds that we hold events, work, we're already changing the situation. That's the main influence. It's not a case of receiving money and being told what to do, although many people see it that way, kind of "you're just laundering money, spending it on gay propaganda," but on the other hand, using money from donors

we can hold roundtables, conferences, conduct research, which is very important. For example we've just done an evaluation for COC and we can present that as evidence that there are real people and this is the real situation. There's data, official data! We didn't just take it from somewhere or other, this is data about Kyrgyzstan, these are the figures, this is situation, this is what needs changing, these are the recommendations.[27]

In effect, as an interviewee from Gender Vektor noted, donors increase local capacity for activism by providing the means to organize and formalize activities aimed at addressing problems faced by the LGBT community.[28]

At the same time, the limits of what funding can achieve directly were also commented upon. Firstly, one respondent questioned what more donors could actually do, given that all material essentials for activism have already been provided thanks to donors: "We've got a house, an internet connection, computer equipment, wages, they sponsor events, what more could they do? We've got everything."[29] Building on this theme, another respondent noted that donor support often takes the form of small seed-corn funding that enables an organization to get established and begin work. However, he went on to observe that recipients need to work hard to build on the support provided and adapt procedures, strategies, and aims to the local context in order to be effective and sustainable. "If there's no adaptation," he observed bluntly, "then it's a waste of money."[30]

Both of these responses point to the reality that more funding does not necessarily result in bigger, or better, results. Rather, the financial support of donors is a necessary but not sufficient condition for effective LGBT activism in Kyrgyzstan. Indeed, receiving large grants early on in an organization's existence often gave rise to unintended consequences that caused as many problems as it solved, as Labrys discovered initially (Wilkinson and Kirey 2010: 493). What respondents, especially those who had been involved in activism for longer periods of time, saw as being far more important was moral support from organizations in other countries and opportunities for knowledge exchange. An activist who began work with Labrys and who recently helped set up TIG explained:

[F]inancial support is important, but this isn't the most important thing for activists themselves, if we're talking about activists then it's moral and political support that is most important. That is, you know that there are resources you can count on, that there's support, that there are information resources, especially if you speak English. Then there's the issue of training and capacity building and that's all foreign organizations.[31]

"Europe" as inspiration

While the response above focuses on the limitations of contact with organizations in other countries for established activists, other responses observed other benefits. Firstly, a member of Labrys described how contact with overseas LGBT organizations could serve to inspire people and empower them to become activists, rather than feeling helpless in often hostile and harsh socio-economic conditions:

[I]f we send a representative of the LGBT communities in Kyrgyzstan to an event that's taking place somewhere in Europe, in America, or wherever – anywhere where they would meet other people like them, activists who are having fun, being fun, being beautiful and whatever, loving each other, being activist-y and stuff like that, it has a very empowering potential. And if even if they might not fully understand everything that's going on there because of language barriers or knowledge barrier, because it could be their first event out there, it's still so empowering for them, usually they come back and go "oh my God, there is life possible outside here and we can work towards it, the shit that we're living here is not the end of it all."[32]

Similarly, for established activists, contact with other organizations, especially when there are opportunities to attend events in person, provides important opportunities to recharge both mentally and physically and reflect on how much has been achieved,[33] rather than feeling as though their work is if not a Sisyphean task, then certainly a dauntingly Herculean one given local and regional constraints.

Secondly, cooperation with foreign organizations can help legitimize the work of local LGBT activists, providing them with greater leverage in advocacy work. A member of Labrys' advocacy team explained:

And it's not so much in relation to financial support, although this is of course important, as in terms of partnerships, for example, it's very important for us that international organizations such as Freedom House and Human Rights Watch cooperate with us on the informational level. For example, we're included in some of their events, or they distribute information for us, or we can get support from them about a particular situation or other, this is very important because if information comes from an international organization it has some sort of weight. For us, whoever says a word in defense of LGBT people, it's worth its weight in gold, because, well, it's important that people hear it – when I say it, that's one thing, but when a representative of an international organization says it, that's already something else.[34]

This approach has proven particularly effective in cases where the government is proving reluctant to engage with local LGBT organizations, as another member of Labrys' advocacy team recounted:

It's often happened that we sent in a question or made a statement about something, but we were ignored and they [the government – CW] didn't answer. But then via these organizations, an official letter was sent, and then they couldn't not answer anymore, because they've signed many international documents, agreements. So yes, they help, it forces the authorities to respond.[35]

"Europe" as a model

Interestingly, while a wide range of organizations and actors were mentioned as advocates for specific norms or values who could exert pressure on the Kyrgyzstani government, even if only by writing letters and/or attempting to publicly embarrass officials, Europe's influence was seen to be somewhat more "by being," rather than "by doing." Respondents from Gender Vektor explained:

Yes, Europe directly influences the situation by being a positive example, let's start with that. For example, with same-sex marriage, it's not discussed here in Kyrgyzstan, Central Asia will stay quiet about it – no people, no problem – they'll just carry on as though nothing is happening. But they've still seen it, that life's in full flow there, while here it is forbidden.[36]

Echoing this view was a respondent from TIG, who also felt that "Europe," in some form that remained unspecified, was capable of exerting some political influence despite the absence of legislative enforcement mechanisms:

Europe is a model, a best example. In principle if we're talking about where we want to go, what we want to see, then we often focus on the results that have been achieved in Europe. Specifically on the results, but not the methods, because conditions are a bit different here. And I think that in principle it's the same politically, the "oh oh oh, what a bad thing you've done, how shameful!", it also has a certain significance, although not as much as one would like because we're not under the jurisdiction of the European Court of Human Rights.[37]

The potential of external actors to exert pressure on the Kyrgyzstani government was commented on especially frequently in relation to the possibility of a Russian-style anti-gay law occurring in Kyrgyzstan.[38] On the one hand, the majority of respondents felt that an initiative to pass a law similar the Russian one was entirely possible, with several noting that politicians often follow Russia's lead with legislation,[39] as demonstrated by attempts to introduce restrictions on NGO activity in 2009 (Mamatov 2009). On the other hand, however, respondents did not think that the actual implementation of an anti-gay law was likely. One respondent gave the following assessment of the situation:

> An anti-gay law is entirely possible here. The real question is how efficiently we react to it. Here we have a pretty nimble, efficient and mobile civil society, and thanks to cooperation with several leading human rights organizations, there is also a certain amount of influence. And what's not insignificant here is that Kyrgyzstan is very dependent on the support of donor organizations. And for us – and not only for LGBT activists but also civil society overall – that's a reason for their influence. The government here won't go for such a measure openly as happened in Russia.[40]

Another respondent was blunter in his assessment of the role of donor financing on Kyrgyzstan's political decisions, as well as suggesting that donors would be willing to "play hardball" in the event of such a law:

> Everyone knows that Kyrgyzstan copies Russia and is dependent on it. But on the other hand, foreign, that is, Western, donors bring in huge amounts of money to the country, and our government doesn't want to lose serious amounts of money, so even if they pass the law, our government will stay quiet and make out that they haven't noticed the LGBT community at all. Kyrgyzstan would be afraid to pass such a law because it receives huge amounts of money for work with MSM [men who sleep with men] for example, and it'll lose that and the donors will leave. It's not beneficial – and this is in our favor.[41]

While these assessments reflect the influence that major donors can have on domestic politics, particularly in the latter's assessment of the willingness of donors to jeopardize programs and relations in practice is arguably overstated. Awareness of the fact that, as a representative of the US Embassy put it, "diplomacy has to be diplomatic,"[42] and that in general the preference is for constructive engagement rather than confrontation – a stance exemplified by the EU – led other respondents to assess the significance of Europe's political influence more conservatively, especially in comparison to that of the US and Russia, which were seen as the two major players in the country:[43]

> It seems to me that Europe plays more of a passive role than an active one. In terms of concrete actions it doesn't play much of a role. But passively in some respects it does. It serves as an example, education, help LGBT activists, on that sort of level. But on in a larger, active sense, no. It's not possible at the moment.[44]

As well as recognizing that financial and moral support from foreign organizations has been fundamental to the growth and sustainment of LGBT activism, several respondents touched upon the downsides of receiving financing from external actors. One commented that activists have not infrequently been accused of misappropriating funds or being "foreign agents" working to promote the interests of America or Israel in Kyrgyzstan at the expense of national interests,[45] while another recounted an incident at a training session in Bishkek during which a local attendee claimed that Labrys was sponsored by a Dutch organization with the aim of sending Kyrgyz children to Europe for organ donation.[46]

Such incidents are indicative of the fact that LGBT activists are unavoidably caught up in ongoing debate surrounding Kyrgyzstan's identity as a state and as a nation. Homosexuality in this respect, as in the rest of the former Soviet Union and in other parts of the world, is viewed as something that is a Western or European phenomenon that is alien to local culture and values. As a result of this "false patriotism," LGBT activism is often popularly viewed as something that must be actively resisted, since it involves the imposition of foreign norms by an aggressive group of morally corrupt deviants who are thought to be demanding special rights.[47]

Activists reject the notion that homosexuality and gender variance are Western or European imports, and challenge the idea that being gay or transgender is incompatible with national identity or local values – an issue that is particularly contentious for ethnic groups that are tradition-ally Muslim. One transgender respondent explained:

> There's the idea that being gay comes from Europe, but there's LGBT people everywhere. In part, my presence here is proof of this – I'm Kyrgyz, I'm in Kyrgyzstan, I've lived all my life here, I hadn't ever been to Europe until after I realized [that I was trans*], and then when I realized and became an activist, I travelled to Europe. That is, I don't believe that Europe has influenced my gender identity.[48]

Assessing Europe's influence

Despite the potential negatives of being associated with Europe, it is impossible to deny that Western or European norms have been influen-tial in the development of LGBT activism, if only because LGBT move-ments in European countries have provided examples of strategies that can be employed. Firstly, as Wilkinson and Kirey (2010) discuss, the appellation "LGBT" has served as a reference point for non-heterosexual and gender variant people to lay claim to sexual citizenship, in the process politicizing sexual orientation and gender identity. Thus, while Europe may not have influenced activists' gender identity or sexuality, it has provided a vocabulary to articulate it as a public identity.

Secondly, the tactic of framing of LGBT rights as human rights that began in the West in the early 1990s (Kollman and Waites 2009) has been employed by local activists to increase the domestic legitimacy of their claims. The success of this move is demonstrated by the gradual shift in attitudes toward LGBT issues in the wider human rights defenders community since the mid-2000s. Initially there was significant resist-ance to the inclusion of the rights of LGBT people within understand-ings of human rights, but increasingly non-LGBT NGOs have been willing to include LGBT issues as an integral part of human rights advo-cacy activities. Reactions to the prosecution of Tolekan Ismailova for allegedly inciting religious hatred by showing the film "I'm Gay and Muslim" at the Bir Duino film festival has arguably been the highest profile example of this to date, indicating how LGBT issues are seen as linked to the wider fight against human rights violations in Kyrgyzstan, as Tolekan Ismailova explained while discussing the case against her:

> I'm cheered that people are coming and preventing [violations by the authorities] – it takes strength and time, but nonetheless there's a huge amount of support from young people, from many journalists

and partner organizations. And it's like we're doing this together, it's a common cause because it is empowering, we need to prove our strength in order to preserve the state's constitutional secularity and the status of human rights that is in the Universal Declaration of Human Rights and in the Constitution.[49]

In addition, this universalization of human rights arguably begins to weaken the association that is often made between human rights and "European values," and the implication that human rights are a luxury that cannot be expected in Kyrgyzstan as a non-European, non-Western country.[50] Rather, as one respondent reflected when considering how Europe influences human rights in Kyrgyzstan, Europe – and Europeans – acts as a conduit for the spread of "universal" norms: "People go to Europe to study or learn, then they come back. Naturally they take on those values, I'm not saying 'European values', but those universal human values, they come back ... And Europeans come here, help us."[51]

As many of the responses in this section highlight, it is difficult to define not only Europe's influence, but also what exactly is meant by Europe. Occasionally the EU was mentioned, yet far more often European organizations such as ILGA-Europe and the OSCE featured, as well as a range of LGBT organizations in Europe, especially in Moldova, Ukraine, and the Balkans. Yet despite – or perhaps because of – the broadness of the term "Europe," all activists felt that Europe has had an influence on LGBT activism in Kyrgyzstan. However, one respondent was quick to clarify this statement: "People think that Europe and America play some sort of role [in LGBT activism in Kyrgyzstan], but in actual fact their role is only in supporting their [LGBT people's] ideas, their rights."[52] This observation highlights the fact that, whether by circumstance or design, to date Europe's overall influence has been predominantly passive – by being, rather than by doing, to use Møller's (2005) phrasing – in relation to LGBT rights in Kyrgyzstan.[53] While this conclusion may be construed as criticism of Europe, as is discussed in the final part of the chapter, the current low-profile approach has had some definite advantages and the EU needs to think carefully about how to maintain the benefits of a more "fuzzy" European identity and its normative power while raising its overall profile in Kyrgyzstan and the rest of Central Asia.

Conclusion: balancing being with doing

While Europe's influence on LGBT activism in Kyrgyzstan is apparent in a number of ways, it remains diffuse and difficult to define precisely.

While this is arguably in keeping with the notion of "normative power," it also presents a problem for the EU as it aims to establish a stronger presence in Kyrgyzstan and become a serious player alongside other external actors, since the "soft power of being" is increasingly seen to be insufficient; political legitimacy and credibility both in Kyrgyzstan and among EU member states demand that visible actions must accompany words (Axyonova 2011; Melvin 2012).

Skepticism over the actual influence of Europe's normative power has most frequently been voiced in relation to debates over Europe's defense and security, with NATO head Anders Fogh Rasmussen declaring that "[w]e Europeans must understand that soft power alone is really no power at all. Without hard capabilities to back up its diplomacy, Europe will lack credibility and influence" (Rettman 2013). However, beyond the narrow confines of military security, such statements miss the power of what Manners (2010: 67) calls "the mythology of 'global Europa' – the EU in the world," which, despite – or perhaps because of – its contradictory, multiple and ideological character, maintains Europe's relevance as a point of reference far beyond its geographical borders. As reflected in interviews with LGBT activists in Bishkek, it is precisely the multiplicity and fluidity of Europe's identity that give it much of its influence: the idea of Europe renders geographical borders fuzzy and porous, thus maintaining its resonance in places such as Kyrgyzstan that are outside of Europe by any common definition and have no realistic prospect of membership, by facilitating the selective incorporation of "Europe" in its different forms into local narratives. Central to this process, as Hudson (2000: 420) observes, is the space that "Europe" has created for "non-territorially defined dimensions of individual identities," which has in turn facilitated "the emergence of various communities of interest in discontinuous spaces within Europe and beyond."

The development of LGBT activism in Kyrgyzstan clearly demonstrates this process, and also confirms its co-constitutive nature, with the idea of Europe being simultaneously maintained and (re)shaped via the use of "Europe" as a point of reference. The result is a largely virtuous circle, whereby even when the (in)actions of Europe as an actor in any of its multiple incarnations are subject to criticism or accusations of working against local interests and values, the ideational power of Europe – the values that it is seen to represent – continues to provide it with legitimacy and salience. The challenge now is how to maintain this dynamic with an increasingly centralized and institutionalized European presence in Central Asia that seeks to harmonize and focus the current diversity of

European influences into unified action aimed at promoting European values and interests.

Although a more forthright and robust presence might be viewed positively by human rights supporters in Europe, local activists were more cautious about this prospect, noting that a sharp increase in political pressure risks "looking like a dictatorship" and could damage relations if engagement is seen solely as criticism. Echoing this, the EU's current "soft but persistent insistence," as Axyonova (2011: 4) calls it, was evaluated positively by one respondent as a way to affect change, as she explained:

> They [the EU] can contribute a lot, and they've been doing that already...the Human Rights Dialogue with the Kyrgyz government, it's a very good instrument, and basically, the more they raise these issues, the more it will become normal – I hate the word normal, but it's the only one that can be used and be understood by people and the government here...the more times the issue is raised in adequate terms, the more adequate the government will become in its attitude towards LGBT people. So if the EU keeps on raising LGBT issues, maybe...Already I think that the government doesn't have the attitude that it used to have four years ago, already it's more like "oh yeah, I know about this issue, we'll work on this issue," and they can start maybe contacting LGBT organizations in a few years.[54]

Both the EU and local LGBT activists are aware of the dangers of being overly strident or seeking to force change. For the EU, the deterioration of relations with the Kyrgyzstani government is likely to result not only in being less able to pursue European strategic interests in the region, but also in reduced capacity for development activities that currently serve as a vehicle for European values. For LGBT activists meanwhile, a more unified and institutionalized identity for Europe risks reducing their ability to employ the idea of Europe as a positive point of reference as the idea itself is increasingly displaced by the more solid and conventional "actorness" of the EU. While the attractiveness of this identity shift is understandable from the perspective of the EEAS, there is a danger that Europe's role in the ongoing development of LGBT activism in Kyrgyzstan may be negatively affected. At present Europe's influence manifests in a wide range of modes and means, with the result that Kyrgyzstan's LGBT activists having become part of a dynamic transnational LGBT network that is strongly European in both origins and values (Ayoub and Paternotte, Chapter 1 in this volume). The fluidity and multiplicity of "Europe" has been central to this process, enabling the idea of Europe not only to travel beyond the bounds of Europe, but also to take root, adapt, and survive in less-hospitable locations such as Kyrgyzstan in a way that a monolithic and institutionalized European identity could not.

Notes

1. Fieldwork for this chapter was funded by Deakin University's 2013 Central Research Grant Scheme (award RM25342) and was approved by Deakin University's Human Research Ethics Committee (reference 2012322). I would like to thank all those people and organizations who assisted with and/or participated in the research and the editors for their thoughtful comments and extended patience as the chapter slowly took its final form. While I have aimed to represent participants' views fairly and accurately, the interpretations and any errors or omissions are mine alone and should be viewed as such. Thirty-two semi-structured interviews were conducted by the author with LGBT and human rights activists and representatives of international organizations. Many interviewees consented to being identified by name. However, the decision has been made to anonymize material from respondents from the local LGBT community in the interests of safety. They are identified by number instead. All translations from Russian are the author's own.
2. http://www.eurodialogue.org/eu-central-asia-strategy/10 (accessed 25 June 2013).
3. Ibid.
4. Ibid.
5. http://eeas.europa.eu/central_asia/docs/factsheet_hr_dialogue_en.pdf (accessed 29 June 2013).
6. Ibid.
7. http://eeas.europa.eu/delegations/kyrgyzstan/documents/eu_kyrgyzstan/press_release_human_rights_dialogue_en.pdf and http://www.donors.kg/en/event/2474/ (accessed 29 June 2013).
8. http://www.consilium.europa.eu/uedocs/cmsUpload/16526.en08.pdf (accessed 29 June 2013).
9. http://eeas.europa.eu/delegations/kyrgyzstan/eu_kyrgyzstan/human_rights/index_en.htm (accessed 29 June 2013).
10. http://eeas.europa.eu/human_rights/dialogues/civil_society/docs/2010_ca_final_report_en.pdf (accessed 29 June 2013).
11. http://www.civilrightsdefenders.org/country-reports/human-rights-in-central-asia/ and http://www.freedomhouse.org/regions/central-and-eastern-europeeurasia (accessed 29 June 2013).
12. Member of the EU Delegation to the Kyrgyz Republic, interview with author, Bishkek, 5 February 2013.
13. Ibid.
14. http://eeas.europa.eu/delegations/kyrgyzstan/documents/eu_kyrgyzstan/development_and_democracy_cooperation_with_civil_society_en.pdf (accessed 29 June 2013).

15. See the final reports from the seminars: http://eeas.europa.eu/delegations/ kyrgyzstan/documents/press_corner/news2012/final_report_english__2_ en.pdf and http://eeas.europa.eu/delegations/kyrgyzstan/documents/eu_ kyrgyzstan/cs_seminar_report_en.pdf (accessed 20 June 2013). It should be noted, however, that a representative of Labrys was present at the regional EU-Central Asia Civil Society Seminar on Women's Rights held in Brussels in 2010.
16. Member of the EU Delegation to the Kyrgyz Republic, interview with author, Bishkek, 5 February 2013.
17. http://eeas.europa.eu/delegations/kyrgyzstan/eu_kyrgyzstan/human_rights/ index_en.htm
18. Respondent 12, interview with author, Bishkek, 16 February 2013.
19. http://www.labrys.kg/index.php?cat=20 (accessed 26 June 2013)
20. http://indigo.kg/o-nas/proektyi (accessed 27 June 2013)
21. http://pathfinder.kloop.kg/o-deyatelnosti-lgbt-organizacii-pathfinder/ (accessed 16 July 2013)
22. http://pathfinder.kloop.kg/my-zhdem-tebya-lgbt-xristianskaya-gruppa/ (accessed 16 July 2013)
23. http://bishkekfeminists.wordpress.com/about/ (accessed 16 July 2013)
24. http://bishkekfeminists.kloop.kg/2013/05/07/ky-rgy-zstan-nedelya-protivos- toyaniya-gomofobii-i-transfobii-2013/ (accessed 16 July 2013)
25. Figure given in Kyrgyz Som (KGS11, 316.5).
26. Respondent 12, interview with author, Bishkek, 21 February 2013.
27. Respondent 8, interview with author, Bishkek, 20 February 2013.
28. Respondent 7, interview with author, Bishkek, 13 February 2013.
29. Respondent 3, interview with author, Bishkek, 13 February 2013.
30. Respondent 7, interview with author, Bishkek, 13 February 2013.
31. Respondent 4, interview with author, Bishkek, 4 February 2013.
32. Respondent 12, interview with author, Bishkek, 16 February 2013.
33. Respondent 11, interview with author, Bishkek, 21 February 2013.
34. Respondent 9, interview with author, Bishkek, 8 February 2013.
35. Respondent 3, interview with author, Bishkek, 13 February 2013.
36. Respondent 7, interview with author, Bishkek, 13 February 2013.
37. Respondent 4, interview with author, Bishkek, 4 February 2013.
38. At the time of interviews, a federal bill prohibiting the "propaganda of homosexuality" had just passed its first reading in the Russian State Duma. The law, which in its final form forbade the "propaganda of non-traditional sexual relations to minors," was subsequently passed on 11 June 2013.
39. Respondent 7, interview with author, Bishkek, 13 February 2013.
40. Respondent 4, interview with author, Bishkek, 4 February 2013.
41. Respondent 7, interview with author, Bishkek, 13 February 2013.
42. Representative of the US Embassy, interview with author, Bishkek, 20 February 2013.
43. Respondent 2, interview with author, Bishkek, 9 February 2013.
44. Respondent 3, interview with author, Bishkek, 13 February 2013.
45. Respondent 10, interview with author, Bishkek, 4 February 2013.
46. Respondent 8, interview with author, Bishkek, 20 February 2013.
47. Respondent 3, interview with author, Bishkek, 13 February 2013.
48. Respondent 2, interview with author, Bishkek, 9 February 2013.

49. Tolekan Ismailova, interview with author, Bishkek, 14 February 2013.
50. Respondent 10, interview with author, Bishkek, 4 February 2013.
51. Respondent 5, interview with author, Bishkek, 4 February 2013.
52. Respondent 1, interview with author, Bishkek, 6 February 2013.
53. Respondent 3, interview with author, Bishkek, 13 February 2013.
54. Respondent 12, interview with author, Bishkek, 16 February 2013.

References

Axyonova, Vera. 2011. "The EU-Central Asia Human Rights Dialogues: Making a Difference?" *Policy Brief* 16. www.fride.org/download/PB_16_EUCAM.pdf (accessed 21 June 2013).

Boonstra, Jos and Jacqueline Hale. 2010. "EU Assistance to Central Asia: Back to the Drawing Board?" EUCAM Working Paper 8.

Cherikov, Sadyrbek. 2014. "Pravozashchitnye NPO v Kyrgyzstane. Rozhdeny, chtoby zashchishchat sodomiyu?" [Human Rights NGOs in Kyrgyzstan. Born to defend sodomy?]*Centrasia.ru*, http://www.centrasia.ru/newsA. php?st=1391440800 (accessed 14 February 2014).

Delcour, Laure. 2011. *Shaping the Post-Soviet Space? EU Policies and Approaches to Region-Building.* Farnham: Ashgate.

European Union Fundamental Rights Agency. 2013. "European Union Lesbian, Gay, Bisexual and Transgender Survey: Results at a Glance." http://fra.europa. eu/sites/default/files/eu-lgbt-survey-results-at-a-glance_en.pdf (accessed 20 June 2013).

Hudson, Ray. 2000. "One Europe or Many? Reflections on Becoming European." *Transactions of the Institute of British Geographers* 25(4): 409–426.

Human Rights Watch. 2008a. "Kyrgyzstan: Halt Anti-Gay Raids." http://www.hrw. org/en/news/2008/04/16/kyrgyzstan-halt-anti-gay-raids (accessed 21 July 2012).

———. 2008b. "These Everyday Humiliations: Violence against Lesbians, Bisexual Women, and Transgender Men in Kyrgyzstan." http://www.hrw.org/ news/2008/10/06/kyrgyzstan-protect-lesbians-and-transgender-men-abuse (accessed 21 July 2012).

———. 2014. "'They Said We Deserved This' Police Violence Against Gay and Bisexual Men in Kyrgyzstan." http://www.hrw.org/node/122474 (accessed 31 January 2013).

Karagapolova, Inga. 2010. *Stories of Gay and Bisexual Men: Kyrgyzstan 2009–2010.* Bishkek: Labrys.

Kim, Younkyoo and Fabio Indeo. 2013. "The New Great Game in Central Asia Post 2014: The US 'New Silk Road' Strategy and Sino-Russian Rivalry." *Communist and Post-Communist Studies* 46(2): 275–286.

Kirey, Anna (ed.). 2007. *Gomoseksualnost: Realii Kyrgyzstana. [Homosexuality: The Reality of Kyrgyzstan]* Bishkek: Labrys.

Kollman, Kelly, and Matthew Waites. 2009. "The Global Politics of Lesbian, Gay, Bisexual and Transgender Human Rights: An Introduction." *Contemporary Politics* 15(1): 1–17.

Mamatov, Arslan. 2009. "Kyrgyzstan: NGOs Assail Proposed Legal Changes as 'Threat to Democracy'." *Eurasianet*, http://www.eurasianet.org/departments/ insightb/articles/eav031009a.shtml (accessed 14 August 2013).

Manners, Ian. 2002. "Normative Power Europe: A Contradiction in Terms?" *Journal of Common Market Studies* 40(2): 235–258.

——. 2010. "Global Europa: Mythology of the European Union in World Politics." *Journal of Common Market Studies* 48(1): 67–87.

——. 2013. "Assessing the Decennial, Reassessing the Global: Understanding European Normative Power in Global Politics." *Cooperation and Conflict* 48(2): 304–329.

Manners, Ian and Richard Whitman. 1998. "Towards Identifying the International Identity of the European Union: A Framework for Analysis of the EU's Network of Relations." *Journal of European Integration* 21(3): 231–249.

Melvin, Neil. 2012. "The EU Needs a New Values-Based Realism for its Central Asia Strategy." *Policy Brief* 28. http://www.fride.org/publication/1075/the-eu-needs-a-new-central-asia-strategy (accessed 14 June 2013).

Møller, Bjorn. 2005. "The EU as a Security Actor." *DIIS Report* 12, Copenhagen: Danish Institute for International Studies.

Rettman, Andrew. 2013. "NATO Chief: EU Soft Power is 'No Power at all'." *EU Observer*, http://euobserver.com/defence/120046 (accessed 20 January 2014).

Rupp, Leila J. 2011. "The Persistence of the Transnational Organizing: The Case of the Homophile Movement." *American Historical Review* 116(4): 1014–1039.

Soros Foundation – Kyrgyzstan. 2007. "Access to Health Care for LGBT People in Kyrgyzstan." http://www.opensocietyfoundations.org/reports/access-health-care-lgbt-people-kyrgyzstan (accessed 20 June 2013).

Trilling, David. 2012. "Kyrgyzstan Bans Documentary about Gay Muslims." *Eurasianet*, 28 September. http://www.eurasianet.org/node/65976 (accessed 30 June 2013).

Van der Veur, Dennis. 2004. *Kyrgyzstan: "The Country of Human Rights"…But Not for Homosexuals!* COC Netherlands/HIVOS. http://www.msmgf.org/index.cfm/id/11/aid/210 (accessed 20 June 2013).

Wilkinson, Cai. 2013. "One Billion Rising Comes to Bishkek." *Eurasianet*, 13 February. http://www.eurasianet.org/node/66557 (accessed 14 August 2013).

Wilkinson, Cai and Anna Kirey. 2010. "What's in a Name? The Personal and Political Meanings of LGBT for Non-Heterosexual and Transgender Youth in Kyrgyzstan." *Central Asian Survey* 29(4): 485–499.

Youngs, Richard. 2010. *The EU's Role in World Politics*. London: Routledge.

4

"In Europe It's Different": Homonationalism and Peripheral Desires for Europe

Gianmaria Colpani and Adriano José Habed

The imperative to resist nationalist and racist co-optations of sexual diversities in Western societies has taken center stage in both queer theory and politics in recent years. In the contemporary Huntingtonian scenario (Huntington 1996) in which cultural differences are mobilized for exclusionary and violent purposes, openness to sexual diversity is being increasingly hailed as a quintessential feature of Western societies that must be defended against racialized others. As Haritaworn et al. (2008: 86) point out:

> Freedom of speech, democracy, women's liberation and gay rights are all invoked to legitimate Islamophobia and attack the rights of all racialised people... [T]hese attacks have direct consequences on the lives of all people of colour, especially those among us whose phenotype is read as "Muslim."

Hence, sexual minorities, once regarded as an inner threat to the social order and Western civilization at large, today enjoy increasing political and cultural recognition at the expense of racialized others. This shift has been termed "homonationalism" (Puar 2007). Today's Europe, perceiving and establishing itself as a fortress constantly under siege, offers particularly fertile ground for the articulation of homonationalist configurations.

Such a racialization of sexual politics has been mainly conceived of as an instrument mobilized within Western nation-states. In this chapter, instead, we try to move beyond methodological nationalism – conceptualized by Ulrich Beck (2005) as the distinctive mark (and limitation) of any production of knowledge that deploys and reproduces the nation-state as a privileged epistemic framework – in order to approach what we may call "European homonationalism." This does not mean that we adopt a comparative perspective and draw different European national settings together in order to highlight the homogenous workings of homonationalism across the continent (homonationalist imaginaries and practices operate heterogeneously, if not contradictorily, in different European locations). We propose rather to understand the *Europeanness* of European homonationalism as anchored to the idea of Europe emerging precisely from such heterogeneity: from the frictions and negotiations between national and European institutions and LGBT social movements.

In particular, these frictions and negotiations manifest themselves at the borders of Europe. We approach them from Italy – peripheral on the European map of liberal sexual politics because of its lack of LGBT civil rights and its rampant homophobia. A widespread Italian imaginary, one that we attempt to track in this chapter, posits Europe as a powerful horizon for those committed to the achievement of sexual rights and social justice. Yet, we suggest, this peripheral orientation toward Europe is one of the mechanisms through which Europe establishes itself as a space of sexual exceptionalism and ultimately as a sexual fortress under siege. Our aim is thus to deconstruct such an orientation – its framing of Europe as sexually exceptionalist and as a powerful rescuer of its own peripheries – by reading legal texts, juridical commentaries, LGBT and queer activist discourses as well as sociological literature.[1] A careful look at those texts shows crucial gaps between the power with which Europe is endowed at its borders, and the power that Europe actually holds. Our readings are located in the interstices between those formative texts and their respective disciplinary boundaries, for such interstices seem to provide the most fertile ground for the crystallization of a certain idea of Europe whose main features and workings we aim to chart.

European homonationalism: beyond methodological nationalism

As soon as the term "homonationalism" appeared within the horizon of feminist, queer, and postcolonial critical theories (Puar 2007), European critics also began to think more carefully about homonationalist formations in Europe (e.g. Haritaworn et al. 2008; Mepschen et al. 2010; Kosnick 2011).[2] However, they have paid little attention to the extent and ways in which homonationalist imaginaries and practices participate in the construction of Europe itself, in the very definition of the continent's Europeanness. For this reason, this chapter aims not to think homonationalism "in" Europe but rather European homonationalism.

Discussing homonationalism in the Netherlands, Mepschen, Duyvendak and Tonkens (2010: 963) observe that the Dutch case provides "quintessential examples of the sexualization of European debates on the vicissitudes of cultural and religious diversity." Yet, the methodological nationalism grounding their own as well as other critics' analyses, while opening up a space for sophisticated questionings of the mechanisms of reproduction of the nation-state, does not thematize Europe itself as a *problematic*:[3] Europe surfaces merely as a background against which complex national histories unfold or, at best, as nothing but the sum of its national singularities. This is indeed how Éric Fassin (2010) qualifies today's Europe – as an assemblage of national identities and not as a peculiar construct of its own. This is so because, according to Fassin, contemporary Europe does not counter but rather sustains nationalist political projects. As he puts it:

> [A] reversal has taken place in the past few years regarding national identities in Europe. Nationalism used to be invoked, in France and elsewhere, in opposition to European institutions...Today, on the contrary,...the European Union is more and more presented as the best guarantee for the protection of national identities. This involves shifting populist resentment from the cosmopolitan Eurocrats (above) to the non-European migrants (outside)...It is in this context that sexual democracy enters the political agenda in Europe. (Fassin 2010: 515)

Thus, for Fassin, homonationalism materializes in Europe insofar as the nation-state maintains a monopoly on our collective imaginaries. Following this perspective, there is no such thing as European homonationalism, but only homonationalisms taking place in different European national settings. In so doing, Fassin sutures the gap between the national and the European scale; Europe *is* its national members. Hence, his emphasis on the European scale tips toward methodological nationalism and proves unable to grasp the Europeanness of European homonationalism, which would account for the role of homonationalism in the making of contemporary Europe. In this chapter, we argue instead that the gap between the European and the national scales cannot be overlooked because it plays a formative role in the making of Europeanness itself.

The tendency to read Europe as the sum of its national members, explicit in Fassin's analysis and implicit in those who take national contexts to be representative of Europe as a whole (Mepschen et al. 2010; Mepschen and Duyvendak 2012), translates into two sympto-matic textual erasures. First, it overshadows the European scale: Europe is never thematized as a material problematic and as an agent itself, but randomly registered as a rhetorical device at work in *national* narra-tives. Hence, it becomes a background against which the nation-state is preserved as a privileged object of analysis. Second, it systematically erases both Eastern and Southern European peripheries. A case in point is Fassin's claim (rooted in the French and the German contexts) that an aversion against the European political project no longer characterizes nationalist projects in Europe as long as Europe has become, in his view, the best guarantor of national identities. Contemporary nationalisms in Central and Eastern Europe and their strong anti-European slant stand in stark contrast to his portrayal.

A pervasive methodological nationalism sustains the disappearance of these peripheries in most attempts to conceptualize homonationalism on a European scale. Insofar as the nation-state remains the privileged epistemological frame to apprehend the territorializing and racializing workings of certain liberal sexual politics, not only will the European scale systematically disappear from view, but few European locations such as France, Germany, or the Netherlands – where elusive princi-ples of "gender equality" and "openness to sexual diversity" are hailed as national cultural legacies and mobilized against the alleged values of migrant communities – will continue to stand metonymically for homonationalist "Europe" as a whole.

We do not suggest that de-centralizing North-Western sexual politics and turning toward European peripheries – where nationalist senti-ments often coagulate around homophobia rather than "sexual democ-racy" – must defy any attempt to profile what we may call "European homonationalism," or even disclose the colonizing effects of the very term "homonationalism" (Kulpa 2011; Kevin Moss, Chapter 10 in this volume). Robert Kulpa, for instance, in polemic with Jasbir Puar, asks almost rhetorically, "what is so necessarily wrong with the willingness to be recognised as a part of the national community." He asserts that "lesbian and gay communities in CEE [Central and Eastern Europe] and elsewhere may well embrace national ideas...as one of the methods of their struggle" (Kulpa 2011: 56). But a de-centralization of the name "Europe" should not mark a departure from recent critical attempts at tracking the forms of connivance between liberal sexual politics and nationalism. A turn toward European peripheries shall rather open up the category "homonationalism" to its contradictory European assemblages; that is, to the contemporary collusions of liberal sexual politics with nationalisms, the European integration and enlargement processes, racism, border policing in fortress Europe, and the policing of Europeanness itself in the negotiations of power between centers and peripheries of the continent. In this chapter we take an early step in this direction by focusing on the sexual exceptionalism marking the emergence of "rainbow Europe" as a powerful object of desire at the borders of the continent.

The term homonationalism itself undeniably deploys a certain emphasis on the workings of national sovereignty. Yet, when coining the term in *Terrorist Assemblages* (2007), focusing on the global landscape shaped by the US "war on terror" and on the US domestic space, Puar addresses a scenario extending beyond the nation-state. More precisely, she considers the national scale as always already exceeding itself and sliding into the biopolitical manufacturing of populations on a broader scale. For her, the rehabilitation of certain homosexual subjects through state benevolence and the concomitant queering of racialized "others" do not take place entirely within the mechanisms of national sovereignty. Rather, state sovereign power operates in concert with, and mutual dependence on, what Michel Foucault has termed "biopolitics" (Puar 2007: xi–xiv, 32–36).

Indeed, in a rough attempt to define biopolitics (or security) vis-à-vis sovereignty and discipline, Foucault suggests that sovereignty is exercised over a territory, discipline over the body, and biopolitics over populations (Foucault 2007: 11). However, he also emphasizes that this schematic rendering of the three does not hold, not only because such a discrete spatialization fails to account for the interventions of each technique of power in all of these spatial domains (territory, body, population), but more generally because the three techniques never operate independently from one another. As he argues:

> There is not the legal age, the disciplinary age, and then the age of security [or biopolitics]…In reality you have a series of complex edifices in which…what above all changes is the dominant characteristic, or more exactly, the system of correlation between juridico-legal mechanisms, disciplinary mechanisms, and mechanisms of security. (Foucault 2007: 8)

Despite the fact that in other passages Foucault more or less unwittingly leaves room for a discrete temporalization of the series sovereignty-discipline-biopolitics, here he suggests to observe the spatially and temporally contingent *systems of correlation* between these different techniques of power, as many of his readers have observed (Agamben 1998; Butler 2004; Schlosser 2008). It is such a reception of Foucault that informs Puar's work on homonationalism: neither a focus on national sovereignty alone, nor a privileging of biopolitics over sovereignty (population over citizenry, the global or transnational over the national); rather, an emphasis on the contemporary arrangements of different scales and techniques of power.

Along these lines, our aim is to suggest a conceptualization of homonationalism and Europeanness that does not neglect the specificities of the European scale and that simultaneously brings into focus the European peripheries that are often invisibilized in these debates. The Italian case is a point of departure that forces us to turn toward the European scale. In Italy, as much as in other European peripheries, LGBT civil rights, or even "sexual freedom" broadly understood, are constantly identified with Europe and Europeanness against the conservative domestic space, thereby inflecting sexual freedom with geopolitically specific boundaries and sustaining an idea of Europe as "the avatar of both freedom and modernity," "the privileged site where sexual radicalism can and does take place" (Butler 2008: 2).

Europe does not hold sovereign power over its territory on matters of sexual politics, but this by no means signals a dematerialization of normative power on the European scale. Indeed, as Kelly Kollman (2009) has shown in her study on the adoption of same-sex unions in different European countries, "soft law hits harder."[4] According to Kollman,

> advocacy groups working at both the national and transnational levels have been able to knit...disparate supranational norms, decisions and policies together to create a soft law norm – a shared, nonbinding principle – for the legal recognition of same-sex relationship. (2009: 38)

In her contribution to this volume (Chapter 5), Kollman stresses that this process is not monolithic and emphasizes the role played by national political subjects of different sorts in crafting European norms and materializing them locally.

Now, a focus on the systems of correlations between sovereignty, discipline, and biopolitics offers a useful lens to start looking at homonationalism on the European scale from a particular (peripheral) perspective. While Kollman considers European "soft law norms" primarily as affirmative means that mediate between the European scale and national sovereignties contributing to implement legal recognition of same-sex relationships in different national settings, we look at those norms critically: as disciplinary and biopolitical mechanisms that foster and sustain, in concert with other texts, European *normativities*.

In Europe it's different

Unsurprisingly, Europe figures as a privileged horizon for the demand of LGBT civil rights in Italy. Europe in the first place establishes itself as a guarantor of such rights. In March 2012 the Italian Court of Cassation (the highest tier of Italy's juridical system) decided on a case of a gay couple who got married in the Netherlands but were refused a transcription of marriage by Italian municipal officers.[5] The ruling confirmed the impossibility of their marriage being registered because same-sex relationships are not recognized by the Italian legislation. Yet, while articulating their decision, Italian magistrates mobilized the idea of Europe in ways that are particularly interesting for our discussion.

The first part of the ruling develops the Court's argument against the registration of same-sex marriage. This argument is constructed around the interpretation of Article 29 of the Italian Constitution, which "establish[es] that partners must be of a different sex." Although many argue that the ambiguous formulation of Article 29 leaves room for marriage to be rethought beyond the heterosexual paradigm (Pugiotto 2010; Gattuso 2012), the Court of Cassation, in the wake of a previous judgment by the Italian Constitutional Court on a similar case,[6] prefers to hold on to "a consolidated and thousand-year notion of marriage [that] postulates sex difference between the partners,"[7] thereby prohibiting the registration of same-sex marriages contracted abroad.

The second part of the ruling, however, offers a more affirmative stance in favor of same-sex marriage. Here, the Court of Cassation turns to Europe, and more specifically to the case *Schalk and Kopf v Austria* by the European Court of Human Rights (ECtHR).[8] According to the Italian Court of Cassation, *Schalk and Kopf* acknowledges that "the right to marry...includes the right for same-sex couples to marry" for the first time.[9] This way, the view of marriage as a "consolidated and thousand-year tradition" preserved in the first part of the ruling is subsequently put into question by means of reference to the European ruling. Consequently, the impossibility to register same-sex marriages is "due not to their non-existence or invalidity, but to their *inaptness* at producing... juridical effects in the Italian legal order."[10]

LGBT activists and jurists in favor of same-sex unions found this ruling to be of enormous significance. The ruling was registered as a double success, for since 2008 the policy activist organization Certi Diritti and the network of lawyers for LGBT rights Rete Lenford have been promoting the campaign "civic affirmation" (*affermazione civile*), consisting precisely of gay and lesbian couples asking for the registration of their marriage (contracted abroad) by their municipality and bringing the case to the Courts after the expected refusal (Certi Diritti 2008). The ruling by the Court of Cassation confirmed, in the view of many, the potential of this strategy. In a radio interview, Paolo Patanè (2012), then president of the leading Italian gay organization Arcigay, referred to it as "a Copernican revolution," because the legislator now cannot ignore what the Court of Cassation (but also the ECtHR) mandates. Similarly, jurist Stefano Rodotà (2012) understood this ruling as "a gift from Europe," while magistrate Marco Gattuso (2012) commented that "who is against the new notion of... marriage should now ask for a turnabout of the European Court." It is thus unsurprising to see Europe also mobilized at Italian Gay Pride demonstrations: "In Europe it's different," read the slogan of the 2009 Turin Gay Pride. Europe is unanimously called upon as a guarantor of same-sex unions against Italy's backwardness.

Such a mobilization of Europe conceals the fact that Europe actually holds little or no ability to implement directly any sort of national legislation concerning gay rights. When LGBT activists and progressive jurists praise the ruling by the Italian Court of Cassation, as well as its use of "Europe" as a step toward the recognition of same-sex unions, not only do they seem to forget that the ruling is ultimately a negative one, but also that the ECtHR itself set the terms for that rejection. Indeed, its stance in favor of the recognition of gay marriage notwithstanding, the *Schalk and Kopf* ruling concluded by stating that "as matters stand, the question whether or not to allow same-sex marriage is left to regulation by the national law,"[11] a principle articulated by Article 12 of the European Convention of Human Rights (ECHR).

The straightforward orientation toward Europe that informs much of the Italian gay liberal discourse is therefore ambiguous. As political scientists make clear, local political subjects often know very well that their mobilization of Europe is of a strategic nature and that the name "Europe" in the context of these disputes over sexual politics is meant to be performative rather than properly referential (Kollman, Chapter 5 in this volume; Ayoub 2013). Yet this strategic deployment of Europe (whose unilateral privileging of gay marriage and other forms of state-sanctioned recognition as central political goals would deserve a critical discussion of its own) also contributes to craft a wider imaginary.

Europe emerges under the sign of sexual exceptionalism: as a space where sexual freedom can and does take place and as a subject able to grant such freedom to others. This emergence depends at least on two disavowals. First, the idea of a "rainbow Europe" must rhetorically erase several European peripheries from its very definition. In this paradox lies the strategic relevance of the idea of Europe for peripheral liberal sexual politics. Second, the idea of Europe as a subject able to grant rights and freedom to others (including its own peripheral members) conceals the limits set to Europe's sovereignty. These limits emerge in the negotiations between European and Italian Courts discussed above.

Focusing on the post-9/11 American "war on terror", Puar (2007: 4, emphasis added) observes that "homosexual subjects who have *limited legal rights* within the US civic context gain *significant representational currency* when situated within the global scene of the war on terror." Such an overrepresentation of LGBT citizens – similar to the overrepresentation of Europe at its borders as an exceptional bearer of sexual freedom and the ultimate guarantor of civil rights – does not merely represent, but accomplishes a disciplinary work that prescribes a particular model of the *representable* subject. The homosexual subject profiled by the European ruling *Schalk and Kopf*, and emerging in all its glory through the negotiations between the ECtHR and the Italian Court of Cassation, is a disciplined and disciplinary gay liberal subject. Granted representational (yet not actual) equality through inclusion into the notions of "marriage" (Article 12 of the ECHR) and "family life" (Article 14 of the same European chart), this subject owes to Europe its disciplinary power; a power emphasized at the borders of the continent where that subject surfaces at the crossroads of a desire for sexual freedom and a feeling of peripherality translating into desire for Europe.

Let us unpack more carefully this particular articulation – that is, the emergence of a European disciplinary gay liberal subject from the periphery of the continent – by turning to Marzio Barbagli and Asher Colombo's sociological work *Omosessuali moderni* [Modern homosexuals] (2007). *Omosessuali moderni* pursues the difficult and to some extent forerunning task of drawing an accurate portrait of the experiences of, and knowledge about, "gays and lesbians in Italy," as reads the subtitle of the publication. The title refers to a "modern" type of homosexual relation distinct from the forms allegedly taken by homosexuality in the past:

> Unlike the previous relations, [those among modern homosexuals] are not structured on the polarization of roles and identities – adult/youngster, active/passive, masculine/feminine. They are no longer characterized by any kind of social or sexual asymmetry. There is no superior and inferior position, nor domination and submission. In principle, both partners hold the same power and status. The sexual relationship no longer involves a subject and an object, but is characterized by versatility and reciprocity. (Barbagli and Colombo 2007: 231)

By terming the homosexuality sketched above as "modern", Barbagli and Colombo posit other forms of homosexual relation as pre-modern. This view not only conceives the model of the "modern homosexual" as naturally overcoming its pre-modern ancestors, but, in so doing, it also cleanses liberal definitions of gay subjectivity from any sort of power dynamic. Pre-modern forms of homosexuality are understood indeed as fostering same-sex relations imbued with power differences (along axes of age and class) and resting on a strict active/passive divide complicit with patriarchal gender patterns. Against such a portrayal of pre-modern homosexuality, the "modern homosexual" functions as a regulatory and desirable ideal. As we will see, that ideal is geopolitically located in Europe.

As an Italian gay website (CulturaGay 2007) puts it to present the second edition of Barbagli and Colombo's work, "'Modern and European homosexuals'…is not the title but certainly the meaning of the new edition of *Omosessuali moderni.*" Indeed, Barbagli and Colombo state that modern homosexuals appeared first in Central-Northern Europe, and only then on the Mediterranean shores. Hence they explain the delay: "maybe over here pederasty and the active/passive dichotomy were more important than elsewhere and survived longer" (Barbagli and Colombo 2007: 274). A curious conversion takes place from the differential temporality suggested by the modern/pre-modern dichotomy to the differential spatiality that posits Central-Northern Europe as the birthplace of modern homosexuals. Italy – and, as we will see, the Mediterranean at large – is configured as one particular spatial and temporal periphery of Europe, where homosexual relationships of "versatility and reciprocity" are haunted by pre-modern forms of queerness.

From the Italian perspective, the "modern homosexual" is the subject we all shall become, while Europe is the place that holds the power to make this phantasy come true. The orientation toward Europe that surfaces in Barbagli and Colombo's account of modern homosexuality echoes segments of the Italian gay liberal discourse, such as in the slogans of the Turin Gay Prides in 2009 ("In Europe it's different"), 2011 ("How far is Piedmont from Europe?"), and 2012 ("We don't ask for the moon...it's Europe that demands it"). If this imaginary binds sexual freedom and sexual rights to Europe and produces the figure of the modern homosexual as a disciplinary subject able to perform Europeanness itself, we must pose a question concerning the boundaries and exclusions that such a performance brings along. In fact, performances are practices of boundary making.

European performativities

Critical theorists of Mediterranean Europe have shown how Europe has historically come to define itself through the abjection of its Mediterranean shores and a denial of the cultural and material continuities between Europe and its others that the Mediterranean represents (Dainotto 2007; Chambers 2008; Cassano 2012).[12] Barbagli and Colombo take part in this particular making of Europe by sketching their "modern homosexual" partly against the background of another figure: the "Mediterranean homosexual" (Dall'Orto 1990). Indeed, at the beginning of their chapter on "The birth of modern homosexuals" (*La nascita degli omosessuali moderni*), the two sociologists observe:

> The system of classification and interpretation that prevails nowadays in Western countries is based on the heterosexual-homosexual dichotomy...Actually, this dichotomy is a historic-social construction that has gradually established itself in the West but has not yet acquired the same importance in other parts of the world. After all, ... also in the southern regions of our country such a system of classification cohabitates with the remains of an earlier one that opposes active to passive. Still today, some people living in Puglia or Sicily consider a man who has sex with another man not to be homosexual but, under certain conditions, to be heterosexual because active. (Barbagli and Colombo 2007: 229)

Although the two authors never explicitly mention Mediterranean homosexuality, their portrayal of these pre-modern understandings and embodiments of same-sex desire coincides with Giovanni Dall'Orto's description of Mediterranean homosexuality: "Its most salient characteristic is the sharp dichotomy between the one who is considered the 'homosexual' in the strict sense, that is the one who plays the insertee role, as against the one who plays the insertor role [the 'active']" (1990: 796). A strict active/passive divide, hence its alignment and complicity with patriarchal gender patterns is what characterizes, according to Dall'Orto, the Mediterranean type of homosexuality.[13]

It is not our aim to dispute the historical and ethnographic merits or flaws of the figure of the "Mediterranean homosexual" or of its modern counterpart. However, it is worth tracking some of the discursive workings of such figures in the contemporary mapping of Europe through liberal sexual politics. Barbagli and Colombo's fiction of modern homosexual relations "based on the principle of equality" (2007: 231) profiles the disciplinary sexual subjectivity to be performed in order to become Europeans. But that figure, especially if read together with Dall'Orto's portrayal of Mediterranean homosexuality, also signals the operation of a discourse that frames the Mediterranean as a limit to Europe and demands a departure from the Mediterranean in order to fully accomplish that performance of Europeanness.

The asymmetry is worth noting: while the "modern homosexual" is framed primarily in *temporal* terms, the Mediterranean one is a figure strongly located in *space*. Such an asymmetry can be easily recomposed as long as "modern" stands for "properly European" while "Mediterranean" carries pre-modern connotations. Yet, it may be even more instructive not to gloss over that space-time distinction so quickly, and ask what the temporal framing of modern homosexuality versus the spatial framing of the Mediterranean type means. If the spatial or geographical framing of the "Mediterranean homosexual" constructs it as a subjectivity bound to its environment, the temporal framing of the "modern homosexual" produces an unbound figure, where time is thought of as an empty container that does not exercise any sort of constraint – while space binds, time and progress set free.

Let us remark that the "modern homosexual" is not disembodied, as a quick turn to standard narratives of modernity (and their critics) may suggest. That figure does have a body, and a very sexualized one. Barbagli and Colombo (2007: 231) go as far as to suggest that modern homosexuals are, in principle, sexually versatile. Thus embodiment is not at stake. The "modern homosexual" is rather *disembedded*. The "Mediterranean homosexual", instead, is fully embedded and bound to its space. Its emergences and disappearances are explained via reference to relations of power other than sexuality (mainly operating along axes of gender and age), and to material modes of production (the

Mediterranean type is allegedly characteristic of pre-industrial societies) (Dall'Orto 1990).[14] This turns the "Mediterranean homosexual" into a metonymic figure of the Mediterranean itself.

It is at this point that discipline and biopolitics fold into one another. While the model of modern homosexuality operates on the scale of the body and prescribes a specific subjectivity able to sexually perform Europeanness and modernity, the "Mediterranean homosexual" operates discursively on the scale of the population. This second figure does not merely identify a particular homosexual type, but marks the Mediterranean space as a whole and its inhabitants as backward and grotesque. Most importantly, the Mediterranean marks a point of contact and continuity of Europe with its others; because, as Dall'Orto (1990: 796) pontificates, the term "Mediterranean homosexuality" "serves to designate a paradigm of homosexual behavior found in the Latin countries of Europe and the Americas, in the Islamic countries of the Mediterranean, as well as in the Balkans." While the concept of modern homosexuality rehabilitates certain homosexual subjects as legitimate inhabitants of the European space, the "Mediterranean homosexual," as a figure, contributes to queering the Mediterranean as a liminal space, a fissure that must be sutured by embracing a straight orientation toward Europe.

At this particular juncture, Italy occupies a position on the European map of liberal sexual politics similar to the position that Merje Kuus (2004) ascribes to Central Europe in the context of the 2004 Europe's eastern enlargement. According to Kuus, both EU and NATO enlargement processes have been framed through a dichotomy between Europe "proper" and its East. Construed in-between the two poles, not-yet fully European yet on their way to Europeanness, Central European accession countries signal the operations of a discourse that re-inscribes, rather than solves, the long-lasting dichotomy between Europe and its (Eastern) other within. This is so because the access of Central European countries to the EU and NATO has not dismantled the divide between East and West; that divide has rather been negotiated by the accession countries themselves through a shifting of Europe's borders further East and the orientalization of their own eastern neighbors (particularly, Russia) (Kuus 2004; see also Bakic-Hayden 1995). More often than not, struggles around sexual politics lie at the core of such re-inscriptions of otherness and, in turn, those geopolitical rearrangements influence the particular unfolding of sexual politics in different locations in Europe (Kulpa and Mizielińska 2011; Ayoub and Paternotte 2014).

This makes both eastern and southern peripheries privileged standpoints to observe the European construction because, as Kuus (2004: 484) argues, "[c]onstructions of Europe from the margins of Europe could indeed provide a particularly useful mirror of the exclusions and divisions that still form an integral part of the idea of Europe." Yet, this mirroring does not merely *reflect* the idea of Europe produced at its power centers. A shift of the critical focus from the centers to the peripheries of the continent works rather *diffractively* and delivers us a different image of Europe, not as a monolith constructed against equally monolithic others, but as a "multitier patchwork Europe with varying degrees of Europeanness" and otherness (Kuus 2004: 475). Contemporary Europe acquires its shape through a constant re-inscription of otherness that "operates through multiple demarcations" (ibid.: 484) and "the reverberation of othering practices" (ibid.: 473) between centers and peripheries of the continent.

A spectacular (and spectacularized) instance of this chain of reverberations can be found in Lady Gaga's performance at the EuroPride in Rome in 2011. As the manifesto of the Pride made clear, Rome was not an accidental location for the European demonstration, for "[the] absence of attention and rights on GLBTQI issues places Italy dramatically outside of Europe, making a EuroPride in Rome particularly [significant]" (Roma EuroPride 2011). Notwithstanding the marketing-led and depoliticizing spirit that made it possible for Lady Gaga to "represent" European queers in Rome, she *did deliver* in fact a political speech:

> I look into the crowd and there is a plethora of European citizens aligned, knowing first hand that some of your governments still block the basic freedom of assembly... We have come so far from the days of Stonewall, but despite the political advances made in terms of our rights and visibility as LGBT people, sadly the truth and the fact is that homophobia and anti-gay violence and bullying are alive and real... I would like to name a few of the governments, right now: Lithuania, Russia, Poland; we stand up for Budapest, for Lebanon, and for Middle Eastern countries. (Lady Gaga 2011)

Italy disappeared from the picture despite the explicit choice of Rome for the European demonstration, which was meant to mark the Italian context vis-à-vis the rest of the continent. One wonders whether gay pride was being celebrated and politically articulated in Rome on a European scale, or rather a European pride (and a specific idea of Europe sustaining it) being manufactured from the southern periphery of the continent at the expense of racialized others and by concealing the internal fractures characterizing today's patchwork Europe.

Conclusion: a southern perspective

The orientation toward Europe informing most of the Italian gay liberal imaginary manifests its disciplinary and biopolitical workings in many of its textual, as well as non-textual, materializations. Running after a largely fictional gay modernity, Italy is supposed to dis-identify from any other imaginable orientation – primarily toward the Mediterranean. As Phillip Ayoub and David Paternotte (2014) have observed in the context of a slightly different yet related discussion on ILGA-Europe, "the European frame has overshadowed other potential frames for political mobilization and organization." The reading of legal, activist, and sociological texts that we have proposed in this chapter shows a chain of reverberations of othering practices. This happens in a process through which the southern periphery of Europe refuses to fully identify as such and pushes instead the European borders further South, sustaining a configuration of Europe that installs the Mediterranean as a limit.

In the first section of this chapter, we have argued that an analysis of European homonationalism (not homonationalisms "in" Europe) must overcome methodological nationalism and foster instead an understanding of the intersections between geopolitics and sexual politics on the European scale. The southern and eastern peripheries of the continent, where claims for sexual rights often translate into desires for Europe, offer privileged perspectives on the making of "rainbow Europe" and its exclusions. Hence, in the second section, we have analyzed a particular instance of the negotiations between Europe and its periphery on the matter of sexual rights: a juridical case involving the Italian Court of Cassation, the European Court of Human Rights and Italian LGBT activists. This case illustrates how the idea of "rainbow Europe" emerges at the borders of the continent hand-in-hand with a disciplinary gay subject able to perform Europeanness itself. That subject largely corresponds to what Italian sociologists Barbagli and Colombo have called "the modern homosexual." In the last section of the chapter, we have argued that the profiling of such a disciplinary subject partly relies on the concomitant framing of the Mediterranean space and its populations as backward and grotesque: a limit posed to the achievement of "proper" Europeanness. Sexual politics proves to be central to the making and negotiations of European boundaries.

Perhaps not by chance, Franco Cassano concludes his *Southern Thought* (2012), a work devoted to returning the Mediterranean to its status as "subject of thought," with a chapter on Italian intellectual Pier Paolo Pasolini (1922–1975). Cassano identifies the roots of Pasolini's radical social critique in what he calls "the diversity of Pasolini's diversity," that is, the substantial gap between Pasolini's homosexuality and the so-called modern "gay culture" (2012: 87–88). Cassano's reading stands in sharp contrast with Barbagli and Colombo's *Omosessuali moderni*, in which they depict Pasolini as one of the most prominent Italian public figures who displayed remnants of a pre-modern understanding and embodiment of homosexuality (2007: 251–252, 272). Hence, they reduce the complexity of Pasolini's trenchant critique of modernity (Pasolini 1975), undeniably intertwined with his own experience of sexuality, to a lack of access to modern homosexuality.

The Mediterranean marks a limit. According to Italian anthropologist Giuseppe Burgio, the Mediterranean is located at the limit (or even *is* the limit) of our very understanding of homosexuality:

> The limit of that continental Europe, of that west that has also labeled, defined, constructed homosexuality as gay identity and from where most of the studies on homosexuality today proceed. Maybe a look from the south…can return unknown shades, perhaps some new questions. (Burgio 2008: 44)

The questions emerging on the Mediterranean shores concern, for Burgio, other forms of identity or, for that matter, of non-identity.[15] This chapter is surely committed to pose similar questions, yet our reading has focused more decisively on the sexualized making of a certain idea of Europe, rather than its possible alternatives. This is so because, while Burgio seems to understand "Europe" merely as the source and location of a particular disciplinary episteme, we argue that such episteme *makes* Europe. Our reading of the negotiations between the European Court of Human Rights and the Italian Court of Cassation, as well as the public debate coagulating around that exchange, shows that Europe acquires its shape through sexual politics. Europe is *both* the source (as Burgio observes) *and* the effect of sexual norms. Consequently, our attention throughout the chapter has oscillated between discipline and biopolitics, the profiling of a certain homosexual subject and the mapping of the European space itself.

A southern perspective, paradoxically located "in and out" of the European map of liberal sexual politics, can unmask not only the disciplinary mechanisms of European gay modernity but also its biopolitical operations – what we may call European homonationalism. The potential of this paradoxical position "in and out" was articulated in the program of the 2011 queer and anti-racist activist-based conference "In and Out of Sexual Democracies," organized in Rome by the collectives Facciamo Breccia and Orgogliosamente LGBTIQ:

> Provocatively, but responsibly, we would like to start up this reflection [on neo-liberal attempts to assimilate gender and sexuality within racist, nationalist and neo-imperialist politics] from our local point of view, Italy, a ghost sexual democracy placed simultaneously inside and outside the map of European sexual democracies: a country that ranks 74 in the gender gap world index, where the process of recognition of the LGBTIQ rights has not even begun, but which nonetheless draws extensively on the repertoires of sexuality and gender to enable nationalist, racist and identitarian rhetoric functional to the definition of thresholds for inclusion and exclusion. The sentence "in and out of sexual democracies" offers a look at these contradictions, from our "privileged" point of view: meaning from the point of view of a periphery which is European and Mediterranean. (Facciamo Breccia 2011)

A southern perspective – understood, as in the passage above, as a peripheral perspective within the continental map of liberal sexual politics – can shed light on the Europeanness of European homonationalism, namely on the ways in which homonationalism participates in the making of contemporary "rainbow Europe." If we *stay* "in and out" of the European map and we hold on to that paradoxical position, we may be able to track down and expose crucial yet otherwise invisible workings of power on the European scale.

Notes

We would like to thank our reading group in Utrecht for commenting on an earlier version of this chapter, particularly Goffredo Polizzi, who introduced to us the concept of "Mediterranean homosexuality" and shared his own critical perspective on it.

1. The translation of all Italian sources is ours, with the exception of Giovanni Dall'Orto's "Mediterranean Homosexuality" (1990), the program of the Italian conference "In and Out of Sexual Democracies" (Facciamo Breccia 2011), and the manifesto of the EuroPride in Rome (Roma EuroPride 2011).

2. Authors also employ notions other than "homonationalism." Some prefer "sexual nationalism" (e.g. Mepschen and Duyvendak 2012). The latter term seems to place more emphasis on the continuities between homonationalism and other articulations of the intersection between sexuality and nationalism. Yet, what gets lost in "sexual nationalism" is precisely the specificity of the access gained by certain queer bodies to the semiotic and material reproductions of the nation. In line with Puar's (2007) work, we maintain that the inclusion of homosexuality into the grammar of nationalism must be read with due attention to its specificities. Éric Fassin frames the problematic of homonationalism as the exclusionary working of what he had already termed "sexual democracy." The term problematically tends to decouple sexual democracy and homonationalism and to frame the latter as a mere cooptation and distortion of the former. Fassin (2011) himself has argued in favor of such a decoupling. This view not only oversimplifies the functioning of power, but, as Jin Haritaworn (2008) has remarked while commenting on Judith Butler's (2008) insistence on the logic of cooptation, it also recomposes too quickly a comfortable space (in theory and practice) for white Western gay constituencies.

3. See Butler 2008; Fassin 2010; El-Tayeb 2011 for partial exceptions.

4. Our analysis here is limited to the workings of European power on matters of sexual politics. Europe exercises its power differently in other domains, first (and importantly for the matter concerning this chapter) in the domain of border control. While we do follow Kollman in considering European sexual norms as "soft laws," laws and norms regulating movement within and across Europe's borders are anything but "soft," though also in this case a Foucauldian framework has proved very useful in analyzing the reconfigurations of power on a European scale. Critical geographers argue that theories of sovereignty alone cannot account for the management of contemporary Europe's borders, and must be supplemented with a focus on scattered operations of biopolitics such as out-sourcing and off-shoring of border control (Walters 2002, 2006; Andrijasevic 2010; Bialasiewicz 2012).

5. Corte di Cassazione, Sezione I Civile, Judgement 4184/2012, 15 March 2012, http://www.giurcost.org/casi_scelti/Cassazione/Cass.sent.4184-2012.htm (accessed 28 November 2013).

6. Corte Costituzionale, Judgement 138/2010, 2 April 2010, http://www.corte-costituzionale.it/actionSchedaPronuncia.do?anno=2010&numero=138 (accessed 28 November 2013).

7. Corte di Cassazione, Sezione I Civile, Judgement 4184/2012.

8. European Court of Human Rights, First Section, *Schalk and Kopf v Austria*, 24 June 2010, http://hudoc.echr.coe.int/sites/eng/pages/search.aspx?i=001-99605#{"itemid":["001-99605"]} (accessed 28 November 2013).

9. Corte di Cassazione, Sezione I Civile, Judgement 4184/2012.

10. Ibid. (Emphasis added).

11. European Court of Human Rights, First Section, *Schalk and Kopf v Austria*.

12. This abjection of the Mediterranean has received new impulse in the context of the current economic crisis. We can certainly read the mobilization of the acronym PIIGS (Portugal, Italy, Ireland, Greece and Spain) as an attempt to naturalize economic injustices; that is, a representational attempt of framing the economic conditions of Southern Europe (and Ireland), not as a structural

consequence of economic and political processes but rather as a symptom of deep-rooted backwardness associated with animality.

13. The figure of the "Mediterranean homosexual" has enjoyed a relatively positive reception even by some Italian critical scholars (Burgio 2008; Benadusi 2007; Ponzanesi 2014). Part of this reception stresses the affirmative potential of such a figure for displacing narratives of Eurocentric (sexual) modernity, yet avoiding the task of deconstructing its orientalist emergence in the first place. It is remarkable that historian Lorenzo Benadusi (2007, 7–8) questions the historical validity of the concept of "Mediterranean homosexuality," but less so that of "modern homosexuality."

14. For a critique of the logic binding patriarchal "cultures of honor" to a lack of industrial development (a logic informing Dall'Orto's account of Mediterranean homosexuality), see Maria Rosa Cutrufelli's *Disoccupata con onore* ("Unemployed with honor") (1975). As feminist historian Liliana Ellena (2011, 31) observes, "*Disoccupata con onore*, published in 1975, aims at reversing the widespread interpretation of the concept of honor as a mark of archaism to which women's subordination would be connected. It highlights instead its genealogy within the process of modernization, in the second half of the nineteenth century."

15. Burgio is among those who mobilize Dall'Orto's concept of "Mediterranean homosexuality" as a potentially affirmative counter-discourse challenging European gay modernity.

References

Agamben, Giorgio. 1998. *Homo Sacer: Sovereign Power and Bare Life*, trans. D. Heller-Roazen. Stanford: Stanford University Press.

Andrijasevic, Rutvica. 2010. "From Exception to Excess: Detention and Deportations across the Mediterranean Space." In *The Deportation Regime: Sovereignty, Space, and the Freedom of Movement*, eds. N. de Genova and N. Peutz. Durham: Duke University Press, 147–165.

Ayoub, Phillip M. 2013. "Cooperative Transnationalism in Contemporary Europe: Europeanization and Political Opportunities in LGBT Mobilization in the European Union." *European Political Science Review* 5(2): 279–310.

Ayoub, Phillip M. and David Paternotte. 2014. "Challenging Borders, Imagining Europe: Transnational LGBT Activism in a New Europe." In *Border Politics, Social Movements and Globalization*, eds. N. Naples and J. Bickham Méndez. New York: New York University Press.

Bakic-Hayden, Milica. 1995. "Nesting Orientalisms: The Case of Former Yugoslavia," *Slavic Review* 54(4): 917–931.

Barbagli, Marzio and Asher Colombo. 2007. *Omosessuali moderni: Gay e lesbiche in Italia*, second edition. Bologna: Il Mulino.

Beck, Ulrich. 2005. *Power in the Global Age*. Cambridge and Malden: Polity Press.

Benadusi, Lorenzo. 2007. "La storia dell'omosessualità maschile: linee di tendenza, spunti di riflessione e prospettive di ricerca." *Rivista di Sessuologia* 31(1): 1–15.

Bialasiewicz, Luiza. 2012. "Off-shoring and Out-sourcing the Borders of Europe: Libya and EU Border Work in the Mediterranean." *Geopolitics* 17(4): 843–866.

Burgio, Giuseppe. 2008. *Mezzi maschi: gli adolescenti gay dell'Italia meridionale. Una ricerca etnopedagogica*. Milano and Udine: Mimesis.

Butler, Judith. 2004. "Indefinite Detention." In *Precarious Life: The Power of Mourning and Violence*. London and New York: Verso, 50–100.

———. 2008. "Sexual Politics, Torture, and Secular Time." *The British Journal of Sociology* 59(1): 1–23.

Cassano, Franco. 2012. *Southern Thought and Other Essays on the Mediterranean*, trans. N. Bouchard and V. Ferme. New York: Fordham University Press.

Certi Diritti. 2008. "Affermazione Civile 2008–2010," 15 April 2008, http://www.certidiritti.it/index.php?option=com_content&task=view&id=41&Itemid=72 (accessed 28 August 2013).

Chambers, Iain. 2008. *Mediterranean Crossings: The Politics of an Interrupted Modernity*. Durham and London: Duke University Press.

CulturaGay. 2007. "Come cambiano i gay," 14 June 2007, http://www.culturagay.it/intervista/364 (accessed 28 August 2013).

Cutrufelli, Maria Rosa. 1975. *Disoccupata con onore. Lavoro e condizione della donna*. Milano: Mazzotta.

Dainotto, Roberto M. 2007. *Europe (in Theory)*. Durham and London: Duke University Press.

Dall'Orto, Giovanni. 1990. "Mediterranean Homosexuality." In *Encyclopedia of Homosexuality*, ed. W.R. Dynes. New York: Garland.

Ellena, Liliana. 2011. "L'invisibile Linea del Colore nel Femminismo Italiano: Viaggi, Traduzioni, Slittamenti." *Genesis: Rivista della Società Italiana delle Storiche* 10(2): 17–39.

El-Tayeb, Fatima. 2011. *European Others: Queering Ethnicity in Postnational Europe*. Minneapolis and London: University of Minnesota Press.

Facciamo Breccia. 2011. "Conference Programme," http://www.facciamobreccia.org/content/view/516/ (accessed 28 August 2013).

Fassin, Éric. 2010. "National Identities and Transnational Intimacies: Sexual Democracy and the Politics of Immigration in Europe." *Public Culture* 22(3): 507–529.

———. 2011. "From Criticism to Critique." *History of the Present* 1(2): 265–274.

Foucault, Michel. 2007. *Security, Territory, Population: Lectures at the Collège de France 1977–78*, trans. G. Burchell. Basingstoke: Palgrave Macmillan.

Gattuso, Marco. 2012. "Dopo la sentenza di Cassazione sulle relazioni affettive fra omosessuali," 19 March 2012, *Persona e Danno*, http://www.personaedanno.it/orientamento-sessuale/dopo-la-sentenza-di-cassazione-sulle-relazioni-affet-tive-fra-omosessuali-marco-gattuso (accessed 28 August 2013).

Haritaworn, Jin. 2008. "Loyal Repetitions of the Nation: Gay Assimilation and the 'War on Terror'," 2 May 2008, *Darkmatter*, http://www.darkmatter101.org/site/2008/05/02/loyal-repetitions-of-the-nation-gay-assimilation-and-the-war-on-terror/ (accessed 28 August 2013).

Haritaworn, Jin, Tamsila Tauqir, and Esra Erdem. 2008. "Gay Imperialism: Gender and Sexuality Discourse in the 'War on Terror'." In *Out of Place: Silences in Queerness/Raciality*, eds. A. Kuntsman and E. Miyake. York: Raw Nerve Books, 9–33.

Huntington, Samuel P. 1996. *The Clash of Civilizations and the Remaking of World Order*. New York: Simon & Schuster.

Kollman, Kelly. 2009. "European Institutions, Transnational Networks and National Same-sex Unions Policy: When Soft Law Hits Harder." *Contemporary Politics* 15(1): 37–53.

Kosnick, Kira. 2011. "Sexuality and Migration Studies: The Invisible, the Oxymoronic and Heteronormative Othering." In *Framing Intersectionality: Debates on a Multi-Faceted Concept in Gender Studies*, eds. H. Lutz, M.T. Herrera Vivar, and L. Supik. Farnham: Ashgate, 121–136.

Kulpa, Robert. 2011. "Nations and Sexualities – 'East' and 'West'." In *De-Centering Western Sexualities: Central and Eastern European Perspectives*, eds. R. Kulpa and J. Mizieliñska. Farnham: Ashgate, 43–62.

Kulpa, Robert and Joanna Mizieliñska, eds. 2011. *De-Centering Western Sexualities: Central and Eastern European Perspectives*. Farnham: Ashgate.

Kuus, Merje. 2004. "Europe's Eastern Expansion and the Reinscription of Otherness in East-Central Europe." *Progress in Human Geography* 28(4): 472–489.

Lady Gaga. 2011. Speech at the EuroPride 2011, http://www.youtube.com/watch?v=L1Tnd0hBihU (accessed 28 August 2013).

Mepschen, Paul and Jan W. Duyvendak. 2012. "European Sexual Nationalisms: The Culturalization of Citizenship and the Sexual Politics of Belonging and Exclusion." *Perspectives on Europe* 42(1): 70–76.

Mepschen, Paul, Jan W. Duyvendak, and Evelien H. Tonkens. 2010. "Sexual Politics, Orientalism and Multicultural Citizenship in the Netherlands." *Sociology* 44(5): 962–979.

Pasolini, Pier Paolo. 1975. *Scritti corsair*. Milano: Garzanti.

Patanè, Paolo. 2012. "Patanè, il presidente di Arcigay, commenta la sentenza della Corte di Cassazione," audio interview, 16 March 2012, http://www.arcigay.it/35008/video-patane-il-presidente-di-arcigay-commenta-la-sentenza-della-corte-di-cassazione/ (accessed 28 August 2013).

Ponzanesi, Sandra. 2014. "Queering European Sexualities through Italy's Fascist Past: Colonialism, Homosexuality and Masculinities." In *What's Queer about Europe? Productive Encounters and Re-enchanting Paradigms*, eds. M. Rosello and S. Dasgupta. New York: Fordham University Press, 81–90.

Puar, Jasbir K. 2007. *Terrorist Assemblages: Homonationalism in Queer Times*. Durham and London: Duke University Press.

Pugiotto, Andrea. 2010. "Una lettura non reticente della sent. 138/2010: il monopolio eterosessuale del matrimonio," *Forum di Quaderni Costituzionali*, http://www.forumcostituzionale.it/site/images/stories/pdf/documenti_forum/paper/0226_pugiotto.pdf (accessed 28 August 2013).

Rodotà, Stefano. 2012. "La Nuova Stagione dei Diritti," 14 May 2012, *MicroMega*, http://temi.repubblica.it/micromega-online/la-nuova-stagione-dei-diritti/ (accessed 28 August 2013).

Roma EuroPride. 2011. "Political Platform," http://www.euprideroma.com/index.php?sezione=54&lang=en (accessed 28 August 2013).

Schlosser, Kolson. 2008. "Bio-Political Geographies." *Geography Compass* 2(5): 1621–1634.

Walters, William. 2002. "Deportation, Expulsion, and the International Police of Aliens." *Citizenship Studies* 6(3): 265–292.

——. 2006. "Border/Control." *European Journal of Social Theory* 9(2):187–203.

Part II

Practicing Europe in LGBTQ Activism

5
Deploying Europe: The Creation of Discursive Imperatives for Same-Sex Unions

Kelly Kollman

Introduction

No fewer than 24 European countries have implemented national same-sex unions (SSU) laws since 1989 (see Table 5.1). This relatively rapid diffusion of SSU policies in the region largely has occurred in the absence of legally binding mandates from either the European Union (EU) or the European Court of Human Rights (ECtHR). The European polity and processes of Europeanization nonetheless have played an important role in these outcomes. In this case Europeanization, defined as the domestic impact of Europe, largely has not occurred through the formal policy decisions of European institutions, but rather through informal processes of social learning fostered by European activist networks and institutions. Throughout the 1990s sympathetic policy elites and lesbian, gay, bisexual and transgender (LGBT) activists became increasingly adept at using European institutions and networks to construct a norm against sexual orientation discrimination and for the right of same-sex couples to participate in state-sanctioned unions. The strength of this same-sex relationship recognition norm lies not only in the resonance of human rights claims more generally, but also crucially, and in line with the theme of this volume, the image of Europe that activists and elites have cultivated as an LGBT community champion and the arbiter of what constitutes legitimate rights in the region.

A number of scholars have examined the ways in which the LGBT rights norms, common movement frames, and legal arguments created by these European actors and activists have catalyzed the adoption of national SSU policies and same-sex marriage laws in the region (Kollman 2009, 2013; Kuhar 2011; Paternotte 2011). Too often, however, these

Table 5.1   National same-sex unions legislation in Europe

Marriage	Registered Partnership	Unregistered Partnership
Netherlands (2001)	Denmark (1989)	Hungary (1996)
Belgium (2003)	Norway (1993–2009)	Portugal (2001)
Spain (2005)	Sweden (1995–2009)	Austria (2003)
Norway (2009)	Iceland (1996)	Croatia (2003)
Sweden (2009)	Greenland (1996)	
Portugal (2010)	Netherlands (1998)	
Iceland (2010)	France (1999)	
Denmark (2012)	Belgium (2000)	
France (2013)	Germany (2001)	
	Finland (2002)	
	Luxembourg (2004)	
	United Kingdom (2004)	
	Andorra (2005)	
	Switzerland (2005)	
	Czech Republic (2006)	
	Slovenia (2006)	
	Austria (2010)	
	Hungary (2010)	
	Ireland (2010)	
	Liechtenstein (2011)	
	Malta (2014)	

Source: ILGA-Europe: http://ilgaeurope.org/home/issues/families/recognition_of_relation-ships/legislation_and_case_law/marriage_and_partnership_rights_for_same_sex_partners_country_by_country. Accessed 21/4/2014. Table modified from Kollman, 2013, p. 2.

accounts portray this European influence as monolithic in nature, although not necessarily in outcomes, in part because scholars tend to focus on the nature of human rights claims rather than the ways in which the image of Europe is used to bolster the appropriateness of such claims in different countries. In this chapter, I seek to add to this work by illustrating the variable ways in which national SSU activists have sought to deploy the image of Europe as a legitimate rights bearer in their attempts to create a "discursive imperative" for same-sex relationship recognition. In so doing, I demonstrate the important mediating and often variable role that national discourses play in bridging the gap between the idea of Europe as an LGBT rights champion and national policy processes.

I examine SSU policy debates in the UK, the Netherlands, and Germany – three countries with very different histories of LGBT politics and very different relationships to the European polity – to tease out the diverse ways in which the idea of Europe is used in these settings to justify the positions of key policy actors. This analysis reveals that although national SSU supporters have invoked a common European norm that defines state relationship recognition as a human right and/or anti-discrimination measure, the extent to and manner in which national policy actors use the image of Europe to legitimize the norm varies across these national settings, sometimes dramatically. In Germany and the Netherlands, SSU advocates have held up other European countries and European institutions as an important benchmark for national human rights practices, one they argue their government should not fall behind. Dutch activists, especially during the debate on opening marriage to same-sex couples in the late 1990s, additionally have portrayed Europe as a common and progressive political project in which the Netherlands itself should play a leading role. In the UK, by contrast, SSU supporters have been much less prone to invoke the idea of Europe and when they do, these activists usually refer to pioneering countries such as Denmark rather than the European polity as whole. Interestingly, the opponents of same-sex marriage in the UK are the ones who have utilized the idea of Europe as the guardian of LGBT rights to argue that future European court mandates for church marriage ceremonies could threaten religious freedom in the UK.

These case studies reveal the important role that national actors play in shaping the nature and extent of Europe's influence in domestic settings. As I seek to demonstrate in this chapter, the idea of Europe is not a uniform structure that is imposed without variation on the region's member states. Rather national policy activists and elites craft discursive imperatives by deploying Europe as an imagined human rights community in variable and creative ways to increase the resonance of their arguments within their particular socio-political setting.

Europeanization, social learning, and domestic discourses

During the early 2000s, there was an explosion of scholarly work that examined the "domestic impact" of the European Union on its member states. This so-called Europeanization literature largely has focused on the effects of formal policy harmonization and the ways in which implementing binding EU directives and legal mandates influence national policy as well as broader political institutions and processes (Börzel and Risse 2006). Far less attention has been paid to non-EU, European institutions such as the Council of Europe and its European Court of Human

Rights or the softer mechanisms of European influence such as social learning. As a growing number of scholars have noted, however, it is precisely these other European actors and softer mechanisms of influence that have played a critical role in the expansion of LGBT rights in the region (Beger 2004; Paternotte 2011; Ayoub 2013; Kollman 2009, 2013). Drawing on constructivist theories of international socialization, these authors illustrate how a largely soft-law norm against sexual orientation discrimination, which has been generated and promoted within the broader European polity since the 1980s, helped to induce social learning among national policymakers and publics by convincing them to internalize and then apply the norm's key principle of equal treatment for gay men, lesbians, bisexuals and transgenders within their own borders.

These accounts of Europeanization via social learning, however, are still incomplete. In particular we remain under-informed about the precise processes by which the creation of European norms and identities induce change in national settings. Here the recent turn toward "discursive" institutionalism developed by scholars such as Vivien Schmidt, Colin Hay and Ben Rosamond can be of help (Schmidt 2008; Hay and Rosamond 2002). These scholars have pointed out that the creation of new norms or ideas is not enough, in and of itself, to bring about political change no matter how compelling the content of these ideas and norms is. Rather change is the result of the nature of the new idea/norm as well as how its supporters fashion arguments to convince policymakers and publics of its merits. Norms and policy ideas need policy actors to make a case for them. How well these actors make these arguments, to whom, with what imagery, and in what venues can make all the difference in policymaking processes and determine which norms succeed in bringing about change (Schmidt 2008).

Constructivist theorists in international relations and Europeanization literatures, of course, recognize the role that discourse plays in international learning processes and many have incorporated a "logic of argumentation" into their theories (Risse 2000). The problem with these accounts is that they often leave the heavy lifting of this argumentation and persuasion work to international actors, generally either intergovernmental organizations such as the EU or transnational networks of experts or activists (Keck and Sikkink 1998; Checkel 2005). Because of this focus on common international actors, there is an implicit assumption that the discourses that introduce new norms into national settings are relatively uniform across countries. Very little of this work gets beneath the surface of national borders to examine how national actors use international norms and imagery during policy debates to get what they want. Thus we miss not only the role that domestic discourses play in the workings of international social learning, but also the mediating and variable role they play in these processes.

In their work, Colin Hay and Ben Rosamond have examined how politicians, interest groups, and important societal actors in different European countries have crafted and then strategically deployed varying "rhetorics" about the threat and opportunities represented by European integration and globalization (Hay and Rosamond 2002). They argue that domestic political actors carve these rhetorics from a broader, transnational discourse and imagery about global and European integration and utilize them to build support for their preferred policies by portraying the latter as necessary or inevitable. These actors often promote unpopular policy reforms by claiming that Europe or global markets "made me do it," thus creating a discursive imperative for such action. What often goes unnoticed is that the rhetorics deployed in each country are the work of local political agents who develop nationally specific arguments to resonate within their particular political settings (ibid.: 147–152).

Hay and Rosamond's concepts of national rhetorics – what I call domestic discourses – and the construction of discursive imperatives help describe how the European soft-law norm for same-sex relationship recognition has catalyzed policy change in the region. As demonstrated below, the particular discourses that national SSU supporters in the Netherlands, Germany, and the UK have utilized to create a policy imperative for such legal reforms vary from country to country. Although SSU supporters in all three countries have used a similar rights-based claim for equal treatment in marriage law and family policy, these activists have deployed the image of Europe as a bearer of human and LGBT rights in different ways and to different extents in their campaigns. The idea of Europe as a champion of LGBT rights is a common but fluid one that takes on different meanings in different national settings, and has been shaped to fit the needs of particular national policy actors.

The creation of European discursive imperatives for same-sex unions in Germany, the Netherlands, and the UK

It goes beyond the scope of this chapter to outline in detail the expansion of LGBT rights within European institutions over the past three decades, but the basic facts can be easily conveyed. Starting in the early 1980s a broad coalition of actors including LGBT rights activists, legal advocates, and supportive bureaucrats within European organizations began to agitate for the incorporation of sexual orientation into the European human rights regime (Beger 2004; Swiebel 2009; Paternotte and Kollman 2013). This coalition's first major victory came with the 1981 European Court of Human Rights' *Dudgeon v. UK* decision, which ruled that the criminalization of sexual activity between two consenting adult men in Northern Ireland violated the European Convention on Human Rights' right to privacy. The Court continued to play an important role in the decriminalization of same-sex sexual activity throughout the region during the 1980s and 1990s and was particularly influential in this area during the Central and East European countries' transitions to democracy after 1989.

The EU did not begin to grapple seriously with the issue of lesbian and gay rights until the 1990s. This engagement with the issue largely was the result of the precedents set by the ECtHR as well as the entrepreneurial actions of certain members of the European Parliament. The latter was home to a strong coalition of LGBT supporters from the Social Democratic and Green Party groupings after direct elections began in 1979 (Swiebel 2009). In 1994 Claudia Roth, a German Member of the Parliament, authored a non-binding report that called on member states to recognize the full equality of gay men and lesbians, including in national marriage laws (European Parliament 1994). The report garnered significant public attention across Europe and pushed the Commission and member state governments to consider sexual orientation discrimination during their negotiations of the Treaty of European Union (Amsterdam Treaty) in the late 1990s. Although controversial, sexual orientation was included in the Treaty's anti-discrimination clause, Article 13, along with protections for age, race or ethnic origin, religion, and disability when it was signed in 1997. The EU translated its new legal competence into binding law by outlawing sexual orientation discrimination in the workplace in the *Employment Equality Directive* in 2000, although unlike race such discrimination is not banned outside the workplace in European law (Swiebel 2009). The ECtHR for its part has continued to outlaw sexual orientation discrimination in certain policy areas such as adoption and serving in national militaries (Bruce-Jones and Itaborahy 2011).

Europe's influence on national same-sex unions policies by contrast has been "soft" in nature with very few and only weak legal mandates for such recognition. Despite European institutions' reluctance to intervene in family policy, LGBT rights activists have been able to use the growing prohibition against sexual orientation discrimination within European law, along with the example of pioneering states such as

Denmark and the Netherlands, to create and disseminate a European norm that defines state (same-sex) relationship recognition as a human right. This norm has become globally prominent in part because of the symbolic value that seems to attach to state recognition of same-sex couples as is evidenced by the media storms that pioneering countries such as Denmark (first RP) and the Netherlands (first same-sex marriage) experienced when implementing these policies (Rydström 2011; van Velde 2009). The legitimacy of the SSU norm and particularly arguments for "marriage equality" have been bolstered further by a transnational network of legal advocates that has developed an expert discourse in which to embed the key principles of the norm (Paternotte 2011).

A number of scholars have demonstrated the ways in which this European norm and legal discourse have influenced national debates and catalyzed the implementation of SSU policies in European countries (Kuhar 2011; Kollman 2009; 2013; Paternotte 2011; Ayoub 2013). These accounts, however, give us only partial insight into how the idea of Europe is used in national settings to bolster claims for relationship recognition rights. As illustrated below, national SSU supporters have incorporated the SSU norm into domestic debates in different ways by deploying the image of Europe strategically to construct a discursive imperative for (and in the UK occasionally against) same-sex relationship that will resonate within their national setting and in particular with their society's view of the European polity. Although Europe is clearly associated with LGBT rights expansion in all three countries, the nature and legitimacy of how this European project is portrayed vary in the political and popular imaginations of their societies. Germany often views itself as a European rights norm taker, the Netherlands as norm shaper, and the UK as a European rights skeptic. The idea of defining state relationship recognition as a (European) right has remained a staple of national SSU discourses in the three countries. What differs is how Europe as a legitimizing image is deployed in each to bolster what was until recently a controversial claim.

Debating same-sex relationship recognition in Germany: Europe as a key benchmark

The newly reunited Germany entered the 1990s with a reputation for being a good European, but the country was no longer considered an LGBT rights pioneer. Although a vibrant homosexual culture and supporting organizations had flourished in the metropolitan centers of the Weimar Republic, lesbian and gay organizing was less successful in the West Germany that emerged in the 1950s, in part because of the Nazis' brutal decimation of the Weimar community. The early dominance of Christian democratic governments in the 1950s and 1960s also made for a difficult atmosphere in which to reestablish strong movements promoting sexual diversity. When communities of lesbians and gay men began to reappear in Germany in the 1970s and 1980s, these movements were heavily influenced by the neo-Marxist and liberationist ideologies of the student protest activism of the era (Herzog 2005). Civil and human rights were seen as conservative in many of these circles as were the occasional calls for opening marriage to same-sex couples (Bruns 2006). No permanent national LGBT rights organization formed until the reunification in the early 1990s when the Schwulen Verband Deutschland (SVD), which was created in East Germany during the transition to democracy, became a German-wide organization. By the mid-1990s SVD had broaden its mandate to include lesbians, thus re-branding itself as Lesben und Schwulenverband in Deutschland (LSVD), and became the driver of the German movement (LSVD 2007). Unlike many of the LGBT organizations of the 1980s, LSVD sought to build connections with other European groups and the institutions of the European human rights regime.

Along with the Green party (Alliance 90/Die Grünen), LSVD thus became one of the first German actors to incorporate European norms into national debates about the expansion of LGBT rights. Europe has been very visible in the discourse that SSU supporters have constructed about state relationship recognition. Indeed SSU supporters first had to convince their own movement that relationship recognition was a worthy goal. In 1986 a fledging national LGBT rights organization, the Bundesverband Homosexualität, disbanded largely over a bitter debate about the desirability of same-sex marriage (Bruns 2006). Unsurprisingly the issue was not broached again in a serious way until after Denmark became the first country to adopt a national SSU law. Manfred Bruns, a member of LSVD and one of the leading campaigners for same-sex relationship rights in Germany, described the influence of Denmark's Registered Partnership (RP) law in this way:

> there was no discussion about the so-called "Homo-marriage" until the implementation of the Danish Registered Partnership Law on October 1st 1989. Only after seeing the pictures of male and female couples registering in the Marriage Hall of the City Chambers in Copenhagen did it gain attention and begin to occupy people's imaginations. (1994: 51; translation by author)

Drawing on the Danish example, LSVD launched the successful *Aktion Standesamt* (Registry Office Campaign) in which over 200 same-sex couples sought to register for a civil marriage with local authorities in several German cities (Bruns 1994). This campaign led to a number of court cases. The legal battle ended in 1993 when the Constitutional Court refused to take a marriage case stating that the plaintiffs had failed to establish that there had been a "fundamental change in the understanding of marriage, one in which the difference in sex no longer played a decisive role" (Constitutional Court cited in Beck 2012: 77–78). Although they were unable to persuade the German courts of the merits of their arguments, the *Aktion Standesamt* garnered the LGBT community a great deal of, largely positive, national media attention and firmly anchored same-sex relationship recognition as a core, although not uncontroversial, goal within the movement (Beck 2012).

After the *Aktion Standesamt*, SSU supporters continued to use the rights-based claims of the European SSU norm and European examples to bolster the norm's legitimacy throughout their decade-long campaign for relationship recognition. There were good strategic reasons for doing so. The rights rhetoric at the heart of the European norm simply found a resonance with the German media and public that earlier, more radical framings of the movement lacked (Bruns 1994). In the early 1990s, however, state relationship recognition, as the Constitutional Court's ruling highlights, was not considered a rights issue. Rather it was perceived as a way to foster an important cultural institution that the state had a compelling interest to promote. In the German case, this thinking was anchored in the Constitution, which calls on the state to provide "special protection of marriage and the family," defined implicitly, but almost universally before 1990, as made up of one man, one woman, and their biological children. For this reason SSU supporters deployed the endorsement of LGBT rights and relationship recognition by European institutions and countries during their campaign. Europe, the EU, and the European human rights regime all enjoyed relatively high levels of legitimacy in Germany at the time (Eurobarometer 2001). SSU supporters sought to use this legitimacy to persuade the public and policymakers that they should follow the examples of their Nordic neighbors and the recommendations of the European Parliament by adopting national SSU legislation and ending sexual orientation discrimination in family policy.

In the discourse that German SSU campaigners constructed to promote their rights-based claims, Europe became an important benchmark that the German state was often portrayed as failing to meet. This motif and legitimizing image of Europe appears in many of the speeches made by parliamentary SSU supporters and in the campaign literature of LGBT rights activists. When the newly elected coalition government made up of the Social Democratic and Green parties stated their intention to implement an RP law in 1998, they justified this goal by saying that it was in keeping with the long-standing recommendations of the European Parliament (SPD/Bündnis '90-Die Grünen 1998). References to Europe were made in a more pointed way during the parliamentary debates that occurred before the RP bill was adopted in 2000. Volker Beck, the backbench Green party MP who helped to shepherd the bill through the lower house of parliament, used the following image of Europe when trying to persuade his fellow MPs to support the controversial bill in 2000:

> From Iceland to the Mediterranean there is legal recognition of same-sex partnerships. Until now there has been a big white spot on the [European] map of civil rights for gay men and lesbians and that is Germany. (Deutscher Bundestag, *Plenarprotokoll 14/115*, 7/7/2000; 10964D [Beck]; translation by author)

The use of the rights framing of the issue is very prevalent. But crucially so too is the use of the idea of Europe as an important benchmark for LGBT rights. Beck used similar language to convince the German public that they should support the law. In an opinion piece published in a national daily newspaper, Beck argued, "[w]hy should something that has existed for years and functioned very well in Denmark, Norway, Sweden, Iceland and the Netherlands be unconstitutional in Germany?" (Beck, *Süddeutsche Zeitung* 10 July 2001; translation by author).

This rhetoric and its deployment of European imagery helped to convince a reluctant Social Democratic party and a slim majority of the German public to support the RP law. Opposition from the Christian democratic parties in both the upper and lower houses of parliament, however, resulted in an RP law that was much less generous in terms of benefits and rights than the Nordic legislation on which it was based when it was implemented in 2001. As a result LGBT rights activists in Germany have campaigned to expand relationship recognition rights further since 2001 and have continued to use Europe as an important benchmark in their arguments. In 2005, LSVD published a press release announcing the opening of marriage to same-sex couples in Canada and Spain with the headline "Canada and Spain are in the Passing

Lane: Equality in Germany Is Long Overdue" (LSVD 2005; translation by author).

Such discourse has proven successful. The RP law has been expanded several times since 2001 – including through a recent decision by the Constitutional Court in 2013 that bestowed the same-tax benefits enjoyed by married couples on registered partners – and now contains most of the rights and privileges of civil marriage (Bundesverfassngsgericht 2013). SSU supporters have continued to use this European imagery in their latest campaign to persuade the government to open marriage to same-sex couples. When the Green and Social Democratic parties, this time as part of the opposition, introduced a bill to open marriage in 2012, Volker Beck taunted Prime Minister Angela Merkel during the parliamentary debate by arguing that she and her Christian Democratic Party should find the courage to support the opening of marriage "with conservative values" that David Cameron, the British prime minister, had used when introducing such legislation in the UK (quoted in Blech, *Queer.de*, 28 June 2012). More than two decades after the issue first came onto the political agenda, supporters of same-sex marriage in Germany continue to deploy European "benchmarks" in both public and elite discourses to add legitimacy to their rights-based claims and to create a discursive imperative for same-sex relationship recognition. In a country where Europe is highly regarded and the public and elites are extremely sensitive about the country's international human rights reputation, this discourse has proven to be extremely effective.[1]

Debating same-sex relationship recognition in the Netherlands: Europe as a common political project

Lesbian and gay activists in the Netherlands were able to recreate a visible community and comparatively strong organizations in the aftermath of WWII. By the late 1970s, the government officially recognized the Centre for Culture and Leisure (Cultuur en Ontspanningscentrum, COC), the largest national lesbian and gay organization then and now, as an official representative of the community (Schuyf and Krouwel 1999). Dutch SSU supporters in the 1990s also inherited a comparatively favorable policy legacy. Unlike in Germany and the UK, sex between two men had been decriminalized in the 19th century and ages of consent for same and different-sex sexual activity were equalized in the 1970s. The latter did not happen until 1994 and 2001 respectively in Germany and the UK (Bruce-Jones and Itaborahy 2011). Further, the Netherlands is often credited with implementing the world's first anti-discrimination legislation to offer gay men and lesbians concrete protections against sexual orientation discrimination in the workplace in 1992 (ibid.). Perhaps most pertinently, as early as 1979, the Dutch government began extending many of the legal and welfare benefits that different-sex domestic cohabitants enjoy in Dutch law to same-sex couples thus creating a proto-SSU law (Waaldijk 2005). It was not until the late 1980s, however, that LGBT rights activists began to focus their attention on more comprehensive relationship recognition rights.

As in Germany, these activists drew on the examples of European countries and European human rights law as an important benchmark to strengthen their rights-based claims for state relationship recognition. In an unsuccessful legal case that challenged the ban against same-sex couples in Dutch marriage law, the plaintiff's lawyer, Lois Gijbels, tried to convince the court of the merits of their legal claim by pointing out that like "the Netherlands, Denmark is also a Member State of the European Community, and, as such, it would not be possible to close our borders to similar [same-sex unions] legislation from abroad" (Lois Gijbels quoted in van Velde, 2009). Activists such as Henk Krol, who as the publisher of a popular gay magazine became the public face of the SSU campaign, also used the example of the adoption of SSU laws by an increasing number of European countries to keep the issue high on the agenda and to highlight the appropriateness of the reform throughout the 1990s (van Velde 2009). This campaigning bore fruit in 1998 when the center-left government adopted a relatively uncontroversial RP law that was open to both same and different-sex partners.

In the Netherlands, however, many SSU activists explicitly rejected the RP model and consistently argued that the latter was an unacceptable and discriminatory form of state relationship recognition. Unlike in Germany in the 1990s, SSU activists were not merely asking for relationship recognition rights, they wanted the Dutch state to become the first to open civil marriage to same-sex couples. To reach this goal, Europe could not be deployed as a benchmark as it had during the debate about general relationship recognition. Marriage advocates, however, still incorporated the image of Europe into the discourse they constructed to persuade policymakers and the public to become the first country to allow same-sex couples to marry. Indeed, in addition to human rights and notions of equal treatment, Europe and the international context became one of the most prominent aspects of this debate. Both opponents and proponents of the reform used references to the latter to bolster their competing claims about what was appropriate.

During the parliamentary hearings on opening marriage to same-sex couples in 1994, MPs from the Christian Democratic Party

(Christen-demokratisch Appel, CDA), who opposed the reform, argued that by radically redefining the institution the government would run the risk of devaluing Dutch marriages in the eyes of foreign governments and societies. It was an argument that the Justice Minister Elizabeth Schmitz of the Labor party (Partij van de Arbeid, PvdA), appeared to take seriously. She used the example of the passage of the discriminatory *Defense of Marriage* acts in the US as an example of what can happen when one jurisdiction redefines marriage ahead of neighboring jurisdictions (*Kamerstukken II 1995/1996* 22 700 no.16; translated by Dorien Keizer). The international context also figured prominently in the deliberations of the Kortmann Commission, which the government formed to examine the legal issues surrounding the opening of marriage in 1996–1997. The minority on this Commission, who recommended against opening marriage, highlighted the potential negative international consequences as one key reason for their refusal to endorse same-sex marriage (Maxwell 2000).

Marriage advocates did not shy away from engaging with these arguments, as is reflected in the following statement made by a member of the Green-Left (GroenLinks) party in a 1994 parliamentary debate. Here the idea of Europe is more prominent:

> My party is therefore in favour of going further and positively putting the possibility of the opening of marriage on the table...I come to the point of the relationship between the Netherlands, Denmark, Sweden and Norway. These are probably the only countries in Europe that [will take] this step on relationships. For the rest the Netherlands will probably, like in the field of drugs, remain isolated within Europe. (*Kamerstukken II 1995/1996* 22 700 no.16; translated by Dorien Keizer)

Mieke van der Burg, one of the leading backbench proponents of same-sex marriage, echoed this point, but put it in a more positive light, "[w]hat the cabinet says on stepping out of pace internationally is correct, but what is wrong with that?" (ibid.). Van der Burg further suggested that the Netherlands could serve as a model for other countries in the region – similar to the Dutch role that Leila Rupp traces back to 1950s homophile organizing in Chapter 2 – by being the first to allow same-sex couples to marry.

Similarly, the majority of the Kortmann Commission came out in favor of the reform and noted that by opening marriage to same-sex couples, the Netherlands "might in fact inspire other countries to extend proper recognition to homosexual couples" (Kortmann Commission quoted in Maxwell 2000). The government clearly picked up on their calls for international leadership. The explanatory memorandum that accompanied the law to open marriage states the following about the international implications of allowing gay and lesbian couples to marry. "Limping legal relations" refer to the diversity of how same-sex couples are treated in the national law of other countries:

> The limping legal relations that can come into existence as a result of the limited recognition of … [same-sex] marriage abroad are a matter the persons involved can consciously accept. Moreover this fact might put extra pressure on the other countries to end the phenomenon of limping legal relations. (*Staatsblad* 2001, no. 9)

Although stated subtly, the ambition to serve as a European and international leader is clearly present.

In these arguments Europe and the international context serve not as a benchmark against which the Netherlands should be measured, but rather as a common political project to which the Netherlands has much to contribute. By acting as a marriage pioneer and example for others to follow, this national discourse posited that the Netherlands could, as they have done in drugs and prostitution policy, add to Europe's reputation for progressive politics and make a significant contribution to the European and global human rights regime. Marriage proponents played on the Netherlands' reputation for social policy innovation to try to create a discursive imperative for marriage equality. In a country where political and social elites have sought to become an influential "middle power" through policy innovation and exporting liberal ideas, deploying the image of Europe as a common normative project resonated with the government and public alike.

Debating same-sex relationship recognition in the United Kingdom: Europe as contested terrain

Unlike Germany and the Netherlands, the United Kingdom has not fostered a reputation for being either a good European or a regional LGBT rights pioneer. Indeed British SSU activists of the 1990s inherited one of the worst policy legacies in the region. Consensual sex between two men was not decriminalized across the UK until 1982, although it had been legalized in England and Wales in 1967. Unequal ages of consent were maintained until 2001 and gay men and lesbians were barred from serving openly in the military until 2000 (Bruce-Jones and Itaborahy 2011). In part because of this poor legacy, British LGBT rights activists frequently have turned toward Europe to advance their agenda. In the 1970s, British organizations such as the Campaign for Homosexual Equality (CHE) played a key role in building and strengthening European activist networks. The founding of what is today the world's largest transnational LGBT rights organization, the International Lesbian and Gay Association, occurred at a CHE conference in Coventry in 1978 (Beger 2004: 33–34). The participation of British LGBT organizations in transnational and European networks has waned, however, since the 1980s as groups such as CHE were replaced by more professionalized lobby organizations such as Stonewall and queer activism, which have been less interested in participating in European activist networks.

Nevertheless, the British movement has made effective use of the institutions of the European human rights regime, especially the European Court of Human Rights. In the 1981 *Dudgeon v. UK* case, the Court ruled that outlawing consensual sex between two adult men violated the Convention's right to privacy. In 1997, the European Commission on Human Rights, a now defunct organ of the Council of Europe, ruled that the unequal ages of consent between different and same-sex sexual activity maintained by the British government violated the European Convention on Human Rights; ages of consent were equalized in 2003. Similarly, in 1999, the ECtHR overturned the ban on gay men, lesbians, and transgenders from serving openly in the British military in the *Smith and Grady v. UK* ruling. These rulings against the UK government helped put LGBT rights onto the political agenda as a human rights issue and, in conjunction with the election of the New Labour government in 1997, made a discussion of same-sex relationship recognition possible by 2000.

Despite the strong influence of the European human rights regime on British LGBT politics, consistently high levels of Euroscepticism appear to have made British SSU supporters more cautious about deploying the image of Europe to bolster their rights-based arguments for relationship recognition (Eurobarometer 2001, 2013). Neither Stonewall nor the Labour government emphasized the example of European SSU pioneer countries or the growing prohibition against sexual orientation within the European human rights regime in their efforts to convince the British public and political establishment of the appropriateness of same-sex relationship recognition. The 2003 White Paper outlining the government's plans to adopt a law that would create a registered civil partnership for same-sex couples did mention the fact that other EU member states had implemented similar legislation, but in passing and with little sense that the UK was becoming a regional laggard (Department of Trade and Industry 2003). Perhaps even more surprisingly, in their submission to the government's consultation on the issue Stonewall mentioned the EU just once, to insist that UK civil partners would be recognized outside the UK. The fact that 14 European countries already had such recognition in place was never mentioned (Stonewall 2003).

When the government presented the bill in parliament for its second reading, the minister responsible for the legislation justified the reform in the following way:

> The Bill ... builds on reforms that began back in 1967 with Leo Abse's private Member's Bill, backed by the then Home Secretary, Roy Jenkins. The Government's commitment to equality has been strong and unequivocal. We have equalised the age of consent, outlawed discrimination in the workplace on the ground of sexual orientation, secured protection from homophobic hate crimes and supported the abolition of Section 28. (UK House of Commons 2004: Column 174)

Although the anti-discrimination language of the European SSU norm is clearly present, Europe itself has been erased from this potted history of LGBT rights expansion in the UK despite the fact that two of the four reforms the minister mentions came about because of European legal mandates. Several backbench MPs, mostly from the Labour and Liberal Democrat parties, did mention the example of other SSU pioneer countries in Europe during this parliamentary debate (UK House of Commons 2004). Unlike in Germany and the Netherlands, however, this was not a discourse that either Stonewall or the government appeared keen to utilize in their efforts to create a discursive imperative for the civil partnership bill.

SSU supporters also were not keen to deploy the image of Europe in the recent debate about opening marriage to same-sex couples that took place in the UK after the Conservative Prime Minister David Cameron and his coalition government announced their intention to implement such a reform in late 2011. Although six European countries have opened marriage to same-sex couples since 2009, the government only rarely referred to this growing trend in justifying their intention to open marriage. In the 2012 public consultation paper published by the government, other European countries that have opened marriage to same-sex couples were only mentioned in an appendix (UK Government Equalities Office 2012). Stonewall, once again, chose not to utilize

European examples or law in their submission to this consultation or in their campaign literature (Stonewall 2012).

Europe nevertheless became a prominent part of the public discourse about opening marriage. Unlike in the Netherlands and Germany, opponents of same-sex marriage primarily deployed it in an attempt to tie an unwanted "European" presence in domestic politics to unwanted LGBT rights. These opponents argued that if the government recognizes same-sex couples in civil marriage law, European courts in the future could invoke the equal treatment logic embedded in European human rights treaties to force religious organizations to perform marriage ceremonies between two men and two women. The bill, which was adopted into law in July 2013 and applies to England and Wales but not Scotland or Northern Ireland, allows religious organizations to opt out of performing such ceremonies and the government has made extensive pledges that it would never force institutions to do so. It is a pledge, however, that many opponents argue the government does not have the authority to keep because of European human rights law. This line of argument and its use of Europe as the purveyor of LGBT rights – in this case as a bogeyman rather than a benchmark – were on prominent display during the Commons debates at the second reading of the marriage bill in February 2013. The following is the first question that the minister introducing the bill received during the parliamentary debate:

> Will the right hon. Lady assure us that, if at any time in the future the European Court of Human Rights ruled that a church not wishing to conduct a gay wedding ceremony was in breach of a discrimination Act, we would defy the European Court? (UK House of Commons. Record of Proceedings, 5 February 2013: Column 128)

Although the government and the other SSU supporters have challenged the likelihood that a European court would issue such a mandate to religious institutions, this became a prominent part of the British discourse.

The use of Europe by SSU opponents as a threat to British values and sovereignty highlights the difficulties of using Europe as a legitimating force in UK political discourse. In a country where Eurobarometer polls consistently register high levels of Euroscepticism and where EU membership is treated with open hostility in the press and a significant part of the political establishment, Europe cannot easily be used to create a discursive imperative for novel political projects (Eurobarometer 2001, 2013). Although the British public, like its German and Dutch

counterparts, associates Europe with LGBT rights expansion, it is difficult for British LGBT rights activists legitimately to portray Europe as a
benchmark by which to measure social progress or as a common polity
to which it should contribute. Rather the image of Europe remains
contested in public discourse, and it often is portrayed as a threat to
the UK. In the SSU case, the power of rights rhetoric was enough to win
the argument, but in the British cultural landscape it is perhaps not
surprising that activists have chosen not to use the image of Europe as
an arbiter of rights LGBT claims to add legitimacy to their campaign.

Conclusions

As many scholars have noted, it is difficult to explain the rapid diffusion
of SSU policies across Europe since 1989 without taking into account
the role that European activists, norms, and institutions have played in
legitimizing the claim that LGBT rights, including relationship recognition, are human rights (Kuhar 2011; Paternotte 2011; Kollman 2009,
2013). In the case of SSU policy this influence has come in the largely
soft form of cross-border social learning rather than through the legal
mandates of the EU or the European Court of Human Rights. The influence of these more normative processes has relied in no small part on
the idea of Europe as the arbiter of legitimate rights claims and as a
global LGBT rights champion. The emphasis in the LGBT politics literature on common European norms, policy frames, and legal arguments,
however, obscures the work that domestic actors do to translate broad
European claims into discourses that are capable of creating imperatives
for change in particular national settings. Here newer work that emphasizes the importance of national policy discourses developed by scholars
such as Vivien Schmidt and Colin Hay can be of help. European structures, both material and normative, often set the parameters of what
can be argued in a domestic setting, but policy change is never inevitable and national actors rarely simply follow a European script without
tailoring it to their own political needs.

As demonstrated above, national LGBT rights activists have incorporated a general European norm against sexual orientation discrimination and for same-sex relationship recognition into domestic policy
debates in very different ways in the UK, the Netherlands, and Germany.
In all three cases national SSU proponents utilized the European framing
of relationship recognition as a human right and anti-discrimination
measure. But activists in the three countries have deployed the image
of Europe as an LGBT rights champion in very different ways in

their attempts to increase the legitimacy of these rights-based claims. In Germany, Europe was portrayed as an important benchmark for national policy. In the Netherlands, Europe was defined as a common and progressive political project that the Dutch should help to shape. And in the UK, Europe and the role it has played in the expansion of LGBT rights often have been erased from British SSU supporters' narratives due to the contested nature of European imagery. This erasure has opened space for SSU opponents to connect a negative image of Europe to LGBT rights expansion and to deploy Europe as a threat to religious organizations as they have done in the recent marriage debate. These distinctive discourses highlight the important, and often overlooked, work that national actors have to do to make European ideas effective in different settings. The image of Europe conjures up different meanings and associations in different countries and policy activists seeking change need to deploy this image strategically to persuade elites and publics of the merits of their arguments.

The evolution of same-sex unions policy in the three countries thus highlights both the extent to which the image of Europe has become linked to LGBT rights expansion as well as how kaleidoscopic this image is. European activists and policymakers have succeeded in building, largely from the bottom up, an image of Europe that defines the polity as an LGBT rights champion. As with many political identities, however, this image is malleable and cannot be controlled by any single political actor. The image of Europe as an LGBT rights bearer that has emerged within the region's member states is a common but manifold one.

Note

1. While Germany often has taken cues about LGBT rights from European institutions and neighbors, it is still reluctant to support the expansion of this regime. It has been widely reported that the German government refused to support an EU Directive that would expand the current ban against sexual orientation discrimination in the workplace into areas such as social policy, education and the provisions of goods and services. See ILGA-Europe 2008 for further details: http://ilga-europe.org/home/news/latest/news_reports_from_ilga_Europe_s_annual_conference_vienna_30_october_2_november/conference_declarations (accessed 20 April 2014).

References

Ayoub, Phillip M. 2013. "Cooperative Transnationalism in Contemporary Europe: Europeanization and Political Opportunities in LGBT Mobilization in the European Union." *European Political Science Review*, 5(2): 279–310.

Beck, Volker. 2001. "Gleiche Liebe, Gleiche Rechte." *Süddeutsche Zeitung*, 10 July. http://www.sueddeutsche.de/politik/pro-gleiche-liebe-gleiche-rechte-1.432696 (accessed 28 August 2010).

———. 2012. "Von der Aktion Standesamt, über die eingetragene Lebenspartnerschaft zur 70 Ehe – Ein gesellschaftlicher Kampf einer Minderheit um Gleichberechtigung." In *Vom Verbot zur Gleichberechtigung: Festschrift für Manfred Bruns*, eds., G. Dworek, A. Hochrein and K. Jetzt. Hirschfeld-Eddy-Stiftung. Stiftung für die Menschenrechte von Lesben, Schwulen, Bisexuellen und Transgender, 70–81.

Beger, Nico. 2004. *Tensions in the Struggle for Sexual Minority Rights in Europe*. Manchester: Manchester University Press.

Blech, N. 2012. "Bundestag stimmt für Beihaltung der Diskriminierung." *Queer. de*, http://www.queer.de/detail.php?article_id=16809 (accessed 6 March 2013).

Börzel, Tanja and Thomas Risse. 2006. "Europeanization: The Domestic Impact of European Union Politics." In *Sage Handbook of European Union Politics*, eds. K. Jorgensen, M. Pollack and B. Rosamond. London: Sage, 483–504.

Bruce-Jones, Eddie and Lucas Itaborahy. 2011. *State-Sponsored Homophobia: A World Survey of Laws Criminalising Same-Sex Sexual Acts between Consulting Adults*. Brussels: International Lesbian, Gay, Sexual, Trans and Intersex Association.

Bruns, Manfred. 1994. "Die 'Aktion Standesamt' des SVD und der 'Schwulen Juristen'." *Lesben.Schwule.Partnerschaften*. Berlin: Berliner Senatsverwaltung für Bildung, Jugend und Sport (Referat fuer gleichgeschlechtliche Lebensweisen), 46–54.

———. 2006. *Schwulenpolitik in der alten Bundesrepublik*. http://old.lsvd.de/bund/schwulenpolitik.html (accessed 3 December 2008).

Checkel, Jeff. 2005. "International Institutions and Socialization in Europe: Introduction and Framework." *International Organization* 59(4): 801–826.

Department of Trade and Industry (United Kingdom). 2003. *Civil Partnerships: A Framework for the Legal Recognition of Same-Sex Couples*. London: DTI.

Deutscher Bundestag [German Parliament]. *Plenarprotokoll 14/115*, 7/7/2000; 10964D.

Eurobarometer. 2001. "Public Opinion in the European Union: Standard Report 55," http://ec.europa.eu/public_opinion/archives/eb/eb55/eb55_en.pdf (accessed 29 July 2013).

———. 2013. "Public Opinion in the European Union: Standard Report Government 80," http://ec.europa.eu/public_opinion/archives/eb/eb80/eb80_first_en.pdf (accessed 10 January 2014).

European Parliament. 1994. *Resolution on Equal Rights for Gays and Lesbians in the EC [Roth]*, A3 – 0028/94, OJ C 61/40, 29.2.1994.

Hay, Colin and Ben Rosamond. 2002. "Globalization, European Integration and the Discursive Construction of Economic Imperatives." *Journal of European Public Policy* 9(2): 147–167.

Herzog, Dagmar. 2005. *Sex after Fascism*. Princeton: Princeton University Press.

Kamerstukken II 1995/1996 22 700 nr. 16. [Dutch Parliament].

Keck, Margret and Kathryn Sikkink. 1998. *Activists beyond Borders: Advocacy Networks in International Politics*. Ithaca: Cornell University Press.

Kollman, Kelly. 2009. "European Institutions, Transnational Networks and National Same-sex Unions Policy: When Soft Law Hits Harder." *Contemporary Politics* 15(1): 37–55.

——. 2013. *Same-sex Unions Revolution: International Norms and Domestic Policy Change.* Manchester: Manchester University Press.

Kuhar, Roman. 2011. "Use of the Europeanization Frame in Same Sex Partnership Issues across Europe." In *The Europeanization of Gender Equality Policies: A Discursive Sociological Approach*, eds. E. Lombardo and M. Forest. Basingstoke: Palgrave Macmillan, 168–191.

Lesben-, und Schwulenverband in Deutschland (LSVD). 2005. *Kanada auf der Überholspur: Gleichstellung in Deutschland laengst Überfaellig.* Berlin: LSVD Pressestelle.

——. 2007. "Chronik," http://typo3.lsvd.de/25.0.html (accessed 5 March 2007).

Maxwell, Nancy. 2000. "Opening Civil Marriage to Same-Gender Couples: A Netherlands-United States Comparison." *Electronic Journal of Comparative Law* 4(3).

Paternotte, David. 2011. *Revendiquer le "mariage gay": Belgique, France, Espagne.* Brussels: Éditions de l'Université de Bruxelles.

Paternotte, David and Kelly Kollman. 2013. "Regulating Intimate Relationships in the European Polity: Same-Sex Unions and Policy Convergence." *Social Politics* 20(4): 510–533.

Risse, Thomas. 2000. "Let's Argue: Communicative Action in World Politics." *International Organization* 54(1): 1–39.

Rydström, Jens. 2011. *Odd Couples: A History of Gay Marriage in Scandinavia.* Amsterdam: Amsterdam University Press (Askand Imprint).

Schmidt, Vivian. 2008. "Discursive Institutionalism: The Explanatory Power of Ideas and Discourse." *Annual Review of Political Science* 11: 303–326.

Schuyf, Judith and André Krouwel. 1999. "The Dutch Gay and Lesbian Movement: The Politics Accommodation." In *The Global Emergence of Gay and Lesbian Politics*, eds. Adam, J. Duyvendak and A. Krouwel. Philadelphia: Temple University Press, 158–183.

SPD/Bündnis '90-Die Grünen. 1998. "Aufbruch und Erneuerung-Deutschlands Weg in 21. Jahrhundert" [on file with the author].

Stonewall (UK). 2003. *Stonewall Response. Civil Partnership: A Framework for the Legal Recognition of Same-sex Couples.* London: Stonewall.

——. 2012. *Equal Civil Marriage: A Consultation. Stonewall Response.* http://www.stonewall.org.uk/documents/stonewall_equal_marriage_consultation_response.pdf (accessed 10 March 2013).

Swiebel, Joke. 2009. "Lesbian, Gay, Bisexual and Transgender Rights: The Search for an International Strategy." *Contemporary Politics* 15(1): 19–35.

UK Government Equalities Office. 2012. *Equal Civil Marriage: A Consultation.* London: HMSO.

UK House of Commons. 2004. *Record of Proceedings (Daily Hansard)*, 12 October.

——. 2013. *Record of Proceedings (Daily Hansard)*, 5 February.

van Velde, H. 2009. *Gay Marriage in the Netherlands.* Friends of *Gay Krant* Foundation. www.gk.nl/index.php?id=222 (accessed 30 April 2009).

Waaldijk, Kees. 2005. "The Netherlands." In *More of Less Together: Levels of Legal Consequences of Marriage, Cohabitation and Registered Partnership for Different-Sex and Same-Sex Partners,* ed. K. Waaldijk. Paris: Institut National d'Etudes Demographiques, 137–154.

Court cases cited

European Court of Human Rights

Dudgeon v. United Kingdom (1981), Series Application No. 45.
Smith and Grady v. The United Kingdom (2002), Application No. 33985/96, 33986/96.
Sutherland v. United Kingdom (1994), Application No. 25186/94 (European Commission of Human Rights).

Bundesverfassungsgericht (German Constitutional Court)

BVerfG, 2 BvR 909/06 vom 7.5.2013, Absatz-Nr. (1–151), 2013.

Legislation cited

Germany

Gesetz zur Beendigung der Diskriminierung gleichgeschlechtlicher Gemeinschaften: Lebenspartnerschaften vom 16.2.2001, BGBl I 2001, 266.
Gesetz zur Überarbeitung des Lebenspartnerschaftsrechts vom 15.12.2004, BGBl I 2004, 3396.

The Netherlands

Amendment of Book 1 of the Civil Code concerning the opening of marriage to persons of the same sex (Staatsblad 2001, No. 9).

The United Kingdom

Civil Partnership Act 2004. London: HMSO.

Local Government Act 1988. London: HMSO.

6

Transnational LGBTI Activism and the European Courts: Constructing the Idea of Europe

Anna van der Vleuten

Introduction

In the famous words of former judge Pierre Pescatore, the Court of Justice of the European Union (ECJ) has always been inspired by "une certaine idée de l'Europe," meaning that the judges defined their mission as contributing to an ever-closer union between the peoples of Europe (Pescatore 1983: 157). This and similar statements have led to criticism among legal scholars, constitutional courts, and governments. They have questioned the activism of the judges, which, it is argued, could turn the ECJ into another European human rights court whereas its mandate was to contribute to market integration by enforcing intergovernmental bargains and resolving trade-related disputes (Garrett 1995).

However, the mission of European judges has been met with praise as well. Activists, including the LGBTI community, have welcomed it, seeing new opportunities for promoting human rights in the European Union (EU). LGBTI activists first began to target the "real" human rights court, the European Court on Human Rights (ECtHR) in Strasbourg, as early as the 1970s.[1] The ECtHR is still the main addressee of LGBTI activism and, despite Pescatore's statement, it remains the more activist court (Helfer and Voeten 2014).

This chapter investigates how activism by the courts and the LGBTI community has constructed a strong LGBTI rights profile in Europe. I find that LGBTI activists have been empowered vis-à-vis their governments by their access to the European courts when access to the national political arena was blocked, and that the ECJ and, to a lesser extent, the ECtHR have been empowered by LGBTI activism. This argument is developed in three parts. The first part presents a model of transnational legal activism that reveals the peculiarities of the European arena. The second part focuses on "the idea of Europe," showing how organizational identities and their underlying logics influence opportunities for LGBTI litigation. The third and final part shows how activism enables the courts to construct a European norm on LGBTI rights.

Transnational legal activism: the LGBTI triangles

While other civil society actors, such as trade unions, have traditionally been rooted in the national context and have yet to come to terms with the multilevel system which has developed in Europe, LGBTI activism acquired a transnational character and a European one early on. After WWII, Europe was considered a special place for the protection of human rights in general and LGBTI rights in particular (Ayoub and Paternotte, Chapter 1 in this volume). Recently, a body of literature has developed on transnational LGBTI activism in the European political arena (see Chapter 1 in this volume; Ayoub 2013; Holzhacker 2012; Kollman 2009; Paternotte and Kollman 2013). Less has been written on LGBTI legal activism, in the sense of activism targeting the courts. Particularly when it comes to LGBTI rights, agenda-setting litigation constitutes an attractive option when the political arena is closed. It is an attempt to stretch existing rules, hoping that the court's rulings may force governments to adopt new legislation. In fact, since member state governments perceive LGBTI issues to be related to basic ordering principles such as citizenship and marriage, they dislike interference from supranational bodies. As a result, LGBTI rights still depend primarily on national politics and there are marked differences between states (Waaldijk and Bonini-Baraldi 2006). Despite mobilization and lobbying, there is still no political will for Europe-wide harmonization in this domain. Nevertheless, the political stagnation has created an impetus for legal activism aimed at the European courts.

In order to map the legal activism of the rainbow community at the European level, I have adapted the concept of the "velvet triangle," shorthand for "a multi-national layered set of triangularly networked actors" (Woodward 2003: 85). The adjective velvet refers to the softness, the informal character of the relationships between the members of the network, and to its relatively elitist character, in the sense that it is a small group of "highly educated, well-travelled and multi-lingual" players (Paternotte and Woodward, 2014: 4). Woodward credits the velvet triangle with the relatively successful trajectory of European gender equality policies. Paternotte and Kollman (2013) found that a similar configuration has developed in the domain of LGBTI policies. They describe how a mixed policy network including activists, academics, and policy elites has promoted same-sex union laws in Europe. They call it a velvet network because of the "importance of personal and informal ties" between members who are defined by their expertise and commitment to the issue and the "porousness of their political, social, and academic spheres, as well as the multipositionality of actors" (Paternotte and Kollman 2013: 9). This velvet network in the European political arena seems to be mirrored by an apparently similar velvet triangle in the legal arena (Figure 6.1). In this section, I will briefly present the different actors involved.

The Courts

The ECJ and the ECtHR are both supranational Courts and their rulings have supremacy over domestic court rulings. However, they differ fundamentally in their competences and, as a result, in their legal opportunity structure (Conant 2006). The ECtHR, which is based in Strasbourg (France), rules on cases brought by individuals, groups of individuals, organizations or states who complain that fundamental rights, as codified in the European Convention on Human Rights (ECHR), have been

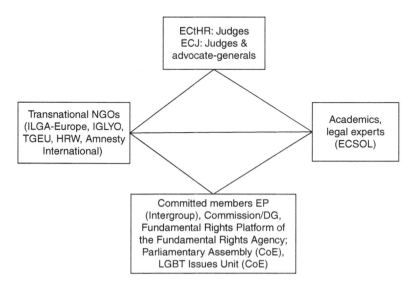

Figure 6.1 Transnational LGBTI legal and political velvet triangles in Europe

violated by a member state and who have exhausted all domestic legal means of recourse. Over the years it has ruled on over 60 LGBTI-related cases (Wintemute 2013). Three articles of the Convention have played a crucial role in most of these LGBTI cases: Article 8 (the right to respect for private and family life), Article 12 (the right to marry and found a family), and Article 14 and Protocol 12 (the prohibition of discrimination) (see Table 6.1).

Table 6.1 ECtHR rulings in LGBTI cases*

		Violation?	ECHR Article
I Lesbian and Gay Legal Issues			
Consensual sex			8
between adult men			
	X v. Germany, 1955	No*	
	Dudgeon v. UK, 1981	Yes	
	Johnson v. UK, 1986	No	
	Norris v. Ireland, 1988	Yes	
	Modinos v. Cyprus, 1993	Yes	
	A.D.T. v. UK, 2000	No	
Consensual			8
sadomasochism			
between adult men			
	Laskey, Jaggard, and Brown v. UK, 1997	No	
Age of consent			8 and 14
	Desmond v. UK, 1984	No*	
	Zukrigl v. Austria, 1992	No*	
	Sutherland v. UK, 1997	Yes	
	L and V v. Austria, 2003	Yes	
	S.L. v. Austria, 2003 and 6 other cases all v. Austria	Yes	
	B.B. v. UK, 2004	Yes	
	Santos Couta v. Portugal, 2010	No	
Serving openly in the			8
armed services			
	B. v. UK, 1983	No*	
	Lustig-Prean and Beckett v. UK, 1999	Yes	
	Smith and Grady v. UK, 1999	Yes	
	Perkins and R v. UK, 2002	Yes	
	Beck, Copp and Bazeley v. UK, 2002	Yes	

Continued

Table 6.1 Continued

		Violation?	ECHR Article
Adoption, parental authority			8 and 14
	Kerkhoven and Hinke v. the Netherlands, 1992	No	
	Fretté v. France, 2002	No	
	E.B. v. France, 2008	Yes	
	Gas and Dubois v. France, 2012	No	
	X and others v. Austria, 2013	Yes	
	Boeckel and Gessner-Boeckel v. Germany, 2013	No	
Child custody	Salgueiro da Silva Mouta v. Portugal, 1999	Yes	
Level of child maintenance	J.M. v. UK, 2010	Yes	
Discrimination unmarried same-sex partners			8 and 14
Housing	Simpson v. UK, 1986	No*	
	Röösli v. Germany, 2008	No*	
	Karner v. Austria, 2003	Yes	
	Kozak v. Poland, 2010	Yes	
Right to marry	Schalk and Kopf v. Austria, 2010	No	12
Refusal of residence permit	X. and Y. v. UK, 1983	No*	
	W.J. and D.P. v. UK, 1986	No*	
	C. and L.M. v. UK, 1989	No*	
	Z.b. v. UK, 1990	No*	
Survivor pension	Mata Estevez v. Spain, 2001	No	
Sickness insurance	P.B. and J.S. v. Austria, 2010	Yes	
Inheritance tax	Courten v. UK	No	
Civil unions	Vallianatos and others v. Greece, 2013	Yes	
Conditions of detention of homosexual prisoners			3 and 14
	Stasi v. France, 2011	No	
	X v. Turkey, 2012	Yes	

Continued

Table 6.1 Continued

		Violation?	ECHR Article
Homosexual asylum seekers			3
	I.I.N. v. the Netherlands, 2004	No	
	A.S.B. v. the Netherlands, 2012	Strike-out	
	M.K.N. v. Sweden, 2013	No	
Freedom of expression			10
	Morissens v. Belgium, 1988	No*	
	Vejdeland and others v. Sweden	No	
Campaigns for LGBTI rights			11, 13, 14
	Baczkowski and others v. Poland, 2007	Yes	
	Alekseyev v. Russia, 2010	Yes	
	Genderdoc-M v. Moldova, 2012	Yes	
II Gender Identity Issues			
Legal recognition of gender reassignment			8, 12, 14
	X v. Germany, 1977	No*	
	Van Oosterwijck v. Belgium, 1980	No	
	B v. France, 1992	Yes	
	Rees v. UK, 1986	No	
	Sheffield and Horsham v. UK, 1998	No	
	Parry v. UK and R and F v. UK, 2006	No	
Transsexual marriage			8 and 12
	Cossey v. UK, 1990	No	
	Christine Goodwin v. UK, 2002	Yes	
	I v. UK, 2002	Yes	
Rights of transsexual parents			8 and 14
	X, Y and Z v. UK, 1997	No	
	P.V. v. Spain, 2010	No	
Gender reassignment			8
	L v. Lithuania, 2007	Yes	
	Van Kück v. Germany, 2003	Yes	

Continued

Table 6.1 Continued

		Violation?	ECHR Article
	Schlumpf v. Switzerland, 2009	Yes	
Pension age transsexual			8
	Grant v. UK, 2006	Yes	

Source: Compiled by author based on ECtHR database, http://hudoc.echr.coe.int/sites/fra/ Pages/search.aspx (accessed 20 April 2014).
*Decision by the Commission (see footnote 1).

The ECJ, which is based in Luxembourg, gives interpretations (known as preliminary rulings) concerning EU law when asked to do so by a domestic court.[2] Accordingly, when some EU rule is applicable to a LGBTI case, individuals and groups are entitled to submit a claim via their own national court, which will ask the ECJ to provide a clarification. Subsequently the domestic court decides on the case.[3] Over the years, the ECJ has given preliminary rulings in 11 LGBTI-related cases. Most of these were framed in terms of a violation of Article 157 (TFEU) on equal pay for men and women or of directives on equal treatment (see Table 6.2).

Both courts require an individual to have approached a domestic court before they can act. However, the Strasbourg Court is perceived as being more accessible, providing an online application form and handing down its final decision without referring back to a domestic court. It is also considered more transparent, since it includes dissenting opinions when it publishes its judgments, whereas the Luxembourg court publishes the judgment only and dissenting voices can only be gleaned from a certain vagueness in its wording. The courts share a peculiarity that strongly dilutes the "velvet potential" of the triangle. Only a limited number from the pool of judges and, in the case of the ECJ, only one of the eight advocates-general, are involved in preparing and judging a case. This means that the identity and the number of judges allotted to a case change from one LGBTI case to the next. The familiarity of judges with sexual orientation and gender identity issues also varies widely. In the ECtHR all judges share a certain expertise in human rights, even though they come from 47 widely differing countries, from Azerbaijan to Iceland. The ECJ judges represent a more coherent community of states, but they differ widely as regards their legal backgrounds. Some of them have shown a strong commitment to human rights during their national career, such as Ninon Colneric and Sacha Prechal. However, Carl Fernlund, for instance, a judge in Case C-81/12 Asociaţia ACCEPT

Table 6.2 ECJ rulings in LGBTI cases

Case	Issue	Legal basis	Sex discrimination?
C-13/94, P. v. S. and Cornwall County Council	Dismissal transsexual	Directive 76/207	Yes
C-249/96, Grant v. South-West Trains	No payment of travel allowance to female partner of woman	Art. 157 TFEU, Directives 75/117 and 76/207	No
C-122/99P and C-125/99P, D. & Sweden v. Council	No household allowance for same-sex partner	Art. 157 TFEU	No
C-117/01, K.B. v. National Health Service Pensions Agency	No surviving spouse pension for transsexual partner of woman	Art. 157 TFEU, Directive 75/117	Yes
C-423/04, Richards v. Secretary of State for Work and Pensions	Pension age transsexual woman	Directive 79/7	Yes
C-267/06, Tadao Maruko v. Versorgungsanstalt der deutschen Bühnen	No surviving spouse pension for male partner of man	Art. 157 TFEU, Directive 2000/78/EC	Yes
C-147/08, Römer v. City of Hamburg	Higher pension for married workers than for workers with registered partner	Art. 157 TFEU, Directive 75/117	Yes
Case F-86/09, W v. European Commission	No household allowance for same-sex partner	Art. 19 TFEU	Yes
C-81/12, Asociaţia ACCEPT v. Consiul Naţional Pentru Combaterea Discriminării	Discrimination of gay football player	Directive 2000/78/EC	Yes
C-267/12 Frédéric Hay v. Crédit agricole	No extra paid holidays and cash bonus for same-sex partners	Directive 2000/78/EC	Yes
C-199/12, C-200/12 and C-201/12, X, Y and Z v. Minister voor Immigratie en Asiel	Conditions for granting refugee status to homosexual applicants for asylum	Directive 2004/83 (right to asylum)	Applicants are not expected to conceal homosexuality in country of origin

Source: Compiled by author based on the ECJ database, http://curia.europa.eu/ (accessed 20 May 2014).

concerning discrimination against a football player portrayed as being gay, is an expert in fiscal law. In addition, both courts have always been aware of the fact that LGBTI cases are sensitive. Therefore, most rulings are delivered by a high number of judges, in order to ensure that they reflect the legal traditions of a large group of the member states; however, this increases the diversity of the court. Combined with the secrecy surrounding the court's deliberations, these practices make it hard for activists to develop personal ties and create a velvet triangle.

Academics and experts

Given the need for specific expertise, a key role is played by the European Commission on Sexual Orientation Law (ECSOL), a transnational network of legal experts that aims to promote equality and recognition for LGBTI persons within Europe (ECSOL Homepage). The network offers an impressive lineup of lawyers who play leading roles in national and international LGBTI movements, while being active in academia and the domestic lower and constitutional courts. They include "big names" such as Suzanne Baer (Germany), Helmut Graupner (Austria), Caroline Mécary (France), Kees Waaldijk (Netherlands), Robert Wintemute (UK), and Andres Ziegler (Switzerland). ECSOL is also member of the Fundamental Rights Platform of the EU Fundamental Rights Agency, linking the legal and political triangles.

ECSOL members are highly active on the legal arena. They submit written observations on behalf of the litigants, setting out the opinion of the LGBTI community to the European judges. For instance, Graupner and Wintemute submitted observations in *Maruko* and *Römer*. Graupner, Wintemute, and Mécary all delivered or drafted oral arguments and third-party interventions in LGBTI cases before the ECtHR. Reimo Mets, the Estonian ECSOL member, sued the Estonian Republic in the ECtHR in a hate crime case. They publish statements, reports, blogs, books, and journal articles and suggest strategic issues for new cases to NGOs, linking two corners of the triangle. There are so many personal ties between these experts and other activists that the ECSOL lawyers are the key players at the intersections of the velvet network.

Transnational NGOs

The third corner of the triangle is home to NGOs. ILGA is the flagship NGO dedicated to the defense of LGBTI rights in Europe and worldwide. It collaborates with the gay, lesbian, bisexual, transgender, and queer youth organization IGLYO, Transgender Europe (TGEU, see Chapter 8 in this volume), and transnational human rights NGOs, such as Amnesty International and Human Rights Watch. ILGA began to create a European-level "political triangle" in 1979, when the first direct elections of the European Parliament (EP) were held. Committed members of the EP, such as LGBTI activist Joke Swiebel, have supported ILGA from the start and in the 1990s personal links were created with the European Commission as well. Since 2010, primary responsibility for LGBTI issues shifted from Social Affairs to the Commissioner for Justice, Fundamental Rights, and Citizenship. This shift strengthens the triangle because of the shared expertise in rights issues. The Fundamental Rights Agency provides the Commissioner and her DG with information; among its experts are LGBTI activists Matteo Bonini-Baraldi (founding member of ECSOL) and Dennis van der Veur (former adviser to the Council of Europe, CoE). The Council of Europe offers access mainly through the Parliamentary Assembly and the LGBTI issues unit. Since its inception, ILGA has not only pursued gay rights in the political arena, but also supported cases brought before the ECtHR, in which the founders of ILGA were often personally involved. The double strategy met an early double success in October 1981, when the Parliamentary Assembly called for the decriminalization of homosexuality and, in the same month, the ECtHR ruled on the *Dudgeon* case. Despite this success, when ILGA applied for consultative status at the CoE in 1989, its application was rejected on the grounds that "ILGA activities are not directly related to the present work programme of the Council of Europe" (Sanders 1996: 81). It was only in 2010 that the Committee of Ministers, referring to ECtHR case law, unequivocally recognized the duty of the CoE and its member states to ensure respect for the human rights of LGBTI people (Committee of Ministers 2010).

In sum, the legal arena is characterized by overlapping membership of committed activists and experts, creating a velvet LGBTI triangle. However, the courts' rules do not enable privileged connections and the courts' secrecy and diversity constitute an obstacle to activism. In order to identify opportunities and constraints, I will now turn to "the idea of Europe" as it relates to the identity of the actors involved.

The "idea of Europe" and the European identity of the actors

It is often argued that Europe is unique because of the existence of two strong supranational courts. Although similar courts have developed in Africa and the Americas, "Europe's courts are in a league of their own" (Alter 2009: 288). But what constitutes this uniqueness, which seems to facilitate the strong defense of human rights? Many have written about the "idea of Europe," trying to determine what the European core is made up of (Pagden 2002). Ash Amin argues that in these writings a common European identity is traditionally based on four "myths of origin," which can be summarized as follows:

> First, the supremacy of a legal system based on Roman law; second, an ethos of social solidarity and common understanding based on Christian piety and humanism; third, a democratic order rooted in recognition of the rights and freedoms of the individual; and fourth, a universalism based on Reason and other Enlightenment principles of cosmopolitan belonging. (2004: 5)

This fourfold idea of Europe helps in understanding the existence of two strong supranational courts in Europe and their potential for defending LGBTI rights.

The first principle refers to the recognition that Roman law "forms a constituent part of the occidental world" (Wieacker 1981: 257). Law is established as a man-made institution rather than "a divine gift or an immemorial custom" (ibid.: 263). Of course, this principle underlies Western legal thought in general, but what makes Europe different is its particular history and the strong desire to overcome the legacy of two world wars – including "the egregious trampling of individual rights" – through political and economic integration, uniting European states "under a rule of law so as to limit any return to authoritarian practices" (Alter 2009: 296). This desire has contributed to the development of two strong courts with a "similar *raison d'être*, namely the replacement of the old world order with an order that would guarantee peace, stability and a high degree of protection of human rights" (Harpaz 2009: 126).

The second myth of origin is referred to in the Preamble of the Treaty of Lisbon as "DRAWING INSPIRATION from the cultural, religious and humanist inheritance of Europe, from which have developed the universal values of the inviolable and inalienable rights of the human person, freedom, democracy, equality and the rule of law" (Council of the European Union 2012: 19). The founding treaty of the Council of Europe refers simply to "the spiritual and moral values which are the common heritage of their peoples and the true source of individual freedom, political liberty and the rule of law" (Council of Europe 1949). We should note that there is no explicit reference to Christianity in the treaties. This dimension of the European idea seems to exclude religious fundamentalism and fosters respect and tolerance vis-à-vis religious, sexual, and other minorities.

The third idea refers to the rights of the individual, as embedded in liberal thought. The EU embodies two types of liberalism: on the one hand, the idea of the "inalienable rights of the human person," and on the other hand, the type of economic governance pursued by the EU, juxtaposing a liberal market economy with a coordinated market economy (Fioretos 2012). Whereas the first type of liberal thinking is embodied in high-level EU support for the principle that "LGBTI persons have the same human rights as all individuals, including the right to non-discrimination" (Foreign Affairs Council 2013: 3), the second type of liberalism underlies EU policies which aim to liberalize the market economy, and for that reason sits uneasily with the need for affirmative action and state intervention in order to address structural inequalities. The Council of Europe has a different legacy in this respect, because it has adopted an open approach to economic and social cooperation.

Finally, the fourth myth refers to universalism, the ideals of the French Revolution and Kantian cosmopolitanism, and more in general to the idea that the European model is suitable for people everywhere (Pagden 2002). Both the EU and the Council of Europe have imposed their values on candidate member states requiring them to absorb the *acquis* in national legislation including norms on nondiscrimination (Ayoub 2013). Still, the idea of the European model as a universal model is contested, because a European mission to spread its norms may easily be perceived as imperialism in a new guise (Van der Vleuten and Hulse 2014).

Having presented these four ideas, the next step is to show how they have contributed to the development of a certain identity for Europe's courts, which has enabled or constrained LGBTI activism.

The EU and the ECJ

The identity of the EU is based on the reconciliation of France and Germany, and on market integration as a means of "locking in" this reconciliation (Van der Vleuten 2007). Market integration is based heavily on deregulation and the removal of barriers to free movement of goods, services, capital, and people. Interventionist policies, such as social policy, are merely add-ons that are pursued as far as necessary to legitimize market integration policies and prepare workers better for an integrated market economy. As a result, the liberal identity of the EU has enabled policymaking in all areas linked to nondiscrimination and equal access to the labor market, but it has constrained policy initiatives that go beyond the labor market and the liberal understanding of equality as "sameness." The predecessors of the EU[4] were organizations that focused on economic integration and that offered individuals and companies economic rights, but they made no provisions for a human rights regime (Harpaz 2009). However, according to former judge Federico Mancini, the court has been tasked with "ensuring that the law is observed in the application of a Treaty whose primary objective is an 'ever closer union among the peoples of Europe'" (Mancini and Keeling 1994: 186). Following this line of reasoning, in *KB* the advocate-general (AG) has argued that:

> If we want Community law to be more than a mere mechanical system of economics…, if we wish it to be a legal system corresponding to the concept of social justice and European integration, not only of the economy but of the people, we cannot fail to live up to what is expected from us. (ECJ 2003: para. 80)

Until 1997, however, the ECJ lacked a treaty base. It therefore set about creating one (Mancini and Keeling 1994). In order to avoid an open fight with the governments and the constitutional courts of some member states (Germany being the most outspoken), which may put its authority and legitimacy at risk, the ECJ advanced carefully, always backing itself with two sets of principles: first, the ECHR and case law by the ECtHR, and second, the "constitutional traditions common to the member states" (ECJ 2011: para. 59). Only in 1997, 40 years after the founding of the European Economic Community (EEC), was the duty to protect fundamental rights inserted into the treaties (Article 6 TEU). This remarkable development reflected concerns over anticipated future enlargement to fragile Central and Eastern European democracies as well as the rejection of racism and xenophobia in the "old" member states (Ribeiro Hoffmann 2007). Moreover, on the initiative of Stonewall, a British LGBTI action group, ILGA, successfully lobbied the EP and the Commission for the inclusion of sexual orientation as one of the grounds for nondiscrimination in the treaty (Bell and Waddington 1996). As a result, Treaty Article 19 allows the European institutions to "take appropriate action to combat discrimination based on sex, racial or ethnic origin, religion or belief, disability, age or sexual orientation" (Council of the European Union 2012: 73). Based on the new treaty article, in 2000 the Council eventually approved a proposal to combat direct and indirect discrimination in employment on all the grounds included in Article 19, including sexual orientation (Employment Equality Directive 2000/78/EC). Furthermore, in 2008 the Commission submitted a draft directive that would extend the prohibition of discrimination based on sexual orientation and the other Article 19 grounds beyond the workplace to education, social security, health, goods and services. Unfortunately, the Council has still not reached agreement on this (Council of the European Union 2013). Indeed, the Employment Equality Directive would now be the only legally binding instrument at EU level on LGBTI rights if it had not been for strategic litigation by the LGBTI community and a few audacious rulings on the part of the ECJ (De Waele and Van der Vleuten 2011).

The EU's identity enables litigation where issues can be framed as discrimination in the labor market, but it constrains litigation on body politics and the private sphere. Also, its neoliberal logic helps to promote Europe's liberal ideas and the rule of law, but it clashes with social policies. It is therefore easier to promote the interests of relatively well-off lesbians and gays in Western Europe than the interests of LGBTI groups who have more to gain from a structural transformation such as "blacks and immigrants, and younger, lower-income, anti-assimilationist 'queers'" (Drucker 2006:4). Given its limited legal basis, ECJ jurisprudence remains limited in number and scope, especially when compared to the ECtHR.

The Council of Europe and the ECtHR

The Council of Europe was also built amid the ruins of WWII, based on the conviction that European states had to cooperate in a range of domains to foster mutual understanding. The Council aims "to achieve a greater unity between its members for the purpose of safeguarding and realising the ideals and principles which are their common heritage and facilitating their economic and social progress" (Council of Europe 1949: Article 1). The centrality of human rights was institutionalized with the adoption of the ECHR in 1950, which is interpreted by the court in Strasbourg, and has resulted in "the most advanced and effective regional human rights regime in the world" (Harpaz 2009: 106). However, notwithstanding the central aim of the Council "to achieve a greater unity between its members, and that this aim may be pursued, in particular, through common action in the field of human rights" (Committee of Ministers 2010), litigation was necessary to bring LGBTI issues onto the political agenda of the Council.

In 1981, the Strasbourg Court delivered its first positive decision in an LGBTI case, *Dudgeon v. United Kingdom*, when it decided that a ban on same-sex sexual activity constituted a violation of the right to private life (Article 8). Since then it has ruled in many cases (see Table 6.1), mainly from countries in which a strong activist movement coexists with conservative laws and political stagnation. In his Stonewall lecture,

Table 6.3 The identities of the EU and the CoE

	European Union	Council of Europe
What they oppose	WWII	WWII
Aim	Transcend Franco-German enmity	Achieve greater unity between the European states
Means	Market integration	Common action in the fields of democracy, human rights, rule of law
Logic state – market	Noninterventionist, eliminate obstacles	Interventionist, develop common standards
LGBTI issues framed as	Nondiscrimination, equality in the labor market	Violation of human rights

Dutch academic and activist Kees Waaldijk recalls how he "was struck by the energy and perseverance of the British members of ILGA. No doubt their emphasis on European lobbying and European litigation was also inspired by Thatcherite hopelessness at the national level" (Waaldijk 2003: 5). However, litigation is constrained because the ECHR does not contain a general provision for equality. It stipulates only "that the rights and freedoms set out in the Convention are to be secured without discrimination" (Sanders 1996: 80).

Table 6.3 summarizes my argument. The identity of the Council of Europe enables LGBTI litigation under the label of human rights violations, whereas the identity of the EU enables LGBTI litigation under the label of unequal treatment in the workplace. Activism is constrained by the absence of a general equality provision in the ECHR; as regards the EU, it is constrained by its market-oriented scope and the absence of any fundamental rights provision in the treaties. In the next section, I will examine how litigation has enabled the courts to contribute to the construction of a "rainbow idea of Europe."

Activism in the European legal arena

Is there a European norm on LGBTI rights, a shared understanding that could be derived from the four "ideas of Europe" that we have outlined? To the extent that there is one, it would seem to favor transnational activism and enable progress in "laggard" states. However, Europe's "normative homogeneity" (Harpaz 2009: 129) concerning LGBTI right is a construction in progress. The courts are able to contribute to the construction of a "Euro-norm," first, when they find reasons to argue that prevailing opinions in European society or a majority of countries have changed. Here, the link with political activism becomes tangible. Second, even if there is no European majority (yet), whenever the ECJ is able to find a source of unequal treatment, it is able to produce a strong ruling. Third, once one of the courts has made a breakthrough, the other court relies on the first one, enabling activists to start a new series of cases. I will discuss the three patterns in this section.

Searching for consensus

First, the ability to find some European majority has resulted in positive rulings in a number of cases. The watershed decision in *Dudgeon* was made possible by the fact that the UK lagged far behind most of Europe, and the law in Northern Ireland even further. Activist Jeff Dudgeon and lawyer Peter Ashman, who were both among the founding members of ILGA, were well aware of this. In its decision, the Strasbourg Court referred to changes in other member states and to the fact that in most countries "homosexual acts in private between adults are no longer criminal" (ECtHR 1981). Judge Walsh, in his partially dissenting opinion, considered the argument "unfortunate if this should lead to the erroneous inference that a Euro-norm in the law concerning homosexual practices has been or can be evolved" (ibid.). However, this is precisely what a "Euro-norm" entails, no more and no less. The ECJ, for its part, has explained that it requires a majority of governments to support change, but not unanimity. In *KB*, AG Ruiz-Jarabo Colomer argued that the right of a transsexual to marry a person of the opposite sex was incorporated into the laws of the vast majority (13 of the then 15) of the member states, and

> That fact must of itself be sufficient for the right to form part of the common legal tradition, since if the general principles are to be determined only when there is complete concordance in all the Member States, this line of inquiry would be rendered nugatory. (ECJ 2003: para. 67)

Judge Skouris stressed that the ECJ does not take the lowest common denominator of constitutional traditions to determine the appropriate level of protection (Skouris 2002). Still, to the amazement of many, in *Grant*, the Court did appear to adopt the lowest common denominator when it argued that:

[I]n the present state of the law within the Community, stable relationships between two persons of the same sex are not regarded as equivalent to marriages or stable relationships outside marriage between persons of opposite sex. (ECJ 1998: para. 35)

Jean-Paul Puissochet, the judge-rapporteur in *Grant*, was very aware of the lack of consensus among member states, exemplified by the then heated debate in his home country, France, concerning gay marriage. He would later defend the Court's decision as not "retrograde" but "a scrupulous picture of the state of law at that moment" (Costa and Puissochet 2001). The ECJ concluded that "in those circumstances, it is for the legislature alone to adopt, if appropriate, measures which may affect that position" (1998: para. 36). Its ruling gave a clear message concerning the urgent need for antidiscrimination legislation. This message was captured by Stonewall, which considered the *Grant* case a success, because it highlighted how unjust existing legislation was and thus encouraged media coverage and mobilization (Vanhala 2009).

In fact, the perceived need for the support of the majority of governments for change has not only contributed to progress in states lagging behind, but it has also constituted an obstacle for those out in front. In 2001 in *D. & Sweden v. Council*, the ECJ found that "according to the definition generally accepted by the Member States, the term 'marriage' means a union between two persons of the opposite sex" (ECJ 2001a: para. 34). The Swedish, Danish, and Dutch governments protested that not the ECJ but their national legislations define the concept of marriage, but the ECJ followed AG Mischo, who argued that the ECJ would have to revise its interpretation only if a "broad social development" changed the situation everywhere in the EU, not just in a single [*sic*] member state (ECJ 2001b: para. 42–44).

As lawyer and activist Wintemute admits, he found it "frustrating at first" that the courts always look for a European consensus (Wintemute 2010). In *Schalk and Kopf*, for instance, the ECtHR decided that as long as (at the time) only seven of 47 member states allowed same-sex couples to marry, the court could not force the views of a small minority on all countries. If it were to do so, governments may threaten to leave the convention system, thus leaving the European human rights regime worse off. Accordingly, Wintemute argues that "if the price of binding human rights law is patience, while consensus builds at the national level, I am happy to pay it" (Wintemute 2010).

Patience was indeed required when it came to the rights of transsexuals, which were the object of a series of cases in the 1980s and

1990s, supported by the LGBTI and human rights network. Stephen Whittle, a trans man, TGEU activist and professor of law, belongs to the people embodying the LGBTI triangles. Being X in the famous case *XYZ v. the UK*, he claimed the right to be recognized as the father of Z. He maintained that there had been significant social development since previous cases (*Van Oosterwijck v. Belgium, Rees v. UK, Cossey v. UK*) because, meanwhile, the EP and the Parliamentary Assembly of the CoE had called for recognition of transsexual identity (Resolution OJ 1989 C256 and Recommendation 1117 of 29 September 1989 respectively) and the ECJ had decided that the dismissal of a transsexual for a reason related to gender reassignment amounted to sex discrimination (*P v. S*). The Strasbourg Court, however, observed that there was "no common European standard with regard to the granting of parental rights to transsexuals" and held by 14 votes to six that there was no violation of Article 8 (ECtHR 1997). Nevertheless the number of dissenting opinions indicated a shift in thinking. Dissenting judge Casadevall pointed out in vain that "more and more States... are taking steps to adapt and harmonise their legislation," whereas dissenting judge Foighel argued that "It is part of our common European heritage that governments are under a duty to take special care of individuals who are disadvantaged in any way... It is the Court's task to balance the rights of the individual against the interests of society as a whole" (ibid.).

The proliferation of dissenting opinions motivated further litigation. In *Sheffield and Horsham v. UK*, the Strasbourg Court still saw no violation, but in 2002, it finally ruled unanimously in *Christine Goodwin v. UK* and *I v. UK* that there was a breach of the Convention when transsexual people were not permitted to marry someone of the opposite sex. It referred to a survey by Liberty, a British human rights organization that intervened as a third party, which indicated that "54% of Contracting States permitted such marriage... while 14% did not... The legal position in the remaining 32% was unclear" (ECtHR 2002). Although obviously there was no consensus among the member states, the Court admitted that "A failure by the Court to maintain a dynamic and evolutive approach would indeed risk rendering it a bar to reform or improvement" (ibid.). Therefore, it "attaches less importance to the lack of evidence of a common European approach... than to the clear and uncontested evidence of a continuing international trend in favour not only of increased social acceptance of transsexuals but of legal recognition of the new sexual identity of post-operative transsexuals" (ibid.). Patience paid off in a series of cases concerning sexual orientation and the army (ECtHR), the age of consent (ECtHR), discrimination of same-sex couples (ECtHR and ECJ), and the rights of trans people (ECJ and ECtHR) (see Tables 6.1 and 6.2).

Stretching norms

The second trajectory that enables the courts to promote the protection of LGBTI rights even in the absence of consensus is associated with their willingness to stretch existing norms. In several cases initiated by Stonewall, the ECJ decided to stretch the principle of equal treatment for men and women and apply it to discrimination arising from gender reassignment (ECJ 1996). In *KB*, the discrimination was hypothetical and related to what would happen if she were to predecease her transsexual partner (ECJ 2003). These (and other) results of legal activism pushed the Council of Ministers to update the equal treatment directive and insert into the Preamble the first ever reference to trans people in an EU legal act, where it states that:

> The Court of Justice has held that the scope of the principle of equal treatment for men and women cannot be confined to the prohibition of discrimination based on the fact that a person is of one or other sex...it also applies to discrimination arising from the gender reassignment of a person. (Directive 2006/54, Article 3)

Here, the neoliberal logic underlying EU identity did not constrain but enabled legal activism. In fact, the principle of nondiscrimination based on nationality as the logical consequence of the free movement of persons has enabled the court to rule on sex discrimination. According to judge Skouris (2002), the ECJ has always considered the "four freedoms" (movement of capital, goods, services, and persons) as fundamental because they represent the driving force for the internal market. From the prohibition of discrimination based on nationality, the ECJ made the step to ruling on discrimination based on sex, which subsequently enabled it to rule on discrimination against transsexuals. In this way the ECJ has been able to develop de facto European matrimonial law. Although the AG has emphasized that "it is true that the Community does not have any powers in the sphere [of national civil rules regulating how a person's sex is registered] but, if the UK rules are found to infringe a fundamental right, such a circumstance cannot easily be ignored" (ECJ 2003: para. 2).

The ECJ accomplished another "stretching" act when it ruled that "equal pay" also includes equal rights as regards pensions and other work-related benefits. In *Maruko* and *Römer*, two German cases on the discrimination of same-sex partners, the ECJ followed the AG who argued that although there was no European norm regarding same-sex marriage, there was a European norm on equal treatment and nondiscrimination, and "there is direct discrimination on the ground of sexual orientation because, under national law, that life partner is in a legal and factual situation comparable to that of a married person as regards that pension" (ECJ 2011: para. 52). The ECJ's rulings strengthened the position of lesbians and gays in member states that already had a partnership regulation. However, in Italy and other member states where same-sex relationships have no legal status at all, lesbians and gays will not even find help in Luxembourg. Worse still, litigation can have an unintended negative boomerang effect, as occurred in the case of Poland, which asked and obtained an opt-out from the Charter of Fundamental Rights, for (legally unfounded) fears that ratification of the Charter could oblige Poland to open up civil marriage to same-sex couples (De Waele and Van der Vleuten 2011).

A final example of stretching embodies the fourth idea of Europe as a model for others. The notion of a European standard is present in the first ECJ case on the rights of LGBTI asylum seekers (joined cases *X, Y and Z*). The AG stated that the ECHR contains no express reference to a right to the expression of sexual orientation, but she was able to read it into the ECHR and the decisions of the ECJ, arguing that an applicant for refugee status should not be expected to conceal his sexual orientation in order to avoid persecution in his country of origin (ECJ 2013). For the first time, the ECJ seems to be willing to read more into the ECHR than it says, which is a promising development, especially against the backdrop of increasingly restrictive immigration policies. At the same time, the AG warned that "the aim is not to export those standards" (ibid.: para. 41), because "[s]uch an export might indeed be regarded as a form of human rights or cultural imperialism" (ibid.: fn. 33). Thus, prudently, the AG limited the duty of the ECJ to safeguard human rights to those within EU borders, but made it clear that precisely this duty makes it impossible to send refugees back to countries where LGBTI people cannot live a decent life as LGBTI people.

Two courts are better than one

The third mechanism regards the mutual use of rulings to back up delicate decisions, and the use of a positive ruling in Strasbourg or Luxembourg by activists in the other court. The ECJ ruling in *P v. S* on the rights of transsexuals was used by activists before the ECtHR in *XYZ v. UK*, while *Goodwin v. UK* (ECtHR) was cited in *KB* (ECJ). In

Maruko, Graupner referred to *Karner* and "the trend in Strasbourg Court law" (Graupner 2007: 13). In fact, as the ECJ needs "common constitutional traditions" or ECtHR jurisprudence to be able to break the political deadlock on LGBTI rights, and given the persistent diversity of the constitutional traditions, the ECtHR has become the main addressee of ILGA-Europe litigation. It perceives the ECtHR as pro-active whereas, in the opinion of Wintemute, the ECJ has to date "done nothing for LGBT individuals … unless the ECtHR had already provided some protection" (Wintemute 2013: 17). ILGA-Europe invites its members to come up with relevant cases that would enable the judges in Strasbourg to develop jurisprudence on new issues (ILGA-Europe). In a further step, a Strasbourg Court decision would enable ILGA organizations to bring cases before their domestic courts, which could then submit these cases to the ECJ for clarification, and the ECJ could then be able to rely on the ECtHR jurisprudence.

Conclusion: legal activism and the idea of Europe

My analysis of legal activism for the promotion of LGBTI rights in Europe has revealed a mixed picture. First, the supranational courts are committed to promoting human rights and have managed to include the defense of LGBTI people in their mission, rooted in the "European idea." Court rulings have empowered LGBTI activists in their dealings with their own governments and have been the catalyst for breakthroughs in countries that were lagging behind their European counterparts. The ECJ has in turn been empowered by its interactions with LGBTI activism and the rulings of the ECtHR, having been able to develop itself as a human rights court despite resistance from governments and constitutional courts. Second, it is clear that the courts, despite their commitment to human rights, are reluctant to uphold cases when there is disagreement among member states. Unfortunately, Europe-wide support is often lacking. In parallel with the increase in the number of member states, diversity has also increased. Progress can be difficult when member-state reluctance to allow for the Europeanization of sensitive domains is coupled with eurosceptic and homophobic public opinion. The need for combined political and legal activism therefore remains pivotal, especially since the legal triangle has one fundamental weakness: it is an uneven triangle, since no stable relationship with supranational judges can develop.

Since its inception in 1978, ILGA has invested in the development of a double velvet triangle that combines lobbying and litigation aimed at issues such as the decriminalization of homosexual acts, an equal age of consent, and, more recently, rights of transsexuals and equality in child custody. Strategic litigation by the LGBTI community has enabled the courts to make rulings that have pressured governments to revise domestic and European law. Conversely, in cases where the courts were unable to find consensus for a positive ruling, as in *Grant*, they mobilized Stonewall and others to lobby the European institutions resulting in the inclusion of sexual orientation in the revised Treaty.

Finally, legal scholars such as Guy Harpaz argue that "the adoption of common human rights standards based, inter alia, on the jurisprudence of the Strasbourg Court may provide the cement for the further construction of the European integration project" (Harpaz 2009: 130). In this respect, the legitimacy crisis of the EU and the questions regarding its *raison d'être* in countries that have been hit hard by the financial crisis may offer a window of opportunity for legal and political activism in favor of LGBTI rights as part of a strengthened EU social profile. In fact, although LGBTI activists and the courts have different missions, they have both gained from their interactions. Activists have used the courts when the national road was blocked; they managed to obtain rights for gays, lesbians, and transsexuals, and have thereby contributed to giving Europe a stronger human rights profile. The courts have used the LGBTI demands to strengthen their own position and signal clearly to member states where legal action was necessary when governments agreed that certain types of differential treatment should be banned. Accordingly, the interaction between activists and the courts has contributed to fortifying the construction of a certain idea of Europe.

Notes

I would like to thank Phil Ayoub and David Paternotte for their comments, confidence, and support.

1. The cases concerning the decriminalization of homosexuality brought in the 1950s and 1960s were decided by the European Commission on Human Rights, which until 1980 assisted the ECtHR. They were all dismissed because state interference in the private sphere with the aim of protecting health or morals was deemed in accordance with the European Convention.
2. Other ECJ competences are of less relevance here.
3. Formally, individuals and groups may also bring legal proceedings directly before the ECJ if they can establish a "direct and individual concern" (Article 236 TfEU). However, the procedures are so strict that this is not considered a serious option for litigation (Chicowski 2007).
4. The European Coal and Steel Community (ECSC) and the European Economic Community (EEC).

References

Alter, Karen, ed. 2009. "Law and Politics in Europe and Beyond." In *The European Court's Political Power: Selected Essays*. Oxford: Oxford University Press, 287–303.

Amin, Ash. 2004. "Multi-Ethnicity and the Idea of Europe." *Theory, Culture & Society* 21(2): 1–24.

Ayoub, Phillip M. 2013. "Cooperative Transnationalism in Contemporary Europe: Europeanization and Political Opportunities for LGBT Mobilization in the European Union." *European Political Science Review* 5(2): 279–310.

Bell, Mark and Lisa Waddington. 1996. "The 1996 Intergovernmental Conference and the Prospects of a Non-Discrimination Treaty Article." *Industrial Law Journal* 25(4): 320–336.

Chicowski, Rachel A. 2007. *The European Court and Civil Society*. Cambridge: Cambridge University Press.

Committee of Ministers. 2010. "Recommendation CM/Rec(2010)5 on Measures to Combat Discrimination on Grounds of Sexual Orientation or Gender Identity," https://wcd.coe.int/ViewDoc.jsp?id=1606669 (accessed 18 April 2014).

Conant, Lisa. 2006. "Individuals, Courts, and the Development of European Social Rights." *Comparative Political Studies* 39(1): 76–100.

Costa, Jean-Paul and Jean-Pierre Puissochet. 2001. "Entretien croisé des juges français." *Pouvoirs* 96(1): 161–175.

Council of Europe. 1949. ETS no. 001. Statute of the Council of Europe, London, 5.V.1949. http://conventions.coe.int/Treaty/en/Treaties/Html/001.htm (accessed 18 April 2014).

Council of the European Union. 2012. Consolidated versions of the Treaty on European Union and the Treaty on the Functioning of the European Union and the Charter of Fundamental Rights of the European Union, 12 November, http://register.consilium.europa.eu/doc/srv?l=EN&f=ST%206655%202008%20REV%207 (accessed 18 April 2014).

——. 2013. Report 16438/13, 22 November, http://register.consilium.europa.eu/doc/srv?l=EN&f=ST%2016438%202013%20INIT (accessed 18 April 2014).

De Waele, Henri and Anna van der Vleuten. 2011. "Judicial Activism in European Court of Justice – The Case of Lesbian, Gay, Bisexual and Transgender Rights." *Michigan State Journal of International Law* 19(3): 639–666.

Directive 2006/54. 2006. "European Parliament and Council Directive of 5 July 2006 on the implementation of the principle of equal opportunities and equal treatment of men and women in matters of employment and occupation (Recast)." *Official Journal* L 204, 26 July, http://eur-lex.europa.eu/LexUriServ/LexUriServ.do?uri=OJ:L:2006:204:0023:01:EN:HTML (accessed 18 April 2014).

Drucker, Peter. 2006. "Same-Sex Marriage and the Neoliberal European Agenda." Paper presented at Socialism and Sexuality Seminar, Paris, October 2006. http://www.europe-solidaire.org/spip.php?article11126 (accessed 18 April 2014).

ECJ. 1996. Judgment Case C-13/94 P v S and Cornwall County Council. http://eur-lex.europa.eu/legal-content/EN/TXT/?uri=CELEX:61994CJ0013 (accessed 31 August 2014).

ECJ. 1998. Judgment. Case C-249/96, Lisa Jacqueline Grant v South-West Trains Ltd. http://eur-lex.europa.eu/legal-content/EN/TXT/?uri=CELEX:61996CJ0249 (accessed 18 April 2014).

——. 2001a. Judgment. Joined cases C-122/99 P and C-125/99 P, D and Kingdom of Sweden v Council of the European Union. http://curia.europa.eu/juris/liste. jsf?language=en&num=C-122/99%20P (accessed 18 April 2014).

——. 2001b. Opinion of Advocate General Mischo. Joined cases C-122/99 P and C-125/99 P, D and Kingdom of Sweden v Council of the European Union. http://curia.europa.eu/juris/liste.jsf?language=en&num=C-122/99%20P (accessed 18 April 2014).

——. 2003. Opinion of Advocate General Ruiz-Jarabo Colomer. Case C-117/01, K.B. v National Health Service Pensions Agency and Secretary of State for Health. http://curia.europa.eu/juris/liste.jsf?language=en&num=C-117/01 (accessed 18 April 2014).

——. 2011. Case 147/08, Jürgen Römer v Freie und Hansestadt Hamburg. http://curia.europa.eu/juris/liste.jsf?language=en&num=C-147/08 (accessed 18 April 2014).

——. 2013. Opinion of Advocate General Sharpston. Joined Cases C-199/12, C-200/12 and C-201/12, X, Y and Z v. Minister voor Immigratie, Integratie en Asiel. http://curia.europa.eu/juris/liste.jsf?language=en&num=C-199/12 (accessed 18 April 2014).

ECSOL Homepage!. http://www.sexualorientationlaw.eu/ (accessed 18 April 2014).

ECtHR. 1981. Dudgeon v. UK. http://hudoc.echr.coe.int/sites/eng/pages/search.aspx?i=001-57473 (accessed 18 April 2014).

——. 1997. X, Y and Z v. UK. http://hudoc.echr.coe.int/sites/eng/pages/search.aspx?i=001-58032 (accessed 18 April 2014).

——. 2002. Christine Goodwin v. The United Kingdom, http://hudoc.echr.coe.int/sites/eng/pages/search.aspx?i=001-60596 (accessed 18 April 2014).

Fioretos, Orfeo. 2012. "Coordinated versus Liberal Market Economies." In *The Oxford Handbook of the European Union*, eds. Erik Jones, Anand Menon and Stephen Weatherill. Oxford: Oxford University Press, 292–305.

Foreign Affairs Council. 2013. Guidelines to Promote and Protect the Enjoyment of All Human Rights by LGBTI Persons, Luxemburg, 24 June. http://www.consilium.europa.eu/uedocs/cms_Data/docs/pressdata/EN/foraff/137584.pdf (accessed 18 April 2014).

Garrett, Geoffrey. 1995. "The Politics of Legal Integration in the European Union." *International Organization* 49(1): 171–181.

Graupner, Helmut. 2007. Oral Observations of Rechtsanwalt Dr. Helmut Graupner on Behalf of Mr. Maruko's Co-representative ILGA-Europe. Draft of 16 June 2007. http://www.ilga-europe.org/media_library/ilga_europe/how_we_work/litigation/ecj (accessed 18 April 2014).

Harpaz, Guy. 2009. "The European Court of Justice and Its Relations with the European Court of Human Rights: The Quest for Enhanced Reliance, Coherence and Legitimacy." *Common Market Law Review* 46(1): 105–141.

Helfer, Laurence R. and Erik Voeten. 2014. "International Courts as Agents of Legal Change: Evidence from LGBT Rights in Europe." *International Organization* 68(1): 77–110.

Holzhacker, Ron. 2012. "National and Transnational Strategies of LGBT Civil Society Organizations in Different Political Environments: Modes of Interaction in Western and Eastern Europe of Equality." *Comparative European Politics* 10(1): 23–47.

ILGA-Europe homepage. Fact Sheet on Strategic Litigation. http://www.ilga-europe.org/home/how_we_work/litigation/resources (accessed 18 April 2014).

Kollman, Kelly. 2009. "European Institutions, Transnational Networks and National Same-Sex Union Policy: When Soft Law Hits Harder." *Contemporary Politics* 15(1): 1–17.

Mancini, Giuseppe F. and David T. Keeling. 1984. "Democracy and the European Court of Justice." *Modern Law Review* 57(2): 175–190.

Pagden, Anthony, ed. 2002. *The Idea of Europe: From Antiquity to the European Union.* Cambridge: Cambridge University Press.

Paternotte, David and Alison Woodward. 2014. "Travelling Concepts: The Velvet Triangle in Motion." Unpublished paper.

Paternotte, David and Kelly Kollman. 2013. "Regulating Intimate Relationships in the European Polity: Same-Sex Unions and Policy Convergence." *Social Politics* 20(4): 510–533.

Pescatore, Pierre. 1983. "The Doctrine of 'Direct Effect': An Infant Disease of Community Law." *European Law Review* 8: 155–177.

Ribeiro Hoffmann, Andrea. 2007. "Political Conditionality and Democratic Clauses in the EU and Mercosur." In *Closing or Widening the Gap? Legitimacy and Democracy in Regional Integration Organizations*, eds. Andrea Ribeiro Hoffmann and Anna van der Vleuten. Farnham: Ashgate, 173–189.

Sanders, Douglas. 1996. "Getting Lesbian and Gay Issues on the International Human Rights Agenda." *Human Rights Quarterly* 18:1, 67–106.

Skouris, Vassilios. 2002. "Speaking Note of Judge Vassilios Skouris," Hearing of 17 September, Working Group II, Working Document 19. http://european-convention.eu.int/docs/wd2/3057.pdf (accessed 18 April 2014).

Van der Vleuten, Anna. 2007. *The Price of Gender Equality: Member States and Governance in the European Union.* Aldershot: Ashgate.

Van der Vleuten, Anna and Merran Hulse. 2014. "Gender mainstreaming in SADC and SADC-EU Trade Relations." In *Gender Equality Norms in Regional Governance: Transnational Dynamics in Europe, South America and Southern Africa*, eds. Anna van der Vleuten, Anouka van Eerdewijk and Conny Roggeband. Basingstoke: Palgrave MacMillan, 165–192.

Vanhala, Lisa. 2009. "Anti-Discrimination Policy Actors and Their Use of Litigation Strategies: The Influence of Identity Politics." *Journal of European Public Policy* 16(5): 738–754.

Waaldijk, Kees. 2003. "Taking Same-Sex Partnerships Seriously: European Experiences as British Perspectives?" https://openaccess.leidenuniv.nl/bitstream/handle/1887/5229/Waaldijk%202003-Taking%20same-sex%20partnerships%20seriously%20%28full%20text%20of%20Stonewall%20lecture%202002%29.pdf?sequence=2 (accessed 18 April 2014).

Waaldijk, Kees and Matteo Bonini-Baraldi. 2006. *Sexual Orientation Discrimination in the European Union: National Laws and the Employment Equality Directive.* The Hague: TMC Asscher Press.

Wieacker, Franz. 1981. "The Importance of Roman Law for Western Civilization and Western Legal Thought." *Boston College International & Comparative Law Review* 4(2): 257–281.

Wintemute, Robert. 2010. "Consensus Is the Right Approach for the European Court of Human Rights." *The Guardian*, 12 August. http://www.theguardian.

com/law/2010/aug/12/european-court-human-rights-consensus (accessed 18 April 2014).

——. 2013. *Sexual Orientation and Gender Identity Discrimination: The Case Law of the European Court of Human Rights and the European Court of Justice.* http://www.ilga-europe.org/home/how_we_work/litigation/cjeu_litigation (accessed 18 April 2014).

Woodward, Alison. 2003. "Building Velvet Triangles: Gender and Informal Governance." In *Informal Governance in the European Union*, eds. Thomas Christiansen and Simona Piattoni. Cheltenham: Edward Elgar: 76–93.

7
Queer Activism and the Idea of "Practicing Europe"
Konstantinos Eleftheriadis

Debates on Europeanization, European identity, and belonging to Europe have primarily addressed relations with the European Union (EU) (Passerini et al. 2007: 4; Borneman and Fowler 1997: 488). Europe is seen as a result of administrative and political processes, which take place from the EU for the EU, "an end in itself" (Borneman and Fowler 1997: 488), while cultural aspects, which equally shape political and social processes, are presented as marginal (Passerini et al. 2007: 5). These institutional approaches have particularly affected social movement studies. Discussions on bottom-up/grassroots mobilization tend to perceive Europe as a frame to gain access to the institutional polity and the official public sphere. The LGBT case is very illustrative of this trend: transnational and local LGBT movements use Europe and its institutions (European Union, Council of Europe) as a strategic channel to claim and gain rights (Ayoub and Paternotte 2012).

Approaching this topic from a nonnominalist and a cultural perspective, I explore the broader idea of what Europe signifies, by encompassing cross-border practices that also transform the European political and social landscape. By shifting attention to social movements – which do not interplay directly with the institutions, do not have access to the official public sphere, and do not use "Europe" as an explicit discursive frame – we can understand better the new configurations of "the idea of Europe" as an extra-institutional construction. Standing outside the institutions, these social movements participate in the building of "the idea of Europe" through the enacting of specific cross-border practices, giving birth to "transnational solidarities" that are "the result of interest convergences and identities of the actors involved beyond national borders" (Dufour 2010: 94, my translation; for a similar perspective see Binnie and Klesse, Chapter 9 in this book).

This chapter focuses on the queer movement, a movement that does not interplay directly with institutions but rather runs counter to dominant cultural narratives. Through the study of a specific form of action, that of queer festivals, I show how these political events are *performed* by cross-border movements, and how these cross-border movements illustrate aspects of "an idea of Europe" that involves noninstitutional relations, giving form to new "transnational solidarities," which move beyond the institutional sphere. In this chapter I will focus on the cross-border practices that are used to set up queer festivals and which help us to understand the ways in which "Europe" as well as being the result of institutionalized and administrative processes is also produced performatively through specific practices going beyond national borders. This focus on queer festivals and cross-border practices therefore helps us reconsider the traditionally established relationships between social movements and transnationalism, and clarifies the new forms of connection developing between activists across Europe.

Queer festivals are political sites that generate new collective identities, which prioritize the idea of breaking the gender and sexual binaries upon which societies have been built: man/woman, gay/straight, cis[1]/trans. By engaging people from across borders, queer festivals build "transnational solidarities" shaped through the realization of specific practices. These practices are performed through physical and digital cross-border movements. They can be strategic, as shown by the use of multiple languages to connect with a wider international public, or they can follow already existing paths of transnational processes, such as the international composition of the organization committees with people who already live or work in one of these cities. The term "cross-border practice" is preferred to avoid binary dilemmas between "acting" and "feeling" transnational, between strategy and practice (Favell et al. 2011: 19). In both cases, queer activists perform a specific kind of transnationalism that is connected to the European space, despite the nonexistence of "Europe" as a frame of action and claim-making.

This specific form of transnationalism is a basic component of queer festivals. The queer movement does not involve European transnational or supranational institutions, since it does not push for policy and legal changes *stricto sensu*. In other words, since queer festivals attempt to construct collective identities that challenge established gender and sexual identities, they can therefore be more usefully placed against the background of the cultural than the institutional arena, particularly since they do not implement any "coordinated actions against fixed targets," similar to other decentralized, oppositional formations (Juris

2008: 201). Moreover, festivals in general (which are particular forms of cultural activity) address *a priori* unknown audiences, and, as a result, can be usefully connected with the idea of a counter-public. As Michael Warner argues:

> A public sets its boundaries and its organization by its own discourse rather than by external frameworks only if it openly addresses people who are identified primarily through their participation in the discourse and who therefore cannot be known in advance. (2002: 56)

These connections can be traced at the socialization level, through friends, acquaintances, and digital networks, or at the participation level in the broader leftist scene of the cities in which festivals take place.

One of the focuses of this study is to see how different forms of activist transnationalism take place. One method of doing this is to check through participant observation: the specific practices that constitute these activist spaces – queer festivals – as transnational arenas. Thus, it is possible to understand how a new form of Europeanness emerges; a "counter"-Europeanness that stands critically against institutionalized politics and attempts to create new forms of sociality and politics. I divide these cross-border practices into four categories, all of which are analyzed below: (i) language, (ii) composition of the organization committees and participants, (iii) links with other leftist movements and cultures, and (iv) digital communication. This list is not exhaustive but allows for a more analytic approach to the topic, since the four categories capture the extra-institutional nature of the processes constructing the festivals as transnational arenas. The way multilingualism is negotiated, for example, helps address a European audience and therefore enhances "inclusive deliberation" (Doerr 2009), thus sustaining transnational solidarities. The international composition of the organization committees and participants follows the already well-established paths of the Europeanization of capital cities, in which intra-European "migrants" are active political participators in their new cities. Moreover, the links of these "migrants" with several European leftist cultures tracks the historical mechanisms of travelling political identities in Europe. Finally, digital networking expands Europe's understanding of nonphysical connections established across the continent.

The analysis relies on an ethnography of queer festivals across Europe. Queer festivals are arenas for an international audience, thus appropriate a transnational political character. They are annual political gatherings, taking place in various European cities. Although queer festivals differ from each other due to their local specificities, there are some common patterns. The queer festivals I study here took place between July 2011 and April 2013 in five European capitals: Copenhagen, Berlin, Oslo, Amsterdam, and Rome. Participant observation is complemented by life stories conducted with activists and participants in the festivals.[2] I use written material, online data, and texts that were circulated in the festivals. Finally, the findings of an online survey (n = 26) which was carried out at the Oslo queer festival will also be presented.[3] The chapter begins with a historical introduction and contextualization of transnational queer politics in Europe. The political and ideological roots of these are described before the case studies are presented.

What is "queer" about European queer festivals: definitions and roots

Unlike the institutionalized activism of the broader LGBT movement, queer activism in Europe has set itself apart from policy-oriented politics. Queer is a "notoriously slippery term" with many ambiguous connotations, due among other things to the ability of the concept to travel and its untranslatability in non-American contexts (Brown forthcoming: 2). In order to clarify how I use the term queer activism, I have adopted Gamson's definition:

> a loose but distinguishable set of political movements and mobilizations ... operat[ing] largely through the decentralized, local, and often anti-organizational cultural activism of street postering, parodic and non-conformist self-presentation, and underground alternative magazines ("zines"). (Gamson 1995: 393)

The main objective of queer politics is to reject identifications with sexual and gender categories, which are viewed as creating new forms of oppression. Influenced by the dialogue with queer theorizing, which also developed in the late 1980s, the challenge against taken-for-granted binaries (e.g. man/woman; gay/straight) has become the core of the queer movement (Brown forthcoming).

Queer politics in Europe

The beginning of the 1990s saw the emergence of queer forms of politics in Europe. It is argued that this diffusion of queer ideas and politics started with the creation of New York-originated ACT-UP branches in several European capitals, such as London, Paris, and Berlin (Brown forthcoming). London saw the birth of some queer groups mobilizing against the Conservative Thatcherite discourses (Bell and Binnie 2000: 44). The most prominent of these, OutRage!, drew upon the legacy of ACT-UP London and was influenced by the direct action protests in response to the Thatcher government's implementation of section 28 of the Local Government Act (1988), which prohibited the use of public funds to "intentionally promote" homosexuality (Brown forthcoming).

ACT-UP Paris is another example of successful transnational diffusion of social movements. As Christophe Broqua explains in his analysis, it was initially journalist Didier Lestrade's articles in the gay magazine *GaiPied* and the daily newspaper *Liberation* that introduced the French public to ACT-UP New York (2005: 66). Lestrade founded ACT-UP Paris with two of his colleagues and they imported new repertoires of action to the Parisian streets, such as die-ins (Broqua 2005: 71). The connections with the USA were close. This is testified by the T-shirts "SILENCE=DEATH"[4] ordered from New York they displayed during their first appearance in the Parisian Gay Pride of 1989. Moreover, regular trips to New York by the Parisian members, as well as various press articles on ACT-UP New York and ACT-UP London, created a space for this sort of anti-AIDS activism in Paris. Although none of the above-mentioned groups utilized "queer" as a mobilizing identity, nearly all of them created the space for a new type of politics to emerge: politics which claims to be angry, confrontational, and beyond sexual identities.

Concerning the ideological bases of queer politics in Europe, the diffusion of queer theory was also crucial. Queer theory quickly found its way into European academia, starting in the UK and later expanding to Germany, France, Scandinavia, Italy, adapting each time to the local context into which it was transposed. Central and Eastern European countries were equally affected by the diffusion of queer theory, although their historical specificities created different "temporal disjunctions" (Kulpa and Mizielinska 2011). In their book *Queer in Europe*, Downing and Gillett argue that the phrase now being used to describe "queer in Europe," should be understood as a tool to describe

> the ways in which strategies that we might call "queer" ... are currently being implemented, discussed, taught or otherwise disseminated in a range of European countries. (Downing and Gillett 2011: 4)

Queer theory is now present in various academic programs across Europe, usually as part of the programs on gender studies, or as specific courses in the humanities and social sciences.

By the end of the 1990s, when the alterglobalization movement began to emerge, many European and American queer groups aligned with anarchist and anti-capitalist strands of the global justice movement (Brown forthcoming; Portwood-Stacer 2010: 487). In 1998, queer activists coming from the anarchist scene of London organized the first Queeruption festival, which went on to function as an annual transnational queer gathering for the next ten years. The following extract was retrieved from Queeruption's website in 2010 just before it shut down:

> We hope this site will convey the diversity of queer life, identity, and politics; provide visibility for a definition of queer that confounds and contradicts the limited representation of the "normal"/consumerist model; and be an active tool for building community that recognises the differences in queerness globally.

Queeruption festivals took place in several cities (New York, San Francisco, London, Berlin, Amsterdam, Sydney, Barcelona, Tel Aviv, and Vancouver) and created a transnational electronic platform whose mailing list functioned as the main channel of communication between queer activists. As well as organizational strategies and actions, identity issues were debated on this list, while hot topics such as Islamophobia and racism were at the frontline of the discussions.

Queeruption festivals were organized in various European capitals. These events had clear links with the alterglobalization movement, which too was developing during that period. Gavin Brown acknowledges that Queeruption festivals were spaces that were "inspired by the anti-capitalist networks of the global justice movement" (2007: 2685). Hence, queer politics in Europe also took the form of pink blocs in big demonstrations (Juris 2008: 74) and the European social forums (Doerr 2007: 82). Membretti and Mudu acknowledge, for instance, that at the demonstration of Genoa in 2001, there were "various blocks oriented towards different uses of space for demonstrating," one of those being the "queer/spectacular" (2013: 88).

Based on anti-authoritarian structures, *Queeruption* was defined with the following words:

> Queeruption is non-commercial! Queeruption is Do-it-Yourself! We draw no line between organisers and participants. We seek to provide a framework (space, co-ordination), which you can fill with your

ideas. It will include workshops, music, demonstrations, film, art, performances, (sex) parties, picnics, games and any other activities your feel like trying! What is Queeruption? What is queer culture? For expression and exploration of identity. Climbing over the artificial boundaries of sexuality, gender, nation, class! Against racism, capitalism, patriarchy and binary gender repression. (cited in Poldervaart, 2003: 6–7)

The aim of all the festivals organized by Queeruption was "to create a DIY [Do-It-Yourself] alternative to a passive, apolitical involvement in the commercial gay scene" (Brown 2007: 2686). While Queeruption is no longer active, it did create the opportunity for new generations of activists to gain experience and develop a specific network. It also contributed to the consolidation of a submerged "anarcho-queer" movement (Hekma 2012: 758) and of a queer feminist transnational movement, which is still active through transnational networks. For instance, Ladyfest Rome draws on the Riot Girls' movement of the 1990s, identifying it as "a solid international network with the main aim of promoting women's art and deconstructing feminine stereotypes, revaluating body and sexuality in its infinite expressions from a queer, feminist and anti-racist perspective."[5]

Contemporary queer festivals are usually urban-based and take place on an annual basis, sharing organizational and framing patterns with those of *Queeruption*. Their urban nature connects with the idea that cities allow "for a radically anti-assimilationist queer identity rejecting the spatio-temporal foundations of the nation-state" (El-Tayeb 2012: 85). Interestingly, Queeruption and these city-based festivals did not follow a linear, successive line, but started to overlap after 2006, the year when the first Copenhagen queer festival took place. In sum, queer politics in Europe developed mainly during the alterglobalization movements. It crystallized as a political identity with the transnational Queeruption festivals. More recently, together with small, locally based groups across the European continent queers in Western European capitals have organized transnational annual events in which solidarities are sustained and enhanced. These events are performed through cross-border practices, which will be analyzed in the next section.

Queer festivals, cross-border practices and "the idea of Europe"

This section describes the different ways in which the idea of "practicing Europe" materializes, and explores how queer festivals are constructed transnationally through specific cross-border practices. These practices are divided into four categories: language, composition of the organization committees and participants, links with other leftist movements and cultures, and digital communication. By analyzing these practices, I show that queer festivals function as transnational arenas, and that they develop an alternative form of Europeanness – that is, a "counter"-Europeanness that attempts to create new forms of transnational solidarities.

Language

One of the strategic and basic aims of queer festivals is to address an international public. This aim is achieved primarily through English. The use of a nonlocal language to address an international audience is important because it exemplifies the attempt of the organizers to transnationalize their events. Language helps to address a (broadly speaking) European public, while it enhances the inclusive deliberation supported by the organizers' arrangements.

One of the first things to notice is that there is a clear attempt on the part of the queer organizers to try to include non-English speakers. Since 2013, for instance, the queer festivals of Amsterdam and Berlin[6] have displayed their callouts in multiple languages, including non-European migrants' languages:

> The call set out is available in other languages including: Nederlands, Deutsch, Español, Português, Italiano, يبرع, & Türkçe. Please specify if you will be conducting your workshop in a language other than English so we can connect you with community translators. (Amsterdam 2013)[7]

By publishing/drafting their callouts in national languages as well as in English and other languages, including migrants' languages, queer festivals illustrate their attempt to reach a wider audience. This audience is not only composed of people who are familiar with the event, but also newcomers. These newcomers cannot be identified in advance. Usually, they are friends or acquaintances of people familiar with the festivals, they participate in digital networks, or in the broader leftist scenes of the cities in which the festivals take place. At the same time, these callouts, given that they are also written in non-European languages, push the linguistic limits of Europe beyond the traditional associations with languages such as English, French, and German.

At the level of practice, queer festivals attempt to create strategies for linguistic inclusion. Due to the lack of financial resources and based on the DIY ethos, organizers attempt to establish translations on an ad hoc basis, asking support from participants. These strategies are therefore less organized than in other political transnational events such as the European social forums (Doerr 2009).

An illustrative example of ad hoc translations comes from the workshop "Queer activism and class" I organized at the Queeristan festival in Amsterdam in May 2012. At the beginning of the workshop, some participants told me that three Spanish activists wanted to participate in the workshop; their understanding of English was, however, very poor. Sara,[8] a Greek participant, standing next to us, took the initiative to translate into Spanish, since she spoke both English and Spanish fluently. The Spanish activists and Sara moved to the back of the room, and while I was presenting the workshop, she quietly translated to them in Spanish. The same thing happened at the 2013 Queer Festival in Rome, where Italian was the predominant language of the event. Translation into and from English functioned similarly for participants or invitees who did not speak Italian. Once again, translations into English happened organically, in order to make non-Italian speakers part of the queer festival.

This awareness of linguistic diversity brings particular benefits to the festivals, since it allows for broader audiences, and thus wider inclusive deliberation. Similar linguistic mechanisms permit transnational political events to be more inclusive than nationally based ones, in which a single linguistic format is usually applied. As Nicole Doerr describes in the case of European social forums:

> inclusive deliberation in the European meetings could be an outcome of the multilingual working practices in these European meetings compared to single language formats in national social forum meetings. (2009: 93)

In this sense, multilingual activist environments are capable of generating inclusiveness, since they favor communication.

Contrary to the European social forums' technical infrastructure and skilled personnel, which assured continuous translation through systems such as Babel (Doerr 2009), queer festivals negotiate multilingualism in a more interpersonal way, supported by the organizers of the events. Although it has been noted that language barriers can constitute a disadvantage for the construction of a European public sphere (Offe 2003), queer activists like their predecessors, such as the alterglobalization movement and the European social forums, have developed strategies to remove, to the greatest possible extent, these barriers.

Multilingualism is becoming a de facto situation in the interactions between activists given the fact that the festivals attract many foreign participants. The tendency, however, is that the basic activities of the festivals take place in English. The daily plenaries and the presentations of the workshops are indicative examples of this trend. Equally, the texts circulating within the spaces are usually in English: fanzines, flyers, programs, advertising posters, rules, and the prices of drinks are displayed in English, together with the local languages. At the same time, personal interactions adapt to the common linguistic knowledge of the people involved, although English is considered the common language *par excellence*.

This does not imply, however, that communication and multilingualism does not generate tension. During my observation, I noticed that there was some concern about the widespread use of English. As Kate, an Australian female participant at the Oslo queer festival put it: "As an English speaker, I see that some are uncomfortable with that."[9] People coming from countries where English is not widely taught and spoken (e.g. Spain and the Ukraine) might have some difficulty in following the everyday interactions or the workshops and performances.

Another concern regarding the linguistic practices relates to the use of specific "queer" academic jargon. Terms such as "heteronormativity," "cis" or "essentialist" all circulate within the everyday discussions at the festivals and constitute a basic part of the theoretical toolkit that is used in the workshops. The problem is that activists with no extensive knowledge of gender studies do not always feel comfortable with these academic terms. This connection between gender studies jargon and queer activism is a recurrent issue within the festivals. As Tobin, a member of the organization committee of the Queeristan festival in Amsterdam, and a PhD candidate in cultural analysis, says:

> the majority of queer theory is presented and published in English. So, it's also like we organize things here only in English. So, that also already appeals that, sort of interpellates [addresses] international, transnational audience.[10]

Vladimir, an employee in a call center in Berlin, who came to the Copenhagen festival, with a basic understanding of queer studies, said:

Yesterday [on the second day of the Copenhagen festival] for example, I realized I was the only person in the ... maybe one of the only persons in the room, who didn't know a term, which was very important [*He does not reveal the word. I ask him*] ... *"cis."*[11]

Gel, an Israeli queer activist, living in Berlin, said at the beginning of her narration:

The queer part came after, like learning more about gender. Maybe I'm the only one you interviewed that didn't study gender studies (laugh). No? [Asking me] [sigh].[12]

This lack of familiarity with the academic jargon, however, motivates some participants to learn more about it. As Giacomo from Oslo says:

I feel I miss elements of the language that I would like to understand more ... I think there is this gap ... that needs to be filled in, in terms of making things more approachable also for the everyday ... I believe that probably our schools, and our basic education should include more for, in terms for example of gender studies and you know also would make people, even people that might not feel directly connected to these issues, I think it would be very helpful for society.[13]

Robin, participating in the Copenhagen festival in 2011, expresses the same motivation:

I want to continue my studies in gender relations and specifically masculinities and femininities. And how masculinities shift and also looking at oppression, and how masculinity shifts under oppression, in different kinds of oppression ... So, I don't find myself in mainstream LGBT frames. And that's why joining this queer collective I found that there are no limits and we got for at least more education, giving more information.[14]

Composition of the organization committees and participants

The international composition of the organizing committees constitutes a further aspect of the idea of "practicing Europe." The international composition of the organization committees and the festivals' participants reflect the already well-established paths that Europeanization has taken in relation to capital cities, in the sense that many nonnationals participating in the organizing committees live, work, and study.

Regarding participants, they tend to come from neighboring countries. Proximity in this sense is very important for the attendance in the events.

Queer festivals are organized horizontally, in that their organizing committees are informally connected through consensus-based deliberation. These organizing committees deal with the setting up of the festivals. Although some of their members are stable, open calls for new members to join always take place a few months before the festivals, as illustrated by the callout for the Oslo queer festival 2013, which states: "Do you want to participate in making this year festival? We have to decide where we want the festival to take place year! Come and help us decide."[15]

Similarly, on 12 January 2013, the Queeristan festival in Amsterdam published a call: "We're starting to organise again for 2013! Meetings every Sunday at the Latin American Center at 17h. If you're interested in organising with us come to our meeting tomorrow."[16] Festivals display these calls mainly through social media (Facebook, mailing lists etc.)

In order to reflect Europe's diversity, the groups organizing the festivals are very keen to create a core with members from diverse backgrounds: national, gender, and sexual. This diversity in the organizing groups reflects the diversity of participants in the events. In fact, many people cross the borders in order to attend queer events. The reasons for attending vary, spanning from a feeling of belonging to an imaginary transnational queer community to affective reasons, such as intimate relationships or friendships. A combination of motivations is also very common. As Tobin, a member of the Amsterdam festival, emphasized:

> Many of them [the old organizational members] are still in the circles; they're still in the network. But like I said, the group is mostly international, so many people do not have Dutch citizenship, most of them students, so they're here for a semester or for two semesters. Or many people leave again. But there is such a commitment that people are still part of the network... This year one of the participants of last year's organization flew over from the USA to give workshops.[17]

The Amsterdam organizing committee is very international, whereas in Oslo, three-quarters of the organizers are Norwegians and in Rome, nearly all the members are Italians.

Diversity in national origins is much more visible among the participants in the events. The pattern is clearly shaped by geographical proximity. Thus, residents from neighboring countries tend to come more than those living further away, making proximity a "critical factor" (this can be seen in Ayoub's (2013: 291) work on Polish sexual minorities mobilizing in Berlin). For instance, several people from Berlin attended the Copenhagen queer festival,[18] while many Scandinavians and British are regular visitors of the Oslo festival. This confirms the results found through my Internet survey on the composition of the activists and participants at the Oslo queer festival: 41.7 % of the respondents live in Oslo, 25% in Sweden, 16.7% in the rest of Norway (this means that 58.4 % of the activists live in Norway in total), 8.3 % in the UK, and 8.3% in other European countries (one of them being Iceland). The national origins of the activists are even more diverse: 45.8 % claim to have been born in Norway, 16.7 % in Sweden, 8.3 % in Korea and Italy, and 20.8 % in other countries (UK, Iceland, Germany, France, and Greece).

In sum, the diversity of the members at the organizational and the participation levels brings us back to the argument of the idea of "practicing Europe." Many nonnational activists who live in the cities where festivals take place play a part in organizing the festivals. Moreover, many people travel to the cities in order to attend the events, thus forming a continuous movement of people beyond institutional channels.

Transnational activist networks: links with other European leftist (sub-)cultures

Transnational links between the festivals allow queer activists to shape a sort of activist map, in which circulation of ideas becomes possible. This kind of mapping is not new for progressive social movements or for the European left in general. Social movements as well as institutional actors, such as political parties, on the left have always connected through networks.

In Western Europe, in particular, actors on the left coordinated and exchanged information and resources and built common identities after WWII and the division of the continent into two blocks. Despite any local differences, European identities of the left circulated very actively in this space, dividing the European left across similar categories. One clear example of how this division of political identities operated across borders can be seen, for instance, in the split of the communist parties into Stalinists/pro-USSR and euro-communists/anti-Stalinists groups, and this split has left its mark on Europe (March and Mudde 2005). The contemporary identity of antifa (antifascist) (Doidge 2013: 258) and the digital network Europeans against the political system are further manifestations of the European trend to make cross-border political identifications available through networks.

Personal link is a crucial factor for the maintenance and strengthening of queer networks. Similarly to what Ayoub refers to as "tactics of European socialization" (2013: 302), queers exploit the networking resources they have from queers across Europe in order to transnationalize their festivals as much as possible. By capitalizing on these networks, organizing committees are able to invite and give space to crews from other festivals. A good example of this is the participation of the crew from the Amsterdam-based Queeristan festival in Rome in April 2013. The personal links between one of the organizers of the Rome festival with the Queeristan group when he was studying in Amsterdam created these ties, which brought the two groups together. The Queeristan crew, composed of eight activists from Amsterdam, gave a speech entitled "Bridging the gap: Beyond the dichotomy theory/practice" in one of the workshops. For this workshop, the organizers had also invited "Pink Panthers," a Portuguese queer organization, Athens Pride from Greece, and Rachele Borghi, an Italian academic and performer who was living in Rennes, France at the time. The organizers' objective was not only to share experiences from queer politics, especially those in Southern Europe, but also, as Andrea Gilbert from Athens Pride mentioned "to create a political network for the future."

Political links across borders are also visible through the discourses at the festivals. For instance, the Copenhagen festival's main slogan "Do it yourself, do it together" is linked to one of the principal characteristics of the leftist extra-parliamentary scenes of Europe, especially those connected to anarchist subcultures. As Leach and Haunss remind us in their study on the Autonomous Movement in Germany, the politics of these subcultures are based on "a rejection of representative politics of any stripe ... they reject the structural hierarchy and ideological dogmatism" (2009: 262). So the links between these subcultures of the left and queer festivals lead us back to the idea of "practicing Europe" through digital networking.

Similarly, when describing the DIY feminism in the European alterglobalization movement, Saskia Poldervaart explains that "Do It Yourself" stands for designing each individual's own life and taking initiatives, without expecting political or social institutions to do so (2006: 8). Moreover, the advertising of the festival is similar to the ways by which leftist events are made public: street posters constitute the main source of information about the event for the inhabitants of the city, as with other leftist events.[19]

Furthermore, interviews with queer activists show that Europe functions as a space in which activists circulate and build different

political subjectivities. These activists construct their political awareness through participating in various movements in different countries.
Their life stories tend to reveal their attraction toward transnational
political trajectories, mainly within leftist political groups, as well as
to different anarchist and leftist scenes around Europe. The interviews
show that the subjects establish political relationships, which they
take them with them when travelling or moving to another country
(Passerini et al. 2007: 3). Since many of these activists have lived in
places other than where the festival takes place, either permanently or
as visitors, they often already have affiliations with groups from other
countries.

Thus, activists and participants can hold several political identities
and membership in different places across Europe. Many come from (or
support) a varied far-leftist ideology (anarchism, anti-authoritarianism,
anti-fascism, leftist libertarianism), while others feel more connected to
the traditional left (environmentalism, social-democracy).

Robin, a member of the Queeristan festival in Amsterdam and an
active member of the Boycotts, Divestment and Sanctions (BDS) movement, the main objective of which is to fight against "Israeli apartheid,"
as they call it, said:

> In the Netherlands I gave different workshops in different venues,
> anarchist venues, or just specific events for Palestinian issues. I give
> talks, mainly about the Palestinian situation, under Israeli occu-
> pation. So, I am very active on that. I am always invited to give
> talks... But now with the queer issue, this is very new, and this is
> where I find myself more and this is where I want to take it more and
> that's why I want to support it with more education so that I can take
> it further.[20]

For Robin, his queer struggle in Amsterdam cannot be separated from his
links with his home nation, Palestine: he is both queer and a Palestinian.
He describes his intersectional identity very well in his interview:

> The queer is part of my personality. But it is very well connected,
> very much connected to the occupation. So that's how it's different
> [from the other Dutch queer activists]. In the Netherlands, the
> queer... and being an international movement, not specifically about
> the Netherlands, but having more international activists brings it to
> [a] more global perspective. Palestinian queer is a very specific [iden-
> tity], [it is] about Palestinian background.[21]

Sergio, a Turkish PhD student in Amsterdam, is also jumping between several activist identities. His basic identity is not queer. He focuses, instead, on radical environmentalism and climate change. He claims that it was the climate summit in Copenhagen in 2009 that changed his mind about radical politics:

> I meet these wonderful people, climate justice action, basically autonomists from all over Europe, who were attracted to this call to Copenhagen. And this was my real contact with autonomia,[22] without really knowing what it is, again you know, being 5 years in France, and you just don't realize what's happening out.[23]

Zoe repeatedly discussed linking queer political identity with other radical subcultures in other parts of Europe in her life narration: she was an organizing member of the 2011 Copenhagen queer festival, and is a singer in a Polish anarcho-punk group:

> I go back and forth for the band, and we have some rehearsals and tours. I don't know how it's going to work now, because now I decided that I wanted to stay in Copenhagen. At least for two more years. I will see how it'll work. I don't know, we didn't want to split, but maybe we'll have a pause or something like this.[24]

Zoe moved to Copenhagen in February 2011, attracted by: "The anarchist movement...and the punk scene. That's why I was very excited about living in Copenhagen." The developed leftist scenes of certain European cities function as sites of attraction for activists who cannot feel at home in their own places of origin. As Zoe says, in her explanation of the differences between Warsaw and Copenhagen activist circles:

> The DIY thing is like priority for me, always. But I can see that it's working a lot better here [In Copenhagen] that I really feel a part of a collective, as a group. And not a leader with all the responsibilities on my head anymore...I really like this kind of very deep reflexivity about politics...that we are so sensitive, and so self-critique, and so open to all these kind of discussion. I've never been to a surrounding that is so open to discuss, and reflect, on things...I was very surprised that we've discussed such issues, and in such a matter.[25,26]

Sergio from Amsterdam explains his links to the other social movements of the left in Amsterdam, where he now lives and includes a description of his relationships with some friends, who were the reason for him moving there:

> My best shot would be to be in the belly of the beast...I came to Amsterdam to look for schools at the same time CJA [Climate Justice Action] had its first post-Copenhagen summit here. Basically because my best friend was studying here. So, I squatted in his place for 1 month. But also, yes, the country of liberties etc. It was attractive. And more important, I wanted to do my research in English. That's why I left France at the first place. I didn't want to do it in French. England, anyway, was out of question; expensive, politically not inspiring, etc. and Netherlands was also attractive about design and culture. So, about for a year after Strasbourg spending a little time in Turkey, Copenhagen, Amsterdam, going back and forth to many places. Going to Strasbourg again for a NATO summit. Again, it was fast tracking of radicalization, which brought me here.[27]

Once again, the image of Amsterdam, as a city that offers the space and the people with whom radical activism can be practiced, lay behind Sergio's decision to move there:

> And it was also going to squats here in Amsterdam for the first time. That kind of stuff. And again, they were meeting in Amsterdam, 'cause there were squats that they could organize this, 'cause there was a good contingency of people here [laughter].[28]

Queer actors often hold multiple activist identities, because of their participating in different social movements on the left across Europe. Moreover, their personal trajectories show that these multiple belongings in various national settings have shaped their political subjectivities. This is not new for Europe. In fact, progressive political identities have always traveled across the continent, especially the Western part of the continent, forming alliances and solidifying networks.

Digital communicative practices

Queer movements tend to involve decentralized network formations supported by technological means of communication, such as mailing lists and social networks. These demonstrate how Europe is equally practiced through extra-institutional digital networks. These networks can sustain the transnational solidarities of the actors avoiding institutional interventions. None of the organizations behind the queer festivals has a formal structure. They are, rather, collectives with an international composition of activists. The festivals, as mentioned in the first part of the chapter, are arenas "where transnational publics can emerge," supported by digital communication tools (Juris 2008: 203):

> The whole collective has a very big international network. I know people here and there, someone else knows people here and there. So, we gather that. And we disseminate the announcement and then we have very standard [public relations] propaganda committee. (Tobin, Amsterdam May 2012)

Apart from mobilizing human, material, and symbolic resources, queer arenas produce self-organized transnational communication. As Juris says, the "exchange regarding tactics, strategies, protests, and campaigns" (2008: 203) is part of this transnational communication, which – in the case of queer festivals – shapes the emergence of these queer transnational counter-publics.

E-mail lists, websites, and Facebook pages provide space for discussions on the organization and the politics of the movement on a Europe-wide scale. One example can be found in the e-mail list queerandnow, which serves as a means to spread information. Older mailing lists, such as that of Queeruption, contributed to the publication of the majority of queer transnational events in Europe before 2010. Digital platforms help the organization and communication of queer activists across the continent.

The festival of Copenhagen illustrates how transnational digital communication operates. The main website for Copenhagen's festival http://www.queerfestival.org/ provides a recent archive with photos (since 2010); it also provides useful information about present and future events. Finally, it constitutes the basic ideological platform of the event, since it displays the festival's manifesto and other policies on the organization, drugs policy, and safe spaces. The information is given in four languages: English, Danish, German, and Spanish. An additional website has been set up on the music platform *MySpace*, which describes the festival's cultural events.[29] It is here that the countercultural character of the queer arena is shaped, through DIY songs. These countercultural songs have titles with sexually explicit vocabulary ("How clean is your penis?"), celebrations of the nonnormative body ("Big-size girl"), and the trash aesthetics[30] promoted within the festivals ("Tina Trasch"). Moreover, a Facebook page also supports the digital infrastructure of the event.

Digital transnational communication also allows for emotional ties generated within the queer festivals to be maintained. As Tobin said: "Over the e-mail correspondence we have still people from previous years giving their thoughts" (Amsterdam 2012). Emotional ties between activists help sustain their digital communication.

Transnational links between queer activists, facilitated by networks and technology, have become very useful for the realization of the festivals. Since queer festivals are autonomous, they are responsible for coordinating and finding all the necessary funding from extra-institutional sources. Hence, Copenhagen's queer festival is dependent on queer activists in Berlin, who organize a party every May, two months before the festival, in order to finance the Copenhagen festival. In turn, Copenhagen's festival advertises various queer festivals taking place around Europe through posters and other material.

Conclusion

In this chapter, I argued that queer festivals function as arenas constituted by a series of cross-border practices that embody a culturally performed Europe, a Europe that moves beyond the institutional and official public spheres. Language, international composition, links with other social movements across borders, and digital communication make up a set of cross-border actions that take place in the shadow of mobility, as promoted or channeled by institutional Europeanization. Approaching counter-public movements from the perspective of politics widens the scope of transnational social movements by exploring how extra-institutional cross-border practices, and the social movements they constitute, contribute to the transformation of the European political and social landscape. These movements lead to new political subjectivities and solidify new activist networks across the borders.

I explored how queer festivals are equally the result of affinities, relationships, and networks, illustrating some of the physical and nonphysical cross-border practices that constitute queer festivals as transnational arenas in Europe. Europeanization is performed by queer activists through their practices, and these practices span across national borders. "Europe" in this sense is not used as a strategy to enhance institutional visibility or to obtain additional resources. "Europe" is rather performatively practiced through cross-border movements. This idea could become the departure point from which to reexamine definitions of "Europe" and the political space that queer festivals open to social movements of gender and sexuality, through the conceptual tool of "practicing Europe."

Notes

1. The word *"cis"* or *"cisgender"* is a neologism used "[instead of the more popular 'gender normative'] to refer to people who do not identify with a gender diverse experience, without enforcing the existence of a 'normative' gender expression" (Green 2006: 247).
2. Since not all of the actors described here define themselves this way, I use the broader term "activist" to define all actors "who share and advance the goals of a social movement organization; individual movement adherents who do not necessarily belong to SMOs; institutionalized movement supporters; alternative institutions, and cultural groups" (Staggenborg 1998: 182).
3. This online survey was conducted through the platform Surveymonkey from October 2012 to February 2013. Since the sample is not highly representative (approximately one out of six participants responded), I simply use the results come to buttress the observations made through my ethnographic participation.
4. 'SILENCE = DEATH' was an exemplary slogan of ACT-UP New York.
5. "Ladyfest Festival," *Ladyfest-Roma.noblogs.org*, lasted modified 11 March 2009, http://ladyfest-roma.noblogs.org/post/2009/03/11/ladyfest-roma/ (accessed 19 April 2014).
6. "Call," *quEAR.org*, http://quear.blogsport.eu/en/call/ (accessed 19 April 2014).
7. "Queeristan 2013 Callout," *Queeristan*.org, last modified 25 February 2013, http://queeristan.org/2013/02/24/queeristan-2013-call-out/#dutch (accessed 19 April 2014).
8. All names were changed for privacy.
9. Intervention in the workshop "Queer activism and Academia," Oslo, 25 September 2011.
10. Respondent A2, interview with author, Amsterdam, 29 May 2012.
11. Respondent C2, interview with author, Copenhagen, 26 July 2011.
12. Respondent B4, interview with author, Berlin, 13 August 2011.
13. Respondent O1, interview with author, Oslo, 25 September 2011.
14. Respondent C1, interview with author, Copenhagen, 25 July 2011.
15. Oslo Queer Festival Meeting 2013, http://www.facebook.com/events/600682553278989/ (accessed 19 April 2014).
16. Queeristan, http://www.facebook.com/permalink.php?id=156441577807398&story_fbid=315900648528156 (accessed 19 April 2014).
17. Respondent A2, interview with author, Amsterdam, 29 May 2012.
18. The distance between Berlin and Copenhagen is only 356 km.
19. As in the case of Berlin, "to find out what is 'really' going on…one does not read the newspapers, one reads the streets" (Leach and Haunss 2009: 263).
20. Respondent C1, interview with author, Copenhagen, 25 July 2011.
21. Ibid.
22. Autonomia is a branch of a far-left extra-parliamentary movement based on theories of Italian workerism and the theories of Toni Negri.

23. Respondent A1, interview with author, Amsterdam, 28 May 2012.
24. Respondent C3, interview with author, Copenhagen, 27 July 2011.
25. She makes reference to the political discussions occurred within the Copenhagen festival (July 2011)
26. Respondent C3, interview with author, Copenhagen, 27 July 2011.
27. Respondent A1, interview with author, Amsterdam, 28 May 2012.
28. Ibid.
29. Copenhagen Queer Festival, http://www.myspace.com/copenhagenqueerfestival (accessed 19 April 2014).
30. This trend of "trash aesthetics" is part of a broader process of clothes styling within youth subcultures, facilitated by commerce, such as vintage shops, from where many activists get these clothes. This process started in the early 1960s when post-hippies, punks, students and others drawn to the subculture obtain a cheaper but more expansive wardrobe. Vintage shops provide old-fashion, trashy clothes of high quality and relatively low prices. This vintage style depends on the "surplus of goods whose use value is not expended when their first owners no longer want them" (McRobbie 1997: 193).

References

Ayoub, Phillip. 2013. "Cooperative Transnationalism in Contemporary Europe: Europeanization and Political Opportunities for LGBT Mobilization in the European Union." *European Political Science Review* 5(2): 279–310.

Ayoub, Phillip and David Paternotte. 2012. "Building Europe: ILGA and LGBT Activism in Central and Eastern Europe." *Perspectives on Europe* 42(1): 50–56.

Bell, David and Jon Binnie. 2000. *The Sexual Citizen: Queer Politics and Beyond*. Cambridge: Polity Press.

Borneman, John and Nick Fowler. 1997. "Europeanization." *Annual Review of Anthropology* 26(1): 487–514.

Broqua, Christophe. 2005. *Agir pour ne pas Mourir! ACT-UP, les Homosexuels, et le Sida*. Paris: Presses de Sciences Po.

Brown, Gavin. 2007. "Mutinous Eruptions: Autonomous Spaces of Radical Queer Activism." *Environment and Planning* 39 (11): 2685–2698.

——. Forthcoming. "Queer Movement." In *Ashgate Research Companion to Lesbian and Gay Activism*, eds. David Paternotte and Manon Tremblay. Farnham: Ashgate.

Doerr, Nicole. 2007. "Is 'Another' Public Space Actually Possible? Deliberative Democracy and the Case of 'Women Without' in the European Social Forum Process." *International Journal of Women's Studies* 8(3): 71–87.

——. 2009. "Listen Carefully: Democracy Brokers at the European Social Forums." PhD Diss. European University Institute.

Doidge, Mark. 2013. "The Birthplace of Italian Communism: Political Identity and Action amongst Livorno Fans." *Soccer & Society* 14(2): 246–261.

Downing, Lisa and Robert Gillett, eds. 2011. *Queer in Europe: Contemporary Case Studies*. Farnham: Ashgate.

Dufour, Pascal. 2010. "Mouvements de Femmes et Pratiques Différenciées de Transnationalisation des Solidarités." In *Au-delà et en deçà de l'Etat: le Genre Entre Dynamiques Transnationales et Multi-niveaux*, eds. Bérengère Marques-Pereira, Petra Meier and David Paternotte. Louvain-la-Neuve: Academia-Bruylant, 93–106.

El-Tayeb, Fatima. 2012. "'Gays Who Cannot Properly Be Gay': Queer Muslims in the Neoliberal European City." *European Journal of Women's Studies* 19(1): 79–95.

Favell, Adrian, Ettore Recchi, Theresa Kuhn, Janne Solgaard Jensen and Juliane Klein. 2011. "The Europeanisation of Everyday Life: Cross-Border Practices and Transnational Identifications among EU and Third-Country Citizens." EUCROSS Working Paper, 1.

Gamson, Joshua. 1995. "Must Identity Movements Self-Destruct: A Queer Dilemma." *Social Problems* 42(3): 390–407.

Green, Eli. 2006. "Debating Trans Inclusion in Feminist Movements: A Trans-Positive Analysis." *Journal of Lesbian Studies* 10(1–2): 231–248.

Hekma, Gert. 2012. "Book Review of Anarchism and Sexuality: Ethics, Relationships and Power by Jamie Heckert and Richard Cleminson, UK: Routledge, 2011." *Journal of Homosexuality* 59(5): 757–759.

Juris, Jeffrey. 2008. *Networking Futures: The Movements against Corporate Globalization*. Durham: Duke University Press.

Kulpa, Robert and Joanna Mizielinska, eds. 2011. *De-centering Western Sexualities: Central and Eastern European Perspectives*. Farnham: Ashgate.

Leach, Darcy, and Sebastian Haunss. 2009. "Scenes and Social Movements." In *Culture, Social Movements and Protest*, ed. Hank Johnston. Farnham: Ashgate, 255–276.

March, Luke and Cas Mudde. (2005). "What's Left of the Radical Left? The European Radical Left since 1989: Decline and Mutation." *Comparative European Politics* 3(1): 23–49.

McRobbie, Angela. 1997. "Second-Hand Dresses and the Role of the Ragmarket." In *The Subcultures Reader*, eds. Ken Gelder and Sarah Thornton. London: Routledge, 191–199.

Membretti, Andrea and Pierpaolo Mudu. 2013. "Where Global Meets Local: Italian Social Centres and the Alterglobalization Movement." In *Understanding European Movements: New Social Movements, Global Justice Struggles, Anti-Austerity Protest*, eds. Cristina Flesher-Fominaya and Laurence Cox. London: Routledge, 76–93.

Offe, Claus. 2003. "Is There, or Can There Be, a 'European Society'?" In *Demokratien in Europa. Der Einfluss der europäischen Integration auf Institutionenwandel und neue Konturen des demokratischen Verfassungsstaates*, eds. Ines Katenhusen and Wolfram Lamping. Opladen: Leske+Budrich, 71–90.

Passerini, Luisa, Dawn Lyon, Enrica Capussotti, and Ioanna Laliotou. 2007. "Editors' Introduction." In *Women Migrants from East to West*, eds. Luisa Passerini, Dawn Lyon, Enrica Capussotti and Ioanna Laliotou. New York: Berghahn Books, 1–20.

Poldervaart, Saskia. 2003. "Utopianism and Sexual Politics in Dutch Social Movements (1830–2003)." Presented at the Conference Past and Present of Radical Sexual Politics, Amsterdam.

———. 2006. "The Utopian Politics of Feminist Alterglobalisation Groups: The Importance of Everyday Life Politics and Personal Change for Utopian Practices." Amsterdam: Amsterdam School for Social Science Research. Working Paper, January 2006.

Portwood-Stacer, Laura. 2010. "Constructing Anarchist Sexuality: Queer Identity, Culture, and Politics in the Anarchist Movement." *Sexualities* 13(4): 479–493.

Staggenborg, Suzanne. 1998. "Social Movement Communities and Cycles of Protest: The Emergence and Maintenance of a Local Women's Movement." *Social Problems* 45(2): 180–204.

Warner, Michael. 2002. "Publics and Counterpublics." *Public Culture* 14(1): 49–90.

Part III

Becoming European

8
Trans Networking in the European Vortex: Between Advocacy and Grassroots Politics

Carsten Balzer and Jan Simon Hutta

Introduction

Since the 2000s, a plethora of local, regional, and transnational trans movements, networks, and organizations have emerged in, and across, different parts of the world (Balzer and Hutta 2012). European trans activism formed an integral part in these wider processes, which is exemplified by the founding of the Transgender Europe (TGEU) network in 2005. Currently counting 74 member organizations in 35 countries in Europe and Central Asia, as well as more than 120 individual members from Europe and beyond,[1] TGEU is the largest regional network of its kind and viewed as the principal voice of trans activism at the European scale. Its expansion is the result of transnational grassroots networking, facilitated by – and increasingly oriented toward – the European arena of institutional politics and legislation ensuing from the so-called political integration through the European Union (EU) and Council of Europe (CoE).

Similarly to ILGA-Europe, TGEU has developed an organizational structure targeted toward professional advocacy. Since 2008, TGEU has oriented itself strongly toward advocacy at the levels of the EU, the CoE, and (to a lesser extent) the Organization for Security and Cooperation in Europe (OSCE) as well as certain UN bodies (World Health Organization, WHO, Office of the United Nations High Commissioner for Human Rights, OHCHR). However, from its inception TGEU has simultaneously cultivated a pronounced grassroots politics of community engagement. Conceived in the spirit of a network of independent groups and individuals joining forces and offering mutual support, its activities have

171

revolved not only around European-scale equality politics and its national implementation, but also around community building, the creation of alternative publics and actions around issues raised by TGEU's members. This has impacted TGEU's campaigns, decision-making procedures, as well as forms of collaboration.

"Europe" has played a significant role at both the institutional and the grassroots levels, opening up political opportunities and providing a set of guiding discourses. Simultaneously, politics reaching beyond Europe has marked TGEU's grassroots dimension of networking. This is evident by its strong engagement in international campaigns, such as the International Transgender Day of Remembrance and the Stop Trans Pathologization campaign. Furthermore, the inclusion of members from non-CoE countries and strong collaborations across other world regions, especially with TGEU's Transrespect versus Transphobia Worldwide research project, exemplify the organization's reach.

Both European-scale advocacy and European/Europe-and-beyond networking have been integral to TGEU, coming together in mutually nurturing as well as conflicting ways at different periods of its development. Their coming together has enabled TGEU to become a hybrid of advocacy and community-oriented politics, of centralized representation and grassroots networking, of unified articulation and multi-sited debate. We argue that Europe has played different roles with respect to institutional advocacy and grassroots networking, and that these differences have come together in both synergistic and conflicting ways, depending on particular constellations in TGEU's history.

In the first part of this chapter, we thus retrace TGEU's development as a hybrid grassroots-advocacy organization in order to discuss some ways in which the scale of Europe has affected trans activism. We propose TGEU's development can best be understood in terms of a dynamic re-composition that occurred under the suction of what we term the "European vortex" and under the impact of an ongoing transnational community networking. With the term "European vortex," we refer to the discursive and political arrangements that operate on institutional levels such as EU, CoE, OSCE, or European Court of Human Rights. These arrangements have opened windows of opportunity that both accelerated and channeled, de- and re-territorialized trans activism. They can be viewed as a vortex – or a set of vortices – that has given trans activism new momentum and around which it has continued to revolve.

After providing an overview of TGEU's development as hybrid grassroots-advocacy network, the second section investigates how embracing advocacy, professionalization, and capacity building fostered by

European opportunity structures has interacted with TGEU's persisting endeavor to engage with and generate grassroots political voices both within Europe and beyond. More specifically, we address challenges that TGEU's double orientation has posed around political strategies, activities, and voice. By considering the European vortex on the one hand and community networking on the other, we then, in the third section, discuss the significance of "Europe" as a simultaneously discursive, material, and social space shaping activism.

On a conceptual level, our discussion calls attention to how political strategies, orientations, and interactions take shape through contingent ensembles of practices and discourses in the context of shifting conditions of possibility for activism. We argue that in order to assess the meaning of Europe with respect to trans activism, one needs to gain a nuanced understanding, not only of the political opportunities, processes, values, or domains in question, but also of how these issues are dynamically assembled in activism's singular trajectory. This focus on contingency, dynamism, and singularity situates our approach in proximity to ethnographic approaches to the study of social movements (e.g. Juris and Khasnabish 2013; Tsing 2005). It moreover leads us to interrogate the very terms that have heretofore guided theoretical discussions, in particular the notions of "horizontal" versus "vertical" politics. Toward the end of the chapter, we thus argue that TGEU's dual orientation of grassroots networking and professionalized advocacy does not easily map onto these apparently resonating terms, which we complement with a notion of "transversality." Methodologically, we draw on our involvement in, and research conducted for, TGEU since its inception, as well as organizational documents and interviews with those who initiated the first network meeting in 2005.

The emergence of a European trans network

The formation of transnational trans activism in Europe needs to be viewed against the backdrop of a number of issues specific to the social situation of trans people, which have started to enter policy discourses over the past ten years. The ongoing pathologization of trans people through diagnostic categories has given rise to extreme degrees of social and political marginalization, posing unique challenges for trans activism. Even in those European countries where trans people are legally recognized, there are so-called gatekeepers in the form of medical specialists who are responsible for diagnosing trans people as subject to "gender identity disorder," thus deciding on a person's ability to change documents. In most countries where legal gender recognition legislation exists, sterilization is required for trans people to achieve their fundamental right of changing documents (TGEU 2013). Marginalization has been further intensified by the fact that many trans people are necessarily "out" in various ways, as their gender expression does not necessarily match normative expectations. These multilayered forms of marginalization is one of the reasons why trans activism's degree of institutionalization and professionalization had been low, in comparison to lesbian, gay, and bisexual activism in Europe, which often excluded trans people and their issues. In this context, TGEU's formation can be viewed as the complex product of emerging opportunities, such as a close cooperation with ILGA-Europe, individual commitments, and a shifting discursive terrain that gave rise to new and self-perpetuating momentum. In the following, we will discuss this interplay by recapitulating TGEU's development in the formative years.

In 2005, activists from the Austrian non-governmental organization (NGO) Trans X invited trans organizations from neighboring countries to Vienna to celebrate Trans X's tenth birthday. They had envisioned a large party as an event for ideas-exchange and networking. Yet, the positive response from activists from across Europe was so tremendous that the Austrian activists altered plans to make the birthday party an occasion for the First European Transgender Council. This event saw more than 120 participants representing 66 organizations from 21 European countries. Over three busy days, apart from sharing experiences on the situation of trans people in various European countries, a set of nine demands were adopted.[2] Twenty-four volunteers from numerous European countries signed on to build a steering committee (SC), 16 of which became active and formally constituted the NGO Transgender Europe. The nine demands were agreed upon after an intense decision-making process that had considered dozens of demands from the participating groups and individuals, sent in weeks before the Council.

Trans X's initiative had clearly touched a nerve. Local organizing and mobilizing around trans issues had in many countries passed a threshold that made a new level of networking vital. Activists were also curious about the situation and political developments in other countries and looked for transnational exchange and collaboration, in particular with individuals from countries with few trans activists. The great diversity of trans identities and trans activists' backgrounds at the Council demonstrated the heterogeneity of the European trans movement in terms of identities, approaches, cultural backgrounds, and other features. A sense of immanent change and continued transnational trans activism pervaded the event, on the backdrop of which this heterogeneity was widely welcomed and perceived as beneficial.

Importantly, this new dynamism was fostered by discursive and political developments on a global scale that had begun to transform trans activisms' conditions of possibility. A broad turn toward conceiving trans issues as issues of human rights was observed, and intensified in the following years. In this context, Europe was often regarded as providing a particularly well-suited space for making political claims. As stated by the website of TGEU's First Council, "The European Transgender Network believes that the acknowledgment and acceptance of gender diversity is a[n] integral part of a modern European society" (2005). This invocation of a European society supportive of gender diversity would subsequently accompany TGEU's advocacy for national and European-scale policy changes. European institutions provided discursive and material frameworks amenable to such advocacy. In parallel, extended forms of grassroots networking took shape, in which Europe was mostly regarded as a privileged space for exchange, resources, and mutual support. An assessment of Europe's significance in European trans activism thus entails an understanding of how the dynamics of advocacy and grassroots networking as well as of European/Europe-and-beyond networking unfolded since TGEU's emergence.

TGEU between grassroots network and advocacy organization

From the beginning, both aspects of advocacy at the level of European institutions and grassroots networking have had a strong presence. However, a permanent oscillation between these two poles was observable in relation to two events from the period between the First Council in 2005 and the Second Council in 2008. The first illustrated the commitment to grassroots activism, while the second demonstrated engagement with European policy.

In February 2006, three months after the First Council, Gisberta Salce Júnior, a trans person who had migrated from Brazil and into a situation of extreme social exclusion in Porto, was tortured for three days, raped, and subsequently murdered in an abandoned construction site. The Portuguese media and criminal justice system approached the crime in the worst possible way. Backed by mainly Portuguese and Austrian activists, TGEU launched the international campaign *Gisberta Liberdade/ [Justice for Gisberta]*, which consisted of informative events, public vigils, manifestations at Portuguese embassies, a documentary film, and further activities in multiple European countries and beyond (e.g. in Australia and Brazil). The campaign had a strong impact on public debate and the LGBT movement in Portugal, backing them in achieving a legal trial on the murder of Gisberta Salce Júnior. It was mainly the commitment by the Austrian activists – who traveled to Portugal to film a self-financed documentary designed as a mobilization tool for the campaign – that boosted the international campaign. Thus, the call for support by the local trans communities in Portugal coincided with a strong commitment toward grassroots activism in the context of the beginning of a European trans network. The transnational connections that developed in the First Council gave rise to new forms of solidarity fostered by a sense of a common cause and an emergent European movement.

On the other hand, the awareness of the need to work with European institutions was growing. As one of the Viennese organizers stated in 2005, the organizers were acutely aware that in order to bring about change some demands relevant to the Austrian context had to be put on the Brussels agenda.[3] This suggests what Keck and Sikkink call a "boomerang pattern" (1998: 12) of advocacy, where domestic groups bypass the national scale of politics by using international allies to pressure their states (see also Imig and Tarrow 2001: 245–249).

In 2007, ILGA-Europe offered to approach the European Commission to apply for funding for a study on the situation of trans people in the EU, which led to the Transgender EuroStudy (Whittle et al. 2008). Conducted under TGEU SC member Stephen Whittle's leadership, the study was launched at the Second Council in Berlin in spring 2008. ILGA-Europe's support and the opportunity to gain funding for an autonomously designed study coincided with Whittle's commitment and competence, as he was able to combine decades of experience as a trans activist with academic work in equalities law. The Transgender EuroStudy not only accelerated the speed at which the terrain of European legislation and institutions gained significance for TGEU, but also paved the way for an advocacy approach that should become one of TGEU's defining characteristics: the use of comprehensive comparative research as a basis for pressuring European and international institutions such as the EU, the CoE, the OSCE, and some UN bodies.

Both events, the grassroots campaign *Gisberta Liberdade* and the advocacy-oriented Transgender EuroStudy, ensued from particular coincidences of individual commitments or competences and emerging needs in the context of social and discursive opportunity structures. An oscillation between the two poles of community networking and institutional advocacy based on such coincidences can be observed throughout the formative years. For instance, a campaign to support the hunger strike of trans women in Spain showed community engagement at the grass-roots level, while participation in several expert meetings by European institutions formed part of the advocacy approach. As a result of this oscillation, in the years following the Second Council, TGEU was able to present itself as both the largest regional membership-based trans network and an increasingly influential European advocacy NGO.

Through the elaboration and adoption of the Malta Declaration in 2009, TGEU went beyond mere oscillation and combined both aspects in a move toward professionalization. In what follows, we trace these changes in order to highlight their implications for TGEU's network character and how the meaning of Europe changed as a consequence. Our focus on contingent articulations of grassroots networking and professional advocacy will then lead us to consider forms of "trans-versal" politics that exceed the common understanding of horizontal and vertical orientations.

New directions related to professionalization

In summer 2009, a team of experts from TGEU and ILGA-Europe formu-lated a declaration draft that was intended to guide the future trans advocacy of both organizations. The document was to be adopted at the Malta Trans Rights Conference, the first and only trans pre-conference at an Annual ILGA-Europe Conference, which took place in fall 2009 in Malta. This draft was first reviewed by TGEU's SC and subsequently, in two loops, by TGEU's constituency. This was achieved in several weeks via TGEU's mailing lists, which at the time included more than 250 participants from Europe and beyond. During the Malta Trans Rights Conference, the final draft was voted on and adopted by more than 90% of the participants. A few days later, the declaration was also adopted by ILGA-Europe.

Since then, the Malta Declaration, which mainly includes recom-mendations and demands toward European institutions (CoE, EU, and OSCE), social partners (trade unions and employers' organizations), national equality bodies, UN bodies (WHO), as well as TGEU and ILGA-Europe, has served as a major guideline for TGEU's and ILGA-Europe's efforts toward trans equality in Europe (TGEU 2009). The Declaration marks TGEU's transition toward a new period in its history, where grassroots networking – rather than forming an autonomous branch of activities – became subsumed more strongly within a rapidly expanding advocacy framework.

In sum, needs, opportunities (ILGA-Europe's offer to finance and co-organize a trans pre-conference), commitments and competences, as well as personal sympathies between actors from TGEU and ILGA-Europe coalesced. However, the boost of professionalized advocacy in the context of the Malta Declaration and Conference occurred after a considerable change within TGEU's structure. This change ensued from a disputed decision at an extraordinary general assembly three months before the Second Council in 2008. It changed TGEU's statutes to reduce TGEU's steering committee from sixteen to nine members. The dispute occurred within TGEU's first SC, as can be inferred from the SC Report for 2005–2008 presented at the Second Council:

> The work of the SC was not always easy. Cultural differences, lack of resources (especially financially!), differences in priorities, strategies and experience lead [*sic*] to many heated discussions and conflict. The latter resulted in the existence of two websites for TransGender Europe, which is hopefully a transitional problem that will be solved with the election of the new SC in Berlin. (TGEU 2008b: 1)

Indeed, the mentioned difficulties and problems diminished with the first democratic election of an SC at the Second Council, where more than 200 trans activists representing 83 groups from 38 countries participated.[4]

The Second Council formed the actual turning point in TGEU's history, not only because of the SC election and the diminishing of substantial conflicts, but also because a multiplicity of opportunities arose that steered the network toward professional advocacy. It was particularly through the intensified cooperation with ILGA-Europe – which received an explicit mandate for trans advocacy by ILGA's general membership in 2008 – that the vortex of European institutions and human rights discourse began absorbing TGEU into an existing advocacy framework, which simultaneously opened the door to a host of new resources and possibilities. There was thus a synergetic interplay between TGEU's establishment as an increasingly professionalized trans network and advocacy organization, and ILGA's new mandate.

The wider processes fostering opportunities in Europe and beyond had to do with "gender identity's" debut on the agenda of international human rights discourses, and with European institutions becoming concerned about the major human rights violations trans people face in Europe. This process implies as a paradigm shift in the perception and framing of the concerns of trans people. The hitherto dominant and globalized Western medical-psychiatric perspective, which defines trans people as a deviation of a "natural" binary gender order, pathologizing and stigmatizing them, had been challenged by a new set of discourses. The new understanding conceives of trans people as equal members of society in the context of the universality of human rights.

A number of significant events expressive of this paradigm change on a global scale coincided with the formation of Transgender Europe. The 2006 Joint Statement on Human Rights Violations Based on Sexual Orientation and Gender Identity was the largest-ever UN statement on these issues and the first to include gender identity. In the same year, the Yogyakarta Principles on the Application of International Human Rights Law in Relation to Sexual Orientation and Gender Identity were drafted by a distinguished group of international human rights experts – referred to in statements by regional bodies such as the EU and the Organization of American States (OAS) in 2008. Also in 2008, a UN declaration on Sexual Orientation, Gender Identity, and Human Rights was adopted by 66 UN member states. Eventually, in 2009, the CoE Commissioner for Human Rights published the Issue Paper "Human Rights and Gender Identity" (Commissioner for Human Rights 2009; see also Balzer 2010: 87, 2014: 133–136; Balzer and Hutta 2012: 20–21).

The embracing of new political opportunities related to European institutions that became available from 2008 introduced new challenges to the balancing or integration of community and advocacy orientation. In this process, TGEU's character as a *network*, which has played a vital role in connecting and mediating between these two orientations since TGEU's inception, gained renewed significance. First, a stronger orientation toward professional advocacy had effects on political representation, decision-making, and campaigning as well as the production of activist knowledge. Influenced by its close cooperation with ILGA-Europe, which served TGEU as a model, the network tended more strongly toward an advocacy organization that acts on behalf of its constituting members, the latter providing political legitimacy.

Second, with the change in organizational structure and increased financial resources, TGEU's network character unfolded in new ways, manifesting in a strong participation of its constituency in TGEU-related workshops (e.g. on Statutes or the Strategic Plan) at the European Transgender Councils or the provision of capacity-building events for its membership and European trans activists. Importantly, TGEU's continued community orientation also led to an increasing diversity in terms of (trans) identities as well as geographical representation.

The persistence or reinvention of a pronounced community orientation tied to transnational networking in the context of increasing professionalization sets TGEU apart from other advocacy organizations such as ILGA-Europe. It signals a distinctive form of transversality, as we explain later. In the next section, we discuss the re-composition of TGEU's network character in relation to the new possibilities and challenges for community mobilizing arising in the context of increasingly influential European vortices.

Trans networking in the context of the European vortex

What is particularly striking of the TGEU's Steering Committee Activity Reports for the years 2008–2010 and 2010–2012 is the intensity and scope of SC activities. These activities included visits to and the support of TGEU member organizations, as well as participation in expert meetings and roundtables of diverse European commissions and institutions, in national conferences organized by TGEU member organizations and/or EU and CoE member states, and in international conferences at the level of EU and CoE on issues around LGBT, gender, equality, or discrimination.

Participation in and organization of such frequent events highlight not only the increasing force of the discursive and material vortex created by European institutions, but also the continued double commitment to advocacy and grassroots networking. How did the increased participation in European institutional politics impact TGEU's format as a network? How did forms of decision-making, campaigning, and knowledge production change? And in what ways did TGEU's community orientation intensify or weaken? We address these questions by discussing, first, an intensified translation between community and European institutions tied to particular forms of knowledge production; second, a change in the relation between TGEU's SC and membership; and, third, the benefit of new resources for TGEU's ongoing networking.

Translating between community and institutions

What strikes us in SC activities since TGEU's change of the SC structure is a permanent translation of issues between trans community and European institutions. Since 2008, SC members made great efforts to re-frame issues relevant to member organizations and the community as a whole – such as depathologization and the legal recognition of trans people's identities – so that they can be articulated within an advocacy discourse of rights and recognition. Such a discourse had already begun to develop in the late 1990s, as civil society organizations such as ILGA-Europe started taking advantage of the EU's and CoE's new focus on social policy and social inclusion (Holzhacker 2009). Backed by the broader turn toward a human rights perspective on trans issues, TGEU's SC became an increasingly important player pushing for and shaping the European advocacy discourse.

One of the most important advocacy tools in European trans activism was the 2009 Issue Paper "Human Rights and Gender Identity," published by the former CoE Commissioner for Human Rights, Thomas Hammarberg. TGEU's activities around this paper, which was perceived as a milestone document by European trans activists, exemplify the back-and-forth translation between European institutions and trans community. As in the case of the Malta Declaration, this implied an integration of, rather than mere oscillation between, advocacy and community networking.

In 2008, TGEU was involved in the preparation of an expert meeting at the CoE on the Human Rights Situation of Transgender People and Discrimination based on Gender Identity. At this meeting, TGEU SC members, as well as several other European trans activists, briefed Commissioner Hammarberg on the human rights situation of trans people in Europe, which eventually led to the publication of the Issue Paper. In this briefing, SC members drew on results from the Transgender EuroStudy and on their sustained consultation of and communication with TGEU's membership and European trans communities. They translated a series of concerns voiced in local, national, and transnational fora into the policy discourse of trans peoples' human rights. In the following years, TGEU published a series of translations of this significant document as part of its new international research project, Transrespect versus Transphobia Worldwide (TvT). The Issue Paper was translated into Spanish, German, Polish, Italian, and Portuguese.

With the translations of the Hammarberg Paper, TGEU interpellated the trans community more strongly into the policy framework, simultaneously providing an activist tool to be used in local and international contexts. TGEU's activities around the Hammarberg Paper are thus symptomatic not only of its dual role as advocacy organization and network, but also of the persistent translations between European institutions and community. Activist knowledge gained through interaction with TGEU's membership and European trans communities fed into the briefing of Commissioner Hammarberg, which shaped the contents of the Issue Paper. This document was then used in meetings, providing TGEU's constituency with a strategic tool for activism.

The SC's capacity to translate issues between trans communities and European institutions came with its absorption into the European vortex. As a consequence, the legal policy discourse of human rights gained prominence as a discourse *into which* issues were translated, shaping and accentuating trans issues in new ways. This also raises questions regarding the production of knowledge tailored specifically to support human rights advocacy. In presupposing an identifiable "trans population," such knowledge actually *constitutes* trans people as discriminated laborers, as excluded consumers, as subject to either transphobia or interlocking systems of oppression, or as in need of state protection (Bernstein 2002: 97; Currah 2006). Where surveys are aimed toward national and European-scale human rights advocacy, such knowledge around trans issues tends to be tailored – in a logic of epistemic supply-and-demand – toward institutional expectations arising in the institutional context of the European vortex.

In many cases, TGEU thus followed the policy path paved by advocacy organizations such as ILGA-Europe. On the other hand, however, TGEU intensified its research activities since 2009 in the context of the TvT project, which has followed the model of producing knowledge within a human rights advocacy framework, but oriented directly toward existing and emergent trans activism. For instance, TGEU mapped mobilizations around the International Transgender Day of Remembrance and the Stop Trans Pathologization campaigns in order to support these campaigns, foster activist networking, and conduct a TvT Legal and Health Care Mapping in collaboration with over 70 international activists (Balzer and Hutta 2012). TvT has thus primarily not addressed institutional European or international actors, but rather trans activists and communities, who can potentially use the knowledge produced in a variety of ways. Interestingly, TGEU's intensified production of knowledge tailored toward human rights advocacy has correlated with and fostered an intensification of community-oriented knowledge production on a scale including, but exceeding, Europe.

The double role of TGEU's membership

The increasing absorption of TGEU's SC into the European vortex also concerns broader challenges in its relations to the membership. In its 2008–2010 *Activity Report*, the SC points out its role as an "interlocutor" with the EU and the CoE:

> The current steering committee has worked hard to strengthen the position of TGEU as interlocutor with decision makers, human rights NGOs and other stakeholders in the European Union and the Council of Europe, as well as forming a network and platform for exchange

for a diverse and ever-growing European trans community. (TGEU 2010a: 5)

The reduction of SC members in 2008 had been followed by professionalization oriented toward European institutional politics, which led to a greater autonomy of the SC in setting agendas and negotiating with the mentioned stakeholders. As a consequence, the role the constituency played in TGEU's activism shifted from the direct proposal and development of activities toward the role of consultation under the lead of the SC. This was exemplified by both the briefing of Commissioner Hammarberg and the development of the 2009 Malta Declaration. Subsequently, membership consultation became a standard element of TGEU's repertoire. For instance, in 2012, TGEU published a *Statement on Social Inclusion through Sustainable Transport* that drew on membership consultation (TGEU 2012).

These consultations indicate the double role played by the constituency with regard to TGEU's function as advocacy organization. On the one hand, the constituency is vital in providing activist knowledge and raising issues of relevance to activists and trans organizations in different local contexts. In that, TGEU's character as a network lives on in the context of new formats that enable extensive communication and exchange. The consultations have also exceeded a mere "filling-in" of details into a set of issues formulated in advance by the SC, comprising, for instance, also votes on the implementation of policies. On the other hand, the constituency now serves as a legitimizing basis for institutional advocacy, featuring as "trans people's voice" in pressures for policy change. To the extent that the constituency is invoked as legitimating basis, its role in the political campaigning and decision-making tends to be circumscribed more strongly by the terms of the debate as set by the SC. Here, the logics of institutional advocacy tend to become the primary discourse *into which* translations between community and European politics occur, with the SC playing a significant role in weighing and specifying the issues.

This double role also shows in TGEU's biennial European Transgender Councils, which are an important platform for exchange of knowledge, the discussion of strategies and the voting on important matters, and simultaneously the legitimating basis for the SC's representation of TGEU and the wider trans community in Europe and beyond. Regarding its Councils, TGEU has adopted various aspects from the annual conferences of ILGA-Europe, which has provided substantive organizational support for the Councils. In that way, the Councils have been one of the major routes through which TGEU assimilated its structure into ILGA's model of professional advocacy.

New capacities for networking

At the same time, within and apart from the Councils, TGEU has kept cultivating the direct and decentralized networking among trans activists. When considering TGEU's networking, a larger number of participants were able to attend the Council meetings with the acquisition of new resources from both European and international institutions and donors. This especially affected participants from Central and Eastern Europe, which subsequently led to the formation of TGEU's Central and Eastern European Working Group (CEEWG) endowed with an independent budget. In this respect, the resources that come with the absorption into the Europe vortex have enabled TGEU to become more inclusive in terms of representation and decision-making through the combination of transnationalization and advocacy-centered professionalization.

In this context, the Trans-Info-Europe mailing list, a list with more than 350 subscribers (as of January 2013) is worth noting. Through this list-based networking, the decentralized involvement of various TGEU members took part in the reform of WHO's International Classification of Diseases (ICD), which classified trans identities in a pathologizing manner as "gender identity disorders." The basis for TGEU's argumentation was established by the sections of the Malta Declaration addressing the ICD reform as well as the expertise gained through workshops at European Transgender Councils and discussions on the Trans-Info-Europe list. Importantly, in cases such as the Malta Declaration and the discussion of the ICD reform, TGEU's community networking has influenced the issues engaged.

Since TGEU's re-composition in 2008, then, the two dimensions of institutional advocacy and grassroots networking have both changed and intensified. TGEU's community orientation has interacted with professional advocacy through persistent back-and-forth translations between trans community and European institutions. Under an increasing pull of the European vortex, professionalized advocacy has gained significance as a discourse *into* which political activities are being translated, with the SC becoming more autonomous and influential. Consequentially, the membership has tended more strongly toward the function of giving TGEU political legitimation, which raises questions regarding the ramifications of such legitimation in light of a highly heterogeneous trans population. Most obviously, participation in the Councils has been heavily restricted by the role of English as lingua franca, which is a fundamental challenge for all European movements. Other issues concern the low degree of involvement of groups such as sex workers and migrants, or significant differences in the representative numbers of participants from different countries. TGEU's continued community orientation is now enacted through consultancy and capacity building. At the same time, networking among activists in Europe and beyond at the grassroots level has benefited from TGEU's access to new resources and materialized especially in the context of the Councils, as well as the Trans-Info-Europe list, both of which have geographically expanded their participants.

A dynamic approach to activism in Europe

Europe has played distinctive roles in regards to both advocacy and community networking. As TGEU reinvented its network character under the pull of the European vortex, the relevance of Europe on discursive, material, and social levels was also reconfigured. We argue that our dynamic approach to European trans activism, which considers TGEU's trajectory in the context of singular constellations of events and shifting conditions of possibility, sheds new light on Europe's changing significance. It also provides new angles on the notions of horizontality and verticality frequently deployed in studies of transnational activism.

Reconsidering the significance of Europe

Since TGEU's inception, Europe has provided a set of productive discourses and resources for its advocacy, in particular in connection with the CoE's work on human rights, but more recently related to some aspects of EU legislation and the work of the OSCE and the European Commission and Parliament. An understanding of Europe as a malleable space open to human rights claims has catalyzed TGEU's engagements with these institutions. Similar to the website of the First Council, in TGEU's "Vision" statement, as approved at the general assembly in 2010,

> Transgender Europe envisions a Europe free from all discrimination – especially including discrimination on grounds of gender identity and gender expression; a Europe where transgender people are respected and valued, a Europe where each and every person can freely choose to live in whichever gender they prefer, without interference. (TGEU 2010b)

In both cases, "Europe" is presented not simply as an ideal space where justice, democracy, and human rights reign; it is rather invoked as a space amenable to claims on rights and justice – claims that can moreover be formulated in terms of concrete policy demands. Importantly, part of TGEU's advocacy has simultaneously occurred on the global scale, for instance the advocacy for reforming the ICD or awareness-raising regarding hate violence against trans and gender variant people at the OSCE and UN OHCHR by means of the TvT project.

In regards to community networking, the significance of Europe was, during TGEU's founding years, mainly related to possibilities of encounter, solidarity, and a sense of potentiality related to an emergent regional movement. With the network's increasing absorption into the European vortex, these aspects have tended to be increasingly tied to a far-reaching policy framework, where – as stated by Cai Wilkinson (Chapter 3) in this volume – even activists in Central Asian countries have, for example, demanded legislative and policy change by appealing to European frameworks of human rights.

Interestingly, rather than a mere ensemble of individual international supporters, the political space of Europe – in the form of the European advocacy network – features as an ally to trans activists within Central Asian countries, which have themselves become part of the network. In the ICD advocacy, boundaries between European and global mobilization blur in a different way, as both activists and the target of advocacy are constituted on a global scale. In both ICD advocacy and TvT's research and advocacy, the dimension of community networking has moreover been vital in creating the epistemic basis for advocacy and simultaneously enabling local trans movements and communities to access new resources.

These issues highlight how an approach tracing the dynamic and intersecting relations of European and international scales on the one hand and advocacy and community networking on the other is needed in order to assess the significance of Europe for TGEU. Such a dynamic approach further entails a reconsideration of the concepts that have so far guided engagements with transnational activism.

New chances for heterogeneity

We now point to a further issue relating to the significance of Europe, as it concerns the effect of transnationalization on the composition of trans activism. Processes of identity construction within trans movements have been highly complex, since the great diversity of trans people's self-understandings has impacted directly on the needs and approaches articulated in political spaces (Balzer 2007: 556–557). Trans movements comprise people socialized in trans, queer, or gay subcultures or in mainstream cultures of gender and sexuality. This heterogeneity of political approaches tied to identities – as well as the rejection of identity in some cases – has posed great challenges, introducing conflicts on the national level, for instance, in regard to emancipation from medical gatekeepers or in regard to the unity of the movements and the inclusion or exclusion of parts of the communities (ibid.: 557–566). Interestingly, these issues have been productively transformed in the context of European-level organizing, as TGEU demonstrates.

With the coming together of activists from different European countries and locations, it was possible to observe a shift from conflicts around different understandings of being trans in the national context to the strategic deployment of "trans" as a broad umbrella term for the purpose of political campaigning. Possibly, the need and desire to have an exchange across a diversity of social and cultural backgrounds in the European context as well as the atmosphere during the initial transnational gathering in Vienna in 2005 also fostered an openness regarding different trans identities. Moreover, the political necessity of joining forces assumed new prominence in an emergent transnational space that was not biased by existing struggles and debates.[5] Since TGEU's inception at the First European Transgender Council in 2005, the tendency toward greater inclusiveness became even more pronounced, in terms of both identities and geography, even if this diversity was also seen as a reason for the dispute of 2008.

Alongside the questions of legitimation and representation discussed earlier, it is thus necessary to consider the very identities and political subjectivities involved in European trans activism, how they have changed in the context of transnationalization, and the implications this has for questions of political participation and representation. European and international levels have fostered trans networking across heterogeneous communities. Taking this further, it can be argued that transnational networking based on heterogeneous subjectivities has also enabled institutional advocacy in Europe to flourish, which has in turn influenced grassroots networking. Considering these interconnections leads to our discussion of the connection between networking and the concept of "horizontality" frequently invoked in discussions of transnational social movements.

Transnational and transversal: key dynamics in TGEU's networking

The notion of "networking" has figured prominently in accounts of transnational activism (Ayoub 2013; della Porta and Caiani 2009; Juris 2008; Juris and Khasnabish 2013; Sitrin 2012). Our discussion of TGEU calls for a reconsideration of the concept of "horizontality" guiding these debates, as the distinction between horizontal and vertical politics is challenged by the ways in which the vortex of European institutions absorbing part of TGEU's activities into an advocacy framework has interacted with a vector of community orientation. Before elaborating this further, conceptual clarification is needed, since "horizontality" has been used in distinct analytical contexts.

In his discussion of networking, Juris (2008) characterizes horizontalism in terms of decentralized collaboration among autonomous elements, connecting it to a grassroots-democratic self-understanding of activism (see also Doerr 2012; Sitrin 2012). He posits the "horizontal" level of organizing as prefiguring a different mode of social organization. This account resonates with TGEU's grassroots and community networking in terms of open circulation of information, decentralized and consensus-based coordination and decision-making, and self-directed networking. Writers focusing on NGOs and advocacy groups also consider the notion of horizontalism as a key feature of transnational activism (Ayoub 2013; Imig and Tarrow 2001; Holzhacker 2009; Keck and Sikkink 1998). These accounts in turn resonate with TGEU's advocacy for legal change in member organizations sharing information and developing joint political strategies. In both cases, the guiding image of horizontality is one of activist groups forming connections and nuclei for the exchange of information and political action. However, while in the first case, the horizontal level of organizing is seen as serving itself to prefigure a different mode of social organization, in the advocacy framework horizontality is deemed vital in establishing the connections necessary to exert "vertical" pressure on states and international institutions.

Both accounts of horizontality, then, resonate with our discussion of TGEU dual orientations. Both community networking and advocacy are constituted through, in part distinctive, forms of horizontality. Moreover, especially with respect to advocacy, the relation between horizontality and a *vertical* dimension of pressuring state and European institutions becomes central. This distinction between horizontal and vertical becomes problematic, however, if we consider how community networking has changed its very format through the pull of Europe's institutional and discursive vortices. TGEU's advocacy, on the other hand, has continued its orientation toward the community.

The dynamic between these different yet coexisting orientations is hard to capture in the language of horizontality versus verticality. In particular, the idea of a network vertically "reaching up" from below toward institutional politics tends to reify a stable location "down there." To the extent that TGEU has started gaining a stake in European institutions, it is not only pressuring "from below," but simultaneously acting "from within" institutional politics, as the SC's briefing of Commissioner Hammarberg highlighted. In developing an advocacy orientation, TGEU has changed, or expanded, its very location on the vertical axis. What needs further conceptual elaboration is TGEU's transformation as it orients itself more heavily toward European institutions while simultaneously continuing its community networking.

This transformation is neither simply a shift from horizontal to vertical activism, nor a straightforward elevation on the vertical axis. Instead, different aspects of both horizontal and vertical organizing and mobilization have been present from TGEU's inception. Its transformations can accordingly be understood as different forms of weighing and re-assembling these aspects, ensuing from contingent articulations of personal commitments, emerging opportunities, and changing discourses. To address these transformations, we propose the notion of "transversality." Transversal dynamics exceed the logics of either horizontality or verticality by assembling heterogeneous strategies and orientations in contingent ways, modifying the very entities that are involved in terms of their horizontal and vertical format and position.

In TGEU, the notion of transversality directs attention to the dynamic relations we have highlighted among TGEU's SC, constituency, political targets and partners, privileged strategies, and forms of decision-making. These relations have been shaped in particular by two sets of vectors: the European vortices absorbing activism into the discourses and practices of professionalized European-level advocacy, expanding TGEU's position upward on the vertical axis; and the networking of the European trans community pulling TGEU toward horizontal grassroots networking. New equilibriums and turbulences have taken shape in the space between the vortex of European institutions and the vector of community networking, as advocacy and grassroots networking have transversally coalesced. These new dynamics comprise both new opportunities, such as additional resources and the productive translation between community and European institutions, and limitations, such as the impossibility to include Europe's heterogeneous trans population within a centralized regime of representation. The notion of transversality, then, asks us to move beyond static understandings of entities located within distinct spheres of civil society or state institutions, and engages with how elements situated in different spheres and at different scales contingently articulate.

Moving toward such a dynamic approach to European trans activism with respect to TGEU, our discussion has sought to call attention to who the subjects voicing particular claims are, on behalf of whom they do so, and how they frame political strategies and issues. In doing so we have demonstrated the role of the European vortex in regards to the specific "European" resources, opportunities, discourse, and practices play in this context. For this purpose, we outlined an important distinction between the levels of institutional advocacy and grassroots networking, in terms of the political and social activities undertaken and the concrete discourses deployed. This has opened up a nuanced understanding of how different levels and scales of politics are being articulated and negotiated, bringing into relief some particularities of TGEU in relation to organizations such as ILGA-Europe as well as some of the ways in which Europe influenced different levels of trans activism. More broadly, we hope that this discussion has contributed to the theorization of transnational activism in and beyond Europe, providing some useful indications regarding its practical opportunities and challenges.

Notes

1. In 2013, TGEU member countries include almost all Western-European countries as well as many Central and Eastern-European countries (Armenia, Croatia, Estonia, Finland, Greece, Hungary, Lithuania, Macedonia, Malta, Montenegro, Poland, Romania, Russia, Serbia, Slovakia, Tajikistan, Ukraine), as well as Iran, Kyrgyzstan, Nigeria, Turkey and the USA.
2. The demands can be viewed at TGEU's former website at http://tgeu.org (accessed 2 December 2013).
3. Interview with Eva Fels, 6 November 2005, Vienna, Austria.
4. The countries included almost all Western-European countries, many Eastern-European countries (among them Armenia and Belarus) as well as Azerbaijan, Israel, Japan, Kyrgyzstan, Namibia, Peru, and the United States. The new SC consisted of activists from Denmark, Germany, Ireland, Italy and the UK (see TGEU 2008a).
5. Doerr (2012) points to a similar shift from relatively closed and hierarchical national debate to more open transnational one in her discussion of the European Social Forum.

References

Ayoub, Phillip M. 2013. "Cooperative Transnationalism in Contemporary Europe: Europeanization and Political Opportunities for LGBT Mobilization in the European Union." *European Political Science Review* 5(2): 279–310.

Balzer, Carsten. 2007. "Gender Outlaw Triptychon – Eine ethnologische Studie zu Selbstbildern und Formen der Selbstorganisation in den Transgender-Subkulturen Rio de Janeiros, New Yorks und Berlins." PhD Diss. Free University Berlin, Germany. www.diss.fu-berlin.de/diss/receive/FUDISS_thesis_000000005722 (accessed 31 August 2013).

———. 2010. "'Eu acho Transexual é Aquele que Disse: Eu sou Transexual!' Reflexiones Etnológicas Sobre la Medicalización Globalizada de las Identidades Trans a Través del Ejemplo de Brasil." In *El Género Desordenado: Críticas en Torno a la Patologización de la Transexualidad*, eds. Miquel Missé and Gerard Coll-Planas. Barcelona-Madrid: Egales, 81–96.

———. 2014. "Human Rights." *Transgender Studies Quarterly* 1(1): 133–136.

Balzer, Carsten and Jan Simon Hutta. 2012. *Transrespect versus Transphobia Worldwide: A Comparative Review of the Human-rights Situation of Gender-variant/Trans People*. Würzburg: Flyerarlarm.

Bernstein, Mary. 2002. "The Contradictions of Gay Ethnicity: Forging Identity in Vermont." In *Social Movements – Identity, Culture, and the State*, eds. David S. Meyer, Nancy E. Whittier, and Belinda Robnett, Oxford: Oxford University Press, 85–104.

Commissioner for Human Rights (Council of Europe). 2009. "Human Rights and Gender Identity." Issue Paper, July 2009. https://wcd.coe.int/ViewDoc.jsp?id=1476365 (accessed 31 August 2013).

Currah, Paisley. 2006. "Gender Pluralism under the Transgender Umbrella." In *Transgender Rights*, eds. Paisley Currah, Richard M. Juang, and Shannon Minter. Minneapolis: University of Minnesota Press, 3–31.

Doerr, Nicole. 2012. "Translating Democracy: How Activists in the European Social Forum Practice Multilingual Deliberation." *European Political Science Review* 4(3): 361–384.

Holzhacker, Ronald. 2009. "Transnational Strategies of Civil Society Organizations Striving for Equality and Nondiscrimination: Exchanging Information on New EU Directives, Coalition Strategies and Strategic Litigation." In *The Transnationalization of Economies, States, and Civil Societies: New Challenges for Governance in Europe*, eds. Laszlo Bruszt and Ronald Holzhacker. New York: Springer, 219–240.

Imig, Doug and Sidney Tarrow, eds. 2001. *Contentious Europeans: Protest and Politics in an Integrating Europe*. Lanham: Rowman & Littlefield.

Juris, Jeffrey S. 2008. *Networking Futures: The Movements against Corporate Globalization, Experimental Futures*. Durham: Duke University Press.

Juris, Jeffrey S. and Alex Khasnabish, eds. 2013. *Insurgent Encounters: Transnational Activism, Ethnography, and the Political*. Durham: Duke University Press.

Keck, Margaret E. and Kathryn Sikkink. 1998. *Activists beyond Borders: Advocacy Networks in International Politics*. Ithaca: Cornell University Press.

della Porta, Donnatella and Manuela Caiani. 2009. *Social Movements and Europeanization*. Oxford: Oxford University Press.

Sitrin, Marina. 2012. *Everyday Revolutions: Horizontalism and Autonomy in Argentina.* London: Zed Books.

TGEU. 2005. "Transgender Europe" [Homepage of the First European Transgender Council]. www.tgeu.net (accessed 31 August 2013).

——. 2008a. "Press Release: 2nd European Transgender Council Transforms into 1st Global Conference of Transgender Activists," 13 May 2008. www.tgeu.org/node/96 (accessed 31 August 2013).

——. 2008b. "Report of the Steering Committee of TransGender Europe 2005 – 2008," presented at the 2nd European Transgender Council, 1–4 May 2008, Berlin.

——. 2009. "Malta Declaration," 28 October 2009. www.tgeu.org/MaltaDeclaration (accessed 31 August 2013).

——. 2010a. "Report of the Executive Board and the Steering Committee of Transgender Europe May 2008– September 2010." www.tgeu.org/sites/default/files/tgeu_report_kleiner3.pdf (accessed 31 August 2013).

——. 2010b. "Vision." http://tgeu.org/missionstatement (accessed 31 August 2013).

——. 2012. "Statement on Realizing Social Inclusion through Sustainable Transport," 19 March 2012. www.tgeu.org/SOCIAL_INCLUSION_THROUGH_SUSTAINABLE_TRANSPORT (accessed 31 August 2013).

——. 2013. "Trans Rights Europe Map & Index 2013," 17 May 2013. www.tgeu.org/Trans_Rights_Map_Europe (accessed 31 August 2013).

Tsing, Anna Lowenhaupt. 2005. *Friction: An Ethnography of Global Connection.* Princeton: Princeton University Press.

Whittle, Stephen Lewis Turner, Ryan Combs, and Stephenne Rhodes. 2008. *Transgender EuroStudy: Legal Survey and Focus on the Transgender Experience of Health Care.* Brussels: Corelio.

9
Transnational Solidarities and LGBTQ Politics in Poland

Jon Binnie and Christian Klesse

Introduction

In this chapter we examine the transnational dimensions of LGBTQ politics and activism in Poland as they relate to the idea of Europe and the politics of Europeanization. We draw on material from an empirical research project we have conducted on contemporary transnational activism and solidarities around gender and sexual politics in Poland, the data collection for which ran from April 2008 to June 2009. Our research focused on the links between activists from abroad and Polish groups and associations organizing LGBTQ-oriented cultural and political events. For this purpose, we participated in a variety of events (mainly cultural festivals and political demonstrations) and interviewed activists in Poland (as well as Germany, the Netherlands, Belgium, and the United Kingdom).

In this discussion, we address the question whether the term "solidarity" is suitable to conceive of elements of this activism and cooperation. We consider the extent to which transnational activism around Polish LGBT politics both reproduces and contests hegemonic political meanings of Europe. Sellar, Staddon, and Young (2009: 253) argue that "European borders and identities and the very idea of 'Europe' itself are perpetually under renegotiation and contestation." We were therefore interested in examining how the activists in our study saw their actions and activism in relation to processes of Europeanization. To what extent did their practices of solidarity reproduce or contest dominant notions of Europeanization? Discussing the impact of the EU on the Polish gay movement, O'Dwyer (2012: 333) suggests that "EU integration brings domestic rights activists into contact and collaboration with West European rights organization in a way not possible before. These transnational linkages, it is argued, increase not only the domestic groups' organisational resources but also their knowledge and self-confidence" (see also Ayoub 2013). We were therefore interested in these transnational linkages as an infrastructure that supports the practicing of solidarity.

Appeals to transnational solidarity formed an important element of the political strategies of Polish LGBT organizations before and after EU accession (Chybisov and Średnicka 2006). Solidarity was also evoked by Western European activist groups, which mobilized for – or otherwise supported – LGBT protest events in Poland. Against this backdrop, we were struck by the fact that although solidarity discourses have been used by some of our research participants, this has not been generally the case. Moreover, solidarity discourses are complex, manifold, and highly contextualized. We advance the argument that an understanding of transnational politics in Poland (and other Central and Eastern European countries) is seriously limited by the operation of an East-West dichotomy. Binary thinking structures many features of current discourses on sexual politics in Central and Eastern Europe, including the dimension of temporality (manifested in the tropes of "progress," "democratization," "modernization," "liberation"). Western European LGBTQ movements (such as those analyzed by Rupp (Chapter 2) and Kollman (Chapter 5) in this volume) tend to be treated as the model case of an advanced political culture around gender and sexual equality, which has significant consequences for the conceptualization of solidarity discourses in the field of transnational politics. Under the influence of an East/West binary, the notion of European solidarity can sometimes be problematically understood to mean Western European activists acting "in support" of struggles in Central and Eastern Europe. Such discourses then reinforce Western European cultural hegemony in sexual politics. Examining and critiquing hegemonic notions of citizenship within Poland based on a political imagination of the nation as homogenous, Catholic, and heterosexual, Keinz (2011: 112) argues that the East-West dichotomy mobilized by some Western activists "draws a sexual division between 'eastern' and 'western' countries, framing the latter as modern and liberal, while stressing the pre-modern and antiliberal character of 'the rest of the world,' in this case Poland. Such images disregard homophobic statements and inequality in many 'western' countries and serve as a kind of continuation of a west-east division along the lines of being modern, democratic, and liberal versus premodern, not yet fully democratized (hence 'civilized'), and traditional (conservative)." The notion of a European solidarity can therefore be problematic if it is simplistically framed in terms of Western support for activists in Central and Eastern Europe.

Many of our respondents in Poland did not use the language of solidarity or even questioned its relevance in the context of their activism. Others did refer to instances of practices of solidarity, but applied it to other and often quite specific forms of collaboration. In this chapter, we draw on Krakow and Poznan based activists' narratives to examine the local and transnational dimensions of solidarity discourses. Furthermore, references to the transnational may not be the most salient feature in many of these understandings of solidarity. Yet, as we will argue throughout this chapter, the local itself tends to be constituted in transnational terms. This insight is obscured through evolutionist thinking along an East/West dichotomy, reinstalling the logic of the *national* in the trans*national*.[1]

Solidarity and transnational gender and sexual politics

Our pilot web-based research of international LGBT activism around events in Poland since 2004 showed the common use of the concept of *solidarity*. At the same time, in the critical literature on transnational sexual politics, the notion of global LGBT solidarity has been widely challenged and criticized for its ethnocentricity; insensitivity to cultural difference in the same way that the concept of global sisterhood has been challenged by postcolonial feminist scholars and activists (see, for instance, Mohanty 2003). Western LGBT activists' will to act in solidarity with LGBT people elsewhere has been criticized for the imposition of Western values often reflecting a neo-colonial mindset (Haritaworn 2008; Haritaworn et al. 2008; Puar 2008). The notion of transnational solidarity is thus often seen as suspect.

We were therefore interested in examining empirically the transnational practices of Western European LGBT activist interventions in Poland. How were they seen by Polish LGBT activists? Postcolonial criticism has drawn attention to the ethnocentricity of Western LGBTQ politics, and the neo-colonial power relations that, for instance characterize connections between activists in the UK and Zimbabwe (Phillips 1997; Stychin 2004). Postcolonial theory and criticism are now being deployed to understand and conceptualize the experiences of post-transition Central and Eastern Europe (Chari and Verdery 2009; Kuus 2004; Light and Young 2009), so we were concerned to understand how a postcolonial theoretical perspective might help us in understanding the transnational politics of sexuality in Poland. By researching the experiences of activists who are differently located within the same transnational activist networks, we aimed to get a sense of what is "good practice" in doing transnational activism, which could contribute to more effective, culturally sensitive cooperation. How do discourses on solidarity figure in transnational gender and sexual politics? Who is using what kind of solidarity discourses and to what ends? In the following we will delve into the tradition of solidarity theory in order to discern a suitable perspective for our project.

Solidarity in social and political theory

Reflecting on academic discussions of solidarity, Jean Harvey (2007: 22) notes: "there seems to be no agreed upon meaning of the term 'solidarity,' nor even a clear consensus as to the kind of item it refers to. Is it an action, a motive, an attitude, a piece of political activism, or something else?" However one dominant framing of solidarity is that solidarity is assumed to designate mutual obligations to aid each other. Yet these positive obligations to act, according to Carol Gould, usually pertain to members of the community to which one belongs oneself (2007: 150). In its history, the term solidarity thus has mostly been defined in terms of an "intragroup solidarity." The idea of "intragroup solidarity" is most nuanced in Emile Durkheim's notion of solidarity as the precondition for social cohesion, as the basic ties, which ground a sense of connectedness and make social forms functional (ibid.).

Durkheim (1964) distinguished between mechanical and organic solidarity. He reserved the first term for the relations in traditional and less-differentiated societies. "Organic solidarity" was supposed to capture the interdependent relations in larger (modern) social formations, which were marked by a significant division of labor. The Durkheimian model of "organic solidarity" (or "social solidarity" in the words of Sally J. Scholz (2007)) could be used to map social relations on different levels, ranging from the "domestic," over small face-to-face networks, to the regional or the national (Brunkhorst 2007; Gould 2007; Gould and Scholz 2007). It fosters the fellow feeling within a certain group context. This notion of intragroup solidarity has often been called upon to promote policies and ethics, which may help to sustain the cohesion of the nation-state. Social solidarity of this kind has been central to the process of nation building (Gellner 1983 Anthias and Yuval-Davis 1992). This is the point, where it left an imprint on civic forms of solidarity, which defined the relationship between the welfare state and its citizens. As we will argue later in more detail, racist and heteronormative practice may be well in tune with such kinds of solidarity. Due to the prominence of an intragroup orientation in modern European solidarity discourses, it is necessary to revise basic tenets of its discourse in order to conceive of transnational or global solidarities. Carol Gould (2007) proceeds in this direction by suggesting the concept of "transnational network" solidarities.

Transnational political and networked solidarities

Transnational activism may be theorized through a model of "network solidarity," since "network solidarity" is understood to be based on plural solidarities (Gould 2007: 150). The term "network" solidarity does not contain any pre-perceived assumptions on group membership or identification and thus is distinct from older identity-based solidarity conceptualizations (ibid.: 159). People of diverse social positioning may partake in network solidarity groups or forms of activism, allowing for the enactment of various and overlapping forms of solidarity. Similar theories of solidarity have been for a long time promoted by anti-racist and anti-colonial feminist activists and scholars. Jacqui Alexander and Chandra Talpade Mohanty (1997), for example, argue that global critical solidarities between women are possible only if they are based on a politics of conscious alliance building. Such politics take account of the differential affects which the current ideologies and politics in the neo-imperial capitalist world order have on women of different positioning and locations.

Similar ideas are expressed in Sally J. Scholz's (2007) definition of "political solidarity." We think the notion of "political solidarity" has a strong relevance for our research, since it refers to forms of solidarity derived from shared commitment to a political project. It lends itself as a tool to think of cooperation and collective action in the context of social movements, since "activism" is a central element of its practice. "Activism is the public side of political solidarity," argues Sally Scholz (2007: 45). "Political solidarity" aims to affect social change. In the ideal case, it is born out of a mutual commitment to a joint struggle to challenge injustice or oppression (Mohanty 2003). It is thus possible to speak of political solidarity, if individuals are prepared to form networks to pursue a political goal by various means of activism. The notion of "shared interest" is relative and limited to the ambition to challenge certain modes of oppression or to pursue a path of liberation: "it is the mutual commitment … that forms the unity of solidarity, not shared feelings, experiences, identities or social locations" (Scholz 2007: 40). Political solidarity is thus represented as a form of coalition politics, which may include dissenting voices and disagreements (including ones regarding the definition of the political goals) (ibid.: 38).

We think that a generalized assumption of the "mutuality" of commitment in coalitional struggles renders this certainly attractive vision of solidarity slightly over-euphemistic, subsuming it to an ultimately liberal understanding of the *political*.[2] The assumption of mutuality obscures to a certain extent the awareness of the various material differences and cultural hegemonies across which solidarity work inevitably needs to be constructed. To what extent do differences in experience and position (in terms of gender, class, race/ethnicity, citizenship, economic power, privileged ideological support, etc.) obstruct balanced mutualities? The assumption of a mutuality of commitment comes along with the connotation that the various commitments at stake are essentially alike and similar in kind. This may go hand in hand with the idea that the motivation for the commitment is the same – that is the struggle for a "good cause." We do not mean to argue that this cannot be the case. Yet the reasons to be engaged in solidarity work may be less "pure" in many instances than the idea of mutuality seems to suggest. In transnational politics, they may include organizational and geo-political considerations and interests, which may intermesh with a dedication to the "good causes" of human rights and equality. We therefore think that the concept of difference has to be placed at an even deeper level close to the core of the theoretical understanding of solidarity discourses and practices. Moreover, it needs to be a concept of difference, which is attuned to the material power relations that structure the field of transnational politics.

Given the way sexuality has been theorized in relation to solidarity, we sought to understand how activists participating in transnational networks conceived their actions in relations to notions of *sameness* and *difference* within the European context. We were therefore interested in what solidarity meant to activists who were differently located (politically, socially, economically, and geographically). What were the practices of solidarity – how certain actions were seen as "solidaristic"? In this chapter, we will concentrate on the thoughts on solidarity by some of the research participants from Poland. It further helps us to recognize the multiple ways in which solidarity has been understood within national polities across Europe.

Solidarity discourses among activists in Poland

The notion of "solidarnosc" has a particular set of meanings in Poland, which sets it apart from other understandings of solidarity in social and political theory (though we also recognize the diverse constructions, legacies, and meanings of solidarity in social democracy and Christian democracy in different national contexts in Europe (Stjerno 2004)). We are more concerned about the way in which contemporary claims for inclusion within Polish civil society try to invoke, or draw upon, the memory of the Solidarnosc movement to promote their political claims. In this context, we are heavily indebted to Anna Gruszczynska's (2009) work on the uses of solidarity in the political claims around the Poznan March of Equality in 2005. In her discussion of the Poznan March in 2005, Gruszczynska (2009: 48) argues that the socially conservative Law and Justice Party claimed the memory of Solidarity in order to promote their political agenda in opposition to that of the left, rooted in the communist past. She argues that "Solidarity functions in the Polish national imaginary very much in the form of hegemonic 'frozen memory'; one of the recurring images of being that of the ZOMO squads breaking up illegal demonstrations" (2009: 49).

Gruszczynska further describes "the emotional spaces of solidarity" associated with the Poznan March in November 2005 in terms of the rallies that were held across Poland in solidarity with the Poznan marchers. Participants in the Poznan March could invoke the memory of the Solidarity movement's protests against an unjust communist state, to legitimize their own spatialized claims for sexual citizenship constituted through walking through urban space to raise the issue of the state's treatment of its gay and lesbian citizens: "The Poznan activists were able to inscribe the Solidarity 'memory package' as relevant to issues of sexual politics" (ibid.). There was therefore a conscious attempt to invoke the memory of "Solidarnosc" in order to create legitimacy for a project of LGBT equality and citizenship. She goes on to argue that:

> by defying the ban of the Poznan mayor, the Poznan March of Equality organizers could be seen as representing the core values of Solidarity, as opposed to newly elected government. Through the spatial and emotional context of the event, the Poznan March organizers could actively challenge what they argued was re-appropriation of Solidarity legacy by the right-wing in power. (Ibid.)

A specific feature of solidarity practice in current sexual politics in Poland can also be identified in the prominence of an approach of intergroup solidarities. In our point of view this becomes most obvious in the organization of the Poznan March for Equality. The march in Poznan is usually organized on the UN International Day of Human Rights. According to our interviews with the organizers of the 2008 march, feminists and anarchist civil rights activists have been influential to the loose networks that are revitalized every year in order to make the march possible. Over the years, the organizing committee has sought to build coalitions with various oppressed groups: women, disabled people, the aged, fat people, and of course lesbians, gay men, bisexuals, and transgender people. The emphasis on solidarity across the boundaries of oppression is most pronounced in the march in Poznan. It is expressed in the title of the march: *Equality March*. For instance, Gruszczynska (2009: 50) notes that "the coalitional aspect of the Poznan Marches in 2006 and 2007 was apparent already in the preparatory phase, where the activists took great care to include representatives of local anarchist, ecologist and disability rights groups among the organizing team." Yet there are similar currents in other localities of Polish activism. Discussions about coalition politics (e.g. with the Jewish community) has been on the agenda of the debates among activists who organize the March for Tolerance in Krakow, too. It could be argued that the choice of political slogans, such as tolerance and equality, has also served to deflect public attention from the sole issue of homosexuality.[3] A recourse to equality and tolerance may also be a conscious strategy to tap into political opportunities opened up by the European Union (EU), its specific anti-discrimination politics and discourses, spread in the course of a "Europeanization" of political discourses during EU accession.

For example, Chybisov and Średnicka (2006) argue that the organizers of 2006 Warsaw "Pride" demonstration opted for the name "Equality Parade" because of its affinities with European values around human rights and anti-discrimination:

> The name of the parade...matches European analogies. The choice of name itself emphasizes the individual rights of human beings, closely matching the tradition of "Human Rights" as codified in Europe following World War II. Specifically, organizers told us that they hoped to invoke the European Convention on Human Rights in support of the parade. (Chybisov and Średnicka 2006)

The common references to tolerance, which Chybisov and Średnicka refer to as "unofficial theme" of the parade, can be interpreted in a similar way. Many protestors wore T-shirts with the slogan "Europe = Tolerancja" [Tolerance].

O'Dwyer (2012) argues that EU accession led to transformation of the framing of debates on homosexuality from one based on personal morality to equality and rights. Yet while Polish activists may have on occasion deployed strategic references to European values to legitimize their cause, their analysis of the material impact of EU policies on the gay rights movement in Poland is more complex and often rather ambivalent. Drawing on his conversations with Polish activists, O'Dwyer argues that the EU has contributed positively toward the development of the movement, not through the practices of conditionality and social learning, but more because of the unintended consequences of EU accession: "the EU has influenced movement development, but more through the unintended consequences of backlash than through the mechanisms of conditionality and social learning" (2012: 334). In an earlier essay on Europeanization and sexual politics in contemporary Poland based on interviews with Polish gay rights activists, O'Dwyer (2010) found that his respondents displayed considerable skepticism about the political will and power of the EU to secure political change in Poland, but they stressed the indirect and mundane influence of Europeanization on sexual politics. For instance, one of his respondents, Tomasz Basiuk suggests: "The main influence if the EU is indirect...through expanded horizons for Poles, through travel, study, work...This is the mechanism for change; not legal solutions" (O'Dwyer 2010: 238).

Elsewhere (Binnie and Klesse 2013a), we have examined the role of East-West migration in the transnational activist networks in our study. We found that while East-West migration was significant in generating inspiration and knowledge for activism in Poland, this was not simply a one-way West-East transfer of knowledge, support, and expertise. We found a number of examples of activists based in Western countries express how much they had learned from activists in Poland, and that they had applied knowledge obtained through collaboration with activists in Poland within their own organizations and national contexts.

Jones and Subotic (2011: 545–546) argue that "the meaning of Europe is fundamentally a relational construct: it emerges out of a series of domestic and international intersections that shape not only how a state views itself, but also how it is viewed by European others." In examining these intersections between the domestic and the international, we need to recognize not only how the concept of solidarity has been practiced and understood within transnational LGBTQ activist networks but also the distinctiveness of solidarity in specific national contexts within Europe. In our study we found that cross-group solidarity was an important element in contemporary sexual politics in Poland. In our interviews, we have seen a commitment to a conscious effort to build bridges and coalitions, rather than an instrumentalist approach to political strategies.

According to Gruszczynska (2009), references to Solidarnosc activate the "frozen memory" of solidarity during oppression under the communist government. It has a strong appeal in many social movement milieus. Yet the legacy of the Solidarnosc movement and of the contemporary connotations of solidarity discourses is contested. Informants in our project saw the value in contesting the dominant meanings of solidarity in Polish society, and seeking to challenge the way it had been appropriated by Law and Justice politicians. This was a dominant theme in our interviews. For instance, Samuel sees solidarity as a term that has been appropriated by the nationalist conservative right to articulate their political vision that excludes many – not just lesbians and gay men:

> The plan is just to show that the way the word is being used excludes a lot of people, except for heterosexual, conservative men and women. It's much more about...stealing the meaning, the essential meaning and to show that...this platform, which was supposed to be a starting point to develop society, was so exclusive. (Samuel, Krakow)

Samuel links the discussion of solidarity with another concept – that of tolerance. He sees an equivalence between the conservative appropriation of the concept of solidarity, with the appropriation of the concept of tolerance for LGBTQ politics:

> So in this case it's not only about solidarity and being...sharing their experience, supporting them. It's a little bit more about fighting with words and stealing the meaning, the essential meaning. Somehow we managed to steal the word tolerance. (Ibid.)

References to solidarity in struggles against homophobia and transphobia thus have specific meaning on the level of re-signification. It is about reclaiming words and histories for a particular political stance. According to Samuel, tolerance has become strongly associated with homosexuality within popular discourse, which he sees as a success of the movement he has been part of. This focus on the politics of representation and contesting terms points toward the power of "solidarity" within Polish political discourse.

One significant and interesting way in which solidarity was conceived by our respondents was that of solidarity as intergroup coalition. The conceptualization of the protest as a coalition-driven multi-issue struggle directly involves the value of solidarity. Aska had linked the concepts equality, tolerance, and solidarity in one sentence earlier in the interview. When we asked her about the significance of solidarity for the larger activist movement around the Poznan protests, she replies:

> *Christian*: Do you think that the work you're doing, you know, organizing this demonstration and this week, do you think that solidarity is...a value which is important in that?
>
> *Aska*: Yeah.
>
> *Christian*: Do you think it has something to do with solidarity?
>
> *Aska*: Yeah. I think, yeah it has a lot to do with solidarity. It stems from this idea that all the discriminated groups are, you know, some kind of minority and the mechanisms of discrimination are the same, so, you know, every group alone could be, you know, fighting discrimination, but if we join in this solidarity, okay solidarity between those groups, you can go do something more.

Solidarity is described as a strategic orientation to build a stronger movement. There are different forms of discriminations. They can be challenged, yet if each group struggles on its own, the effectivity of their struggle will ultimately be limited. Aska's view further rests on the assumptions that discriminations work along similar mechanisms. Even if she does not elaborate on this issue, we can draw from this point that the advantage of a politics of solidarity is not simply as question of strength based on numbers. People who are faced with certain forms of discrimination can learn from each other's experiences and utilize these experiences in their own or independent struggles. Political struggles are then a matter of mutual learning and collaboration.

This notion of solidarity as based on coalition between different groups that are marginalized by the conservative political mainstream is articulated by other activists. For instance, Pawel talks of a "new Polish solidarity," which involves around the coalitions of feminists, lesbians, gay men, bisexuals, left-wing groups, including anti-globalization actors and anarchists, democratic actors from within previous periods of anti-communist movement struggles, artists and curators, progressive academics, and sometimes workers, too. This new solidarity is a networked solidarity, based on the readiness to engage in forms of collective action or to address in local forms of support work for other groups. In particular, the marches become rallying points for the articulation of this new kind of solidarity:

> They [that is the marches] gathered people from many left wing groups...You will have, in the Polish parade, many straight men,...you

will have, like, left wing straight men, or anarchists, participating in these activities. They have this gathering of left wing, intellectual activists...young people mostly, but not only, or people who are against [the] Church, against Catholicism in Poland...But the critics of the parade and people who attack the parade, they see only the gay ingredient, and they attack the parade because of the gay ingredient.

Pawel sees a new kind of solidarity emerging which is born out of a general dissatisfaction with the cultural conservatism and the political authoritarianism, which drives far right's government politics. It gives birth to a social movement (or a coalition of social movements) which go far beyond the issue of homosexuality, even if solidarity with LGB(T) people is a theme around which these various groups and actors fight together. The understandings of solidarity articulated by Pawel and Aska demonstrate elements of both intergroup and intragroup discourses on solidarity in the sense that the members of these coalitions of different activist groups share a common conservative, authoritarian enemy while they recognize the variety of distinctive political actors and projects that make up these coalitions.

We find it noteworthy that the primary frame of reference encompasses the collaboration between various groups within Polish society. Pawel refers to the most striking solidarity he has experienced over recent years of LGBTQ struggle as the "new Polish solidarity." This does not mean the accounts of our informants did not contain references to "transnational solidarities." The transnational dimension may add a further element. The emphasis on "transnational solidarities" would vary according to the context of the event or context under consideration. The march in Poznan, for example, has seen few participants from abroad over the years and has been organized without any financial support from abroad, whereas other events, such as the Krakow Culture for Tolerance Festival and the associated march have been attended and supported in manifold ways by various groups and institutions from other countries. David Featherstone (2008: 44) has argued that: "Solidarities are not produced on a smooth surface between discretely bounded struggles, but rather are part of ongoing connections, relations and articulations between places. Further, they are interventions in the social and material relations between places." In our project, we sought to understand the nature of these connections between places and how they were imagined by our respondents. In this concluding section, we wish to draw the discussion of transnational activist solidarities together by focusing on their spatial politics. We found major differences in character between the marches and associated cultural festivals in Krakow,

Warsaw, and Poznan. Each city is differently embedded within transnational networks. In a similar way, each respondent deployed different imaginaries of solidarity, which linked different groups and places with each other. For Western European activists, transnational dimension of European solidarity was the primary frame, whereas for activist in Poland, it was secondary. For many of them, Western Europe was not necessarily the dominant reference.

When we asked Samuel and Ania about their ideas on the relevance of transnational solidarity in the current moment of struggle, Samuel's reply made quite clear that their political strategy is primarily designed to respond to "local" discourses:

> *Christian*: Yes, the question for us would be... "How is it possible to conceive of something like queer, or lesbian, gay, bisexual solidarity? Is there something [like that] and what are the emotions underpinning it"? [Or]... would you suggest, [that]... it's not an appropriate concept... to carry to the field of sexual politics in Poland at all. You know, maybe we should just discard it... let's stop... thinking there's solidarity we need to find.
>
> *Samuel*: I'm sorry to disappoint you, but to be honest our perspective is quite narrow here. We don't think that much on the global scale. I think we should start, but it's still like we really created measures to deal with the local issues and that's why sometimes one might find us a little bit narrow minded. (Samuel/Krakow)

Samuel goes on then to talk about the international orientation of the art festival, but his point about priorities and orientations are quite clear. For Samuel, LGBTQ politics in Poland, first, need to find a response to the specific construction of Polish national identity. All transnational strategies need to be mediated via the requirements defined by this basic conditionality.

Multiple solidarities

Another interesting observation is that many respondents saw solidarity as something that is not one-dimensional. This means that even if activists referred to what could be called "transnational" acts of solidarity, it was not necessarily the transnational dimension in that encounter and interaction, which people found most noteworthy. At the start of the project we had envisaged that activists would conceive of solidarity as being constituted primarily in across cultural or national differences. However, our respondents pointed toward other lines of difference that were at least as significant as national, or intercultural difference that we had not envisaged, or could not have anticipated from the outset of our project. These were differences along lines of age and sexual orientation. For example, Bettina, one of the organizers of the 2008 Krakow Festival for Tolerance, suggested that the difficulties of transnational cooperation are aggravated by gender, intergenerational, and cultural differences:

> *Christian*: would you say the co-operation turned difficult because of primarily personal, emotional or political issues ... or a mixture of it?
>
> *Bettina*: ... I think it's more about personal ... but I think it was just misunderstandings because of culture and because of generation, because the activists who came, they were all, like fifty years old. They were all like twice the age of the average Polish activist's age ... and they were also sometimes, like ... because our activists are almost all women ... and it was a little, sometimes, strange. It was like the fifty year old German gays come and tell the young, Polish lesbian feminist women what to do ... Germans have this tendency, maybe, to discuss everything and to make it clear and Polish people don't have, maybe, this much this culture ... and then the generational thing, that they have the experience of twenty, thirty years activism.

Bettina argued that the interplay of various factors and positions resulted in a situation in which some (female) Polish activists read the behavior of some (male) German activists as patronizing and domineering. Cultural differences in styles of communication, androcentrism and gender-normative behaviors, age differences, and differences in experience are the perspectives through which Bettina interprets certain "transnational" dynamics. Geo-political hegemony is reinforced through uneven geo-temporalities (here with regard to the histories of social movement activism) and forms of gender power. While Bettina talks of generational difference as a source of problems in this quote, she sees them as an inspiration a specific articulation of (positive) solidarity in other parts of the interview (Binnie and Klesse 2013b). Apart from intergenerational solidarity, Bettina also stresses a moment of solidarity across sexual identities:

> And I think there is also within the march a big solidarity because most people marching with us are heterosexual like 50% so it's like a real a big issue because the majority of lesbians and gay from Krakow

don't go to the march...so therefore other heterosexual people are coming because they are in favor of tolerance and equal rights. This is really positive I think but on the other hand it is also a little problem in that...the march is even hetero dominated...in that there are very few gay and lesbian couples visible...and there are even heterosexual couples visible – like holding hands and may be kissing...so this is also a little strange because it would be also nice to have a visibility of gay and lesbian people in Krakow which is the only day where we are visible in the whole year...but...it's just great that they are coming because...there are very very many gay people who don't come because of being afraid of being seen and so it's good that we have these groups like Social Democratic and Green Party, anarchists and feminists who support us...it's great we have these groups who support us. (Bettina, Krakow)

Bettina, like many others, emphasizes that the support by heterosexual participants was vital to the early marches. At the same time, the quote reveals grains of ambiguity about heterosexual and LGBTQ visibilities. Solidarities across sexual orientation, too, are enacted across uneven terrain. Many activists from Poland described an understanding of solidarity as a complex and multilayered process of intersecting inter-and intra- group solidarities. The transnational is one element among them and often not the most prominent. This calls into question hegemonic understandings of solidarity in gender and sexual politics in Poland, as operating along East/West binary and center on cross-national flows and links, which structures popular, media, and activist discourses on sexuality and sexual politics in Europe.

Conclusion

In this chapter, we have examined the way in which the concept of solidarity has been used by the research participants within our study on transnational activism around contemporary LGBTQ politics in Poland. We have seen that the key terms in our study, such as "transnational" and "solidarity," have multiple and contested meanings and that we have sought to understand how our informants have understood and used them. We have argued that notions of sameness and difference have been central in social and political theories of solidarity. Concentrating on interviews with respondents in Poznan and Krakow, we found that many of them did not use the term solidarity directly to articulate their sense of connection to others involved in common projects to challenge heteronormativity in Polish society. Because of the hegemonic meaning of Solidarnosc within contemporary Polish politics and its appropriation by socially conservative Law and Justice politicians we noted that some respondents saw the need to contest the dominant meanings associated with terms such as "solidarity" and "tolerance."

These terms have been remodeled and appropriated for an LGBT-rights agenda through discursive links with European human rights and anti-discrimination frameworks. Transnational activism was key to this process, which took place at a moment when EU accession seemed to have shifted political opportunity structures. Yet the transnational dimension does not exhaust the operational meanings of solidarity discourses in Polish LGBTQ politics in this historical conjuncture. The implicit plurality of solidarity discourse is well captured in the following quote by Chybisov and Średnicka (2006): "When we combine the idea of political struggle (including transnational activism) with our notion of solidarity (with a lower-case s), we believe the result is an effective solution for creating social change."

One of the most significant ways in which solidarity was envisaged within our respondents was the notion of solidarity as intergroup coalition. This is particularly true of the activists in Poznan where there was evidence of a conscious attempt to establish and mobilize connections between different, but related, groups of activists focusing on diverse political projects with roots in feminism, anarchism, anti-capitalism, age awareness, and fat activism.[4] The references here were often primarily local. In terms of the transnational dimensions of activism (which was the primary focus of our project) we saw that our understanding of the transnational basis of solidarity needs to be set in context of other and overlapping forms of solidarity which we had not envisaged at the outset of our project such as intergenerational solidarities. We also recognize that it is imperative that the transnational mobility of the respondents in our project is not overstated, and that more research needs to be conducted on the transnational dimensions of the Christian Right and Far Right activism within Poland.

Notes

An earlier version was published as 'Researching transnational activism around LGBTQ politics in Central and Eastern Europe: Activist solidarities and spatial imaginings', in Robert Kulpa and Joanna Mizielinska (eds.) *De-Centring Western Sexualities: Central and Eastern European Perspectives*, Farnham: Ashgate: 107–129.

1. In total we interviewed 35 activists in Poland, Germany, the Netherlands, Belgium, and the United Kingdom. These included a wide range of activists

from diverse backgrounds affiliated with different types of organizations from professional LGB(T) rights organizations to queer anarchist groups; those working in trade unions to those who were not affiliated with any formal organization. We also participated in the equality marches and cultural festivals in Warsaw and Poznan in 2008; the Krakow Culture for Tolerance Festival in 2008 and 2009; the Krakow Queer in May event in 2009, as well as the Krakow March for Tolerance in 2008 and 2009. In addition we took part in the 2007 Get Bent Festival in 2007; and the 2008 Queer Up North event (both in Manchester), as well as the 2009 Pink Saturday Event in The Hague. We also took part in international networking events of Dutch COC local organizations in The Hague and Arnhem in 2009. In addition we conducted archive research on Polish LGBTQ politics in IHLIA (the international gay and lesbian information centre and archive) in Amsterdam.

2. We are grateful to the feedback from Jenny Petzen and our discussions with Sarah Lamble, who encouraged us to develop our analysis along these lines.

3. According to Robert Kulpa (personal communication), the attempts to deflect from a pure focus on (homo- or bi-) and to build strong coalitions across sexual identities played a role in the creation of the name 'Equality Parade' for the events that took place in Warsaw since 2001. The Equality theme further resonates with European – and other transnational – Equality and Human Rights discourses. (See Ayoub 2013 and Binnie and Klesse 2012 for further discussion of the latter argument).

4. The 2008 Poznan Equality and Tolerance event and Equality March included a specific commitment to age awareness and fat activism, as evidenced by the declaration on organization's website that: "This year we want to put up a problem of women over 50 and talk about discrimination of overweight women" (Organizational Committee of the Equality and Tolerance Days in Poznan 2008).

References

Alexander, Jacqui M. and Chandra Talpade Mohanty. 1997. "Introduction: Genealogies, Legacies, Movements." In *Feminist Genealogies, Colonial Legacies, Democratic Futures*, eds. Jacqui M. Alexander and Chandra Talpade Mohanty. New York: Routledge, xiii–xlii.

Anthias, Floya and Nira Yuval-Davis. 1992. *Racialized Boundaries: Race, Nation, Gender, Colour and Class*. New York: Routledge.

Ayoub, Phillip M. 2013. "Cooperative Transnationalism in Contemporary Europe: Europeanization and Political Opportunities for LGBT Mobilization in the European Union." *European Political Science Review* 5(2): 279–310.

Binnie, Jon and Christian Klesse. 2012. "Solidarities and Tensions: Feminism and Transnational LGBTQ Rights Politics in Poland." *European Journal of Women's Studies* 19(4): 444–459.

——. 2013a. "'Like a Bomb in the Gasoline Station': East-West Activism Around Lesbian, Gay, Bisexual, Transgender and Queer Politics in Poland." *Journal of Ethnic and Migration Studies* 39(7): 1107–1124.

——. 2013b. "The Politics of Age, Temporality and Intergenerationality in Transnational Lesbian, Gay, Bisexual, Transgender and Queer Networks." *Sociology* 47(3): 580–595.

Brunkhorst, Hauke. 2007. "Globalizing Solidarity: The Destiny of Democratic Solidarity in the Times of Global Capitalism, Global Religion, and Global Public." *Journal of Social Philosophy* 38(1): 93–11.

Chari, Sharad and Katherine Verdery. 2009. "Thinking Between the Posts: Postcolonialism, Postsocialism, and Ethnography after the Cold War." *Comparative Studies in Society and History* 51(1): 6–34.

Chybisov, Dmytro and Jesse Van Tol Średnicka (2006). "From 'Imagined' Homogeneity to Sexual Solidarity." *Humanity in Action.* http://www.humanityinaction.org/knowledgebase/215-from-imagined-homogeneity-to-sexual-solidarity-the-struggle-over-lgbt-rights-in-poland (accessed 14 March 2014).

Durkheim, Emile. 1964. *The Division of Labor in Society.* New York: Free Press.

Featherstone, David. 2008. *Resistance, Space and Political Identities: The Making of Counter-Global Networks.* Chichester: Wiley-Blackwell.

Gellner, Ernest. 1983. *Nations and Nationalism.* Oxford: Basil Blackwell.

Gould, Carol C. 2007. "Transnational Solidarities." *Journal of Social Philosophy* 38(1): 148–164.

Gould, Carol C. and Sally J. Scholz. 2007. "Introduction." *Journal of Social Philosophy* 8(1): 3–6.

Gruszczynska, Anna. 2009. "'I Was Mad About It All, About the Ban': Emotional Spaces of Solidarity in the Poznan March of Equality." *Emotion, Space and Society* 2(1): 44–51.

Haritaworn, Jin. 2008. "Loyal Repetitions of the Nation: Gay Assimilation and the 'War on Terror'." *Darkmatter* 3. http://www.darkmatter101.org/site/author/jin/ (accessed 20 December 2009).

Haritaworn, Jin, Tamsila Tauqir, and Esra Erdem. 2008. "Gay Imperialism: Gender and Sexuality Discourse in the 'War on Terror'." In *Out of Place: Interrogating the Silences of Queerness/Raciality*, eds. Adi Kuntsman and Esperanza Miyake. Centre of Women's Studies, York University: Raw Nerve Books, 71–98.

Harvey, Jean. 2007. "Moral Solidarity and Empathetic Understanding: The Oral Value and Scope of the Relationship." *Journal of Social Philosophy* 38(1): 22–37.

Jones, Shannon and Jelena Subotic. 2011. "Fantasies of Power: Performing Europeanization on the European Periphery." *European Journal of Cultural Studies* 14(5): 542–557.

Keinz, Anika 2011. "National Bedrooms and European Desires? Negotiating Normalcy in Postsocialist Poland." *Central European History* 44(1): 92–117.

Kuus, Merje. 2004. "Europe's Eastern Expansion and the Reinscription of Otherness in East-Central Europe." *Progress in Human Geography* 28(4): 472–489.

Light, Duncan and Craig Young. 2009. "European Union Enlargement, Post-Accession Migration and Imaginative Geographies of the 'New Europe': Media Discourses in Romania and the United Kingdom." *Journal of Cultural Geography* 26(3): 283–305.

Mohanty, Chandra Talpade. 2003. *Feminism without Borders: Decolonizing Theory, Practicing Solidarity.* Durham: Duke University Press.

O'Dwyer, Conor. 2010. "From Conditionality to Persuasion? Europeanization and the Rights of Sexual Minorities in Post-Accession Poland." *Journal of European Integration* 32(3): 229–247.

———. 2012. "Does the EU Help or Hinder Gay-Rights Movements in Post-Communist Europe? The Case of Poland." *East European Politics* 28(4): 332–352.

Organizational Committee of the Equality and Tolerance Days in Poznan. 2008. "Equality and Tolerance Days in Poznan, Poland (10–16 November 2008)." http://www.dnirownosci.most.org.pl (accessed 10 March 2010).

Phillips, Oliver. 1997. "Zimbabwean Law and the Production of a White Man's Disease." *Social and Legal Studies* 6(4): 471–491.

Puar, Jasbir. 2008. "Homonationalism and Biopolitics." In *Out of Place: Interrogating the Silences of Queerness/Raciality*, eds. Adi Kuntsman and Esperanza Miyake. York: Raw Nerve Books, 13–70.

Scholz, Sally J. 2007. "Political Solidarity and Violent Resistance." *Journal of Social Philosophy* 38(1): 38–52.

Sellar, Christian, Caedmon Staddon, and Craig Young. 2009. "Twenty Years after the Wall: Geographical Imaginaries of 'Europe' during European Union Enlargement." *Journal of Cultural Geography* 26(3): 253–258.

Stjerno, Steinar. 2004. *Solidarity in Europe*. Cambridge: Cambridge University Press.

Stychin, Carl. 2004. "Same-Sex Sexualities and the Globalization of Human Rights Discourse." *McGill Law Journal* 49: 951–968.

10

Split Europe: Homonationalism and Homophobia in Croatia

Kevin Moss

In Central and Eastern Europe (CEE), tolerance of homosexuality has been portrayed as a value associated with the idea of Europe (or the West, or America) both by local queers aspiring to attaining rights in their own countries and perhaps even more by nationalists who want to exclude homosexuals from the nation by portraying homosexuality as a foreign import. It is part of a tradition I have followed since the early 1990s (Moss 1995). I have found numerous examples of right-wing nationalists in Czech Republic, Hungary, Russia, and Yugoslavia defining national identity as purely heterosexual, while portraying homosexuality as an import from Western Europe. Wiktor Grodecki's three pseudo-documentaries about Prague rent boys, for example, present the boys as innocent straight Czechs who fall into the clutches of depraved gay clients from Western Europe (Moss 2006). Recently the best analysis of this kind of mapping has come from Agnieszka Graff in Poland (Graff 2006, 2008, 2010). Anxieties about joining the European Union (EU) were expressed in Poland via attitudes toward lesbians and gay men, and for the nationalists "homophobia" became a mark of national difference. The conflict, she writes, "was more about cultural identity and national pride than about sexual orientation or public morality" (Graff 2010: 584). In other words, Poles were homophobes not because they were Catholic or because homosexuality is immoral or unnatural, but because they were Poles, and homophobia is a sign of patriotism. Tolerance of gay people became a litmus test for attitudes toward EU accession.

This chapter will examine the case of Split Pride 2011 to show how the idea of Europe was deployed in Croatia the same week that the country was approved for entry in the EU by the European Commission. Croatia is a useful focus both because of the timeline of its entry into the EU and because it is in the Balkans, a region with a fraught relationship to Europe and its others. The same can be said for Central and Eastern Europe as a whole, which provides a fertile ground for testing theories about deployment of European ideas of tolerance. While some scholars argue that claims for tolerance of LGBT identities reproduce Orientalizing discourse that establishes (Western) Europe as the wiser, more progressed culture to be imitated by local, more backward peoples, I will claim that refusal to allow local LGBT citizens to identify as they choose is equally, if not more, problematic. In fact the critics of homonationalism erase local CEE queer experience and ignore CEE in their analysis, which focuses instead on (Western) Europe and its colonial/Oriental other.

The conflict between European tolerance and local nationalist exclusion becomes particularly salient when queers attempt to occupy public space through gay pride demonstrations. These have often provoked either violent reactions on the part of local populations or bans by local authorities, who cite the risk of violence or local tradition or both as a justification for the bans. Attempts by LGBT activists in CEE have encountered violence or official bans or both in Moscow, Belgrade, Vilnius, Riga, Budapest, Warsaw, Krakow, Zagreb, and Split. Three of these, Belgrade, Vilnius, and Budapest have been analyzed in depth in a special edition of *Sextures* edited by Anna Gruszczynska tellingly titled *Parades of Pride or Shame* (Gruszczynska 2012). For the LGBT participants they were parades of pride, while for the local nationalists they were parades of shame and European decadence. The same mapping was deployed on all sides: by Western Europeans reporting on pride parades, by local LGBT marchers, who appealed to European values in demanding the state protect their right to march, and by right-wing nationalist opponents. The only difference was that for the opponents, "tolerance" and "Europeanness" were given a negative value. Dana Johnson writes about the discourse around Belgrade Pride 2009, which was ultimately canceled: anti-gay graffiti by the group Obraz emphasized its Serbianness by using old-fashioned Cyrillic letters and religious imagery, while counter-graffiti used Latin letters and modern images such as Batman and Robin, which Johnson claims discursively constructs Pride as a "demonstration of Europeanness" (2012: 13). A year later the Tadić government would allow and protect pride to show its own commitment to Europeanness and desire to join the EU.

Dorottya Rédai analyzes similar phenomena in the reporting on the 2008 Budapest Gay Pride. Homophobia was presented in the Hungarian press as anti-"European" or "sub-European" (Rédai 2012: 55), which for the mainstream pro-European press was seen as bad, but for the right-wing press was seen as virtuous. For the right-wing press "(Western)

Europe is a morally decaying world which Hungary should not follow. Gay people are seen as non-Hungarians, diseased/immoral foreigners who penetrate the body of virtuous Hungary, whose morality is presented as historically integral" (ibid.: 59). Rédai cites Hadley Renkin, who complicates the idea of a simplistic association of LGBT people as the nation's transnational "Others" – primarily "Europe" and "the West" (2009: 24). Renkin points out that this reading, while informative, can erase the agency of actual Hungarian LGBT activists on the ground, who have consciously queered Hungarian public spaces by marching in historically and culturally significant parts of Budapest and claiming Hungarian historical figures, such as Kertbeny, for the international gay movement. It is because the LGBT activists "challenge the traditionally heteronormative boundaries of national belonging, asserting that they too, although both 'gay' and globally connected, are members of the Nation" that the right-wing nationalists react with increasing violence (ibid.: 31).

It is easy to split Europe through analysis of homonegativity or of the availability of rights or of protections from discrimination of LGBT citizens. Eastern Europe (post-Socialist Europe, Europe in transition, the newer or future members of the Eurozone) has, for the most part, a higher level of homonegativity than Western Europe (the original EU). Štulhofer and Rimac analyzed social distance (would not want a homosexual as a neighbor) toward homosexuals and disapproval of homosexuality in the 1999 European Values Survey of 32 countries and drew the following conclusions: "In comparison to the old EU countries (the EU-15), participants from the countries that recently joined the EU and the non-EU countries (with the exception of Iceland) were found to be more homonegative" (2009: 28). Takács and Szalma (2011) reach similar conclusions through analysis of the European Social Survey dataset from 2010. Their table of the average acceptance of gay men and lesbian women shows that newer or prospective/non-EU members account for the ten least accepting societies (Ukraine, Russia, Romania, Croatia, Latvia, Estonia, Slovakia, Hungary, Bulgaria, and Poland), while the remainder of CEE countries in the analysis (Slovenia, Czech Republic) fall in the middle. The most accepting societies are all in "old Europe" (Takács and Szalma: 2011: 362). Their main argument is that institutionalization of same-sex relationships has a positive effect on the social acceptance of gay men and lesbians, but they also find a correlation between social acceptance and satisfaction with democracy. It is interesting to note, as they point out, that the two countries in "new Europe" that have the highest level of acceptance, Slovenia and Czech

Republic, are also the two post-Socialist countries that have legalized registered same-sex partnerships (ibid.: 369). It is no accident, then, that the common assumption is that "the West" is more tolerant and grants more rights, while "the East" is more homophobic and grants fewer. A glance at ILGA-Europe's May 2013 Rainbow Map confirms this assumption, with green on the West (for more rights) and red in the East (for fewer), while Central Europe is yellow (in between).

European tolerance and its discontents

In recent years scholars of queer theory have developed a critique of the abuse of the idea of tolerance of sexual difference as a way to exclude other groups from full rights. Critics such as Judith Butler and Jasbir Puar object to the use of sexual freedom – specifically the freedom of gay people – as an instrument of bigotry (Butler 2008; Puar 2007). Puar writes about how the folding into citizenship of homonormative queers comes at a cost: the production of queer terrorist bodies targeted for dying. Joseph Massad, on whose work Puar builds, takes the postcolonial critique of Orientalism even further, arguing that LGBT identity in the Arab world is a foreign import, and that the "Gay International" causes more problems than it solves when it meddles in the Middle East (Massad 2002, 2007). Conferences such as the Sexual Nationalisms conference in Amsterdam (January 2011) and the Center for Lesbian and Gay Studies (CLAGS) Homonationalism and Pinkwashing conference (April 2013) pay lip service to including all of Europe, but while presenters do find that tolerance in CEE is presented as "European" or "Western," this idea is deployed against local nationalists and neo-Nazis, not against immigrants. According to the CLAGS conference program, "Homonationalism is increasingly present in Nationalist ideologies across the globe, as secular right-wing forces increasingly leave anti-gay politics to organized religion." But this critique of homonationalism seems at best completely irrelevant for much of Eastern Europe, where good old-fashioned heteronationalism continues to flourish. In Serbia, for example, it was the Serbian Prime Minister and party leader Ivica Dačić (2012), not a representative of organized religion (which is hardly marginalized in Serbia or Russia anyway), who said he "hated any Union where a gay parade is the ticket in."

Some scholars have attempted to expand the homonationalist critique to the region. Robert Kulpa and Joanna Mizielinska (2011) claim, following Jon Binnie, in Central and Eastern Europe there is a problem with the hegemony of Western Europe in general vis-a-vis Eastern Europe, with the interventions of Western LGBT activists in the East, and with the hegemony of Western and mostly American queer academic work. Kulpa (2013) expands this critique in his article on "leveraged pedagogy," by which he means, I think, the idea that Europe or "the West" knows more about gay rights and can therefore "teach" our "less progressed" brothers and sisters in Central and Eastern Europe. Binnie (2004: 76) explains it as follows: "The logic goes something like this: you are less developed than us because you treat your gays badly. Thus the western state becomes the guarantor of lesbian and gay rights versus the threat constituted by the savage brutal other." Nicole Butterfield (2013) applies a similar critique to Croatia in an article that covers much the same material as this chapter, but with a different spin: "Sexual Rights as a Tool for Mapping Europe." What neither Kulpa nor Butterfield shows, in my opinion, is an actual negative effect of deploying a European ideal of tolerance on local activists or local queer citizens. Quite the contrary: it seems that local activists are only too happy to demand tolerance à l'européenne and local queers are only happy to enjoy it. In his earlier book Kulpa asked, "What is so necessarily wrong with the willingness to be recognized as part of the national community, to build one's own identification in relation to other nationals and not be left aside as encapsulated and self-contained ab/sub/ob/ject?" (Kulpa 2011: 56). What, indeed, is wrong with it? Butterfield (2013: 25) argues that "discrimination based on sexual orientation or Pride parades in Europe...have become key issues like many other women's issues before through which activists and governments are (re)fortifying the boundaries between so-called developed and undeveloped societies." But are they not rather breaking down those boundaries by claiming a global LGBT identity rather than a specific exemption for the "undeveloped" society to discriminate? In grasping for possible negative effects, Butterfield concludes with a quotation from Carl Stychin: "Same-sex sexual communities must themselves continue to be interrogated for their own exclusions and marginalizations (such as around race, gender, and social class)" (Butterfield 2013: 28). None of these really apply to Croatia, where activists are scrupulously attentive to inclusion of all ethnicities (there is no race), women are more visible than men (see Split Pride), and class divides are not nearly as prominent as in the "developed" West.

It seems that the result of expansion of homonationalist analysis is either erasure of the realities of LGBT citizens in CEE or their distortion by forcing them onto the procrustean bed of Western theory. As Roman Kuhar suggests in his introduction to a recent edition of *Southeastern Europe* on homophobia in CEE, homonationalism may not be a pan-European project, and there are "countries where homophobia remains a 'family value' and the gay and lesbian human rights cannot serve as a litmus test for the selection of immigrants" (2013: 1–2). What we find in the East is really the heteronationalism first described by George Mosse (1985). I would argue that it is the queer theorists here who in their eagerness to find homonationalism everywhere do an injustice to the multiplicity of real-life experiences of local queers through a kind of neocolonialism and Orientalizing projection onto them. Yes, we should be vigilant about the potential downsides of including LGBT people into the nation or into Europe through appeals to European values, but only if those downsides really materialize. Otherwise, why should we deny to Croatians or other "Eastern" or "Balkan" people the same kind of identities and freedoms demanded by those in Old Europe? Is it because they are primitive and tribal?

The nesting Balkans between East and West

This simple East/West binary, however, becomes even more complicated in the case of Croatia. Yugoslavia famously straddles the fault line between East and West. The resulting confusion was already noted by St. Sava in the 13th century: "At first we were confused. The East thought that we were West, while the West considered us to be East. Some of us misunderstood our place in the clash of currents, so they cried that we belong to neither side, and others that we belong exclusively to one side or the other. But I tell you, Ireneus, we are doomed by fate to be the East in the West and the West in the East" (St. Sava, Letter to Ireneus, 1221 [possibly apocryphal], quoted in Bakić-Hayden and Hayden 1992: 1). The region that came to be known as the Balkans has a complicated relation to the East and to the West's project of Orientalism. Among the first to apply Said's Orientalism to the still existing Yugoslavia were Milica Bakić-Hayden and Robert M. Hayden in "Orientalist Variations on the Theme 'Balkans'" (1992). They pointed to an Orientalist framework of analysis being used by Yugoslavs from the North and West of the country, and by some foreign observers. Slovenes and Croatians were represented as inherently more democratic and advanced than the inhabitants of the republics to the south and east of them (1992: 3). These distinctions privilege the predominantly Catholic, formerly Hapsburg territories, as "European," while condemning the predominantly Orthodox or Muslim, formerly Ottoman territories, as Balkan, non-European, and Other. Bakić-Hayden and Hayden describe a system of "'nesting' orientalisms, in which there exists a tendency for each region to view cultures and religions to the south and east of it as more conservative or primitive" (ibid.: 4). Maria Todorova elaborates on this analysis, but points out that "Balkanization" came to mean not only parcelization of viable political units, but also "a synonym for a reversion to the tribal, the backward, the primitive, the barbarian" (1994: 453). In fact, the Orientalist projection of the West onto the Balkans in the 1990s can largely be attributed to the Western imagining of the Balkans as a place of tribal primitivism and "centuries old ethnic hatreds," which allowed Europe and the US to avoid intervening until the last minute in the bloodiest conflict in Europe since 1945.

That conflict also complicates any simplistic analysis of the region in terms of European values of tolerance toward LGBT citizens, which are inextricably tied to heteronormativity and gender roles. During the wars of succession, nationalist politicians on all sides invoked traditional patriarchal gender roles and demonized queers as traitors to the nation. The effect of this repatriarchalization was strongest where the conflict was longer and more intense: Serbia, Croatia, Bosnia, and Herzegovina. Queers were called traitors to the nation for not contributing to the population of national citizens, and pacifists were labeled queers for not participating in the wars.

In her later book, *Imagining the Balkans*, Todorova writes of Balkanism as a variation of Orientalism, where the difference is mapped along gender lines. Whereas the Orient was perceived as a realm of wealth and femininity, with sexually available women and men, the Balkans were a male world of brutality and primitive barbarism (Todorova 1997: 13–14). This gendered version of Europe/Balkan as female/male is also described by Marina Blagojević in her description of the Serbian cultural imaginary in the 1990s (2000: 305–306). Women are aligned with Europe, while only men (she uses mužjaci here – real men, males) are Serbs. She quotes Jovo Toševski, who writes, "It is obvious that Serbs represent the masculine principle, while Europe has always like today represented the feminine principle" (2000: 301–302).

That sexuality is deeply implicated in perceptions of nationality can be gauged by the different positions on homosexuality in the former Yugoslavia, where the "nesting Balkans" mean that tolerance of queer citizens increases as one moves North and West. Slovenia, always the most European and least Balkan republic, had the first gay and lesbian festival in all of Eastern Europe in 1984. Slovene tolerance of homosexuality was used by Serb nationalists to fan anti-Slovene sentiment already in 1987, as Roman Kuhar and Alenka Švab (2013) document. "The scandal was blown up to the extent that Yugoslav media started to report that Slovenia would host 'the world congress of faggots'" (Kuhar and Švab 2013: 26). They write that coverage in the Slovenian media was spun exactly the opposite way: "Slovenian media used the scandal to show that Slovenia indeed does not belong to the Yugoslav federation anymore. In other words: the scandal can be seen as a cultural war between allegedly progressed and westernized Slovenia and the backward Balkan nations, which do not 'understand' homosexuality and condemn it" (ibid.: 27).

Slovenia's first gay pride parade went off without a hitch in 2001. When Belgrade held its first gay pride parade the same year, on the other hand, the gay bashers far outnumbered the gay marchers. The reaction on both sides was cast in terms of the idea of Europe: pro-gay spokesmen lamented that the counter-protests show how far Serbia is from democracy and from readiness to join Europe: "Serbia will never enter Europe with such behavior towards the freedom of the individual...How is it that all Europe accepts as normal gay, bisexual, and lesbians, etc., while Serbia takes a step backwards?" (Queeria 2002) Anti-gay protesters, on the other hand, took pride in the idea that Serbia is an oasis of patriarchal values: "If this is a part of what we have to do to become part of Europe, then better we should never become that" (ibid.). Both sides frame the conflict in terms of the idea of Europe and its relation to Serbia/the Balkans.

Croatia and Split Pride 2011

Croatia falls between the extremes of Slovenia and Serbia. It is positioned this way in many mappings: on the imaginary sliding scale of the nesting Balkans (from Europe to Balkan), in the schedule of joining the EU (Slovenia joined in 2004, Croatia in 2013, Serbia is a candidate), in the length and legacy of the violence in the 1990s, and in terms of gay rights and homophobia (as measured by the level of violence at the first pride parades in 2001 and 2002). Pride parades have been held in Zagreb since 2002, and the major LGBT rights groups were also (with the exception of LORI – Lesbian Organization Rijeka) based in the capital. The parades were often regional, with attendees coming not only from all over Croatia but also from the wider region, including Slovenia and Serbia. The current website of Zagreb Pride even claims that the event in 2002 was in response to the violence experienced at Belgrade Pride in 2001, and "for exactly that reason has a strong regional character and supports collaboration with LGBTIQ people from the Western Balkan region at the Zagreb Pride March" (Zagreb Pride 2013). Zagreb, in spite of some opposition and incidents of violence, was a relatively safe place for queers from the former Yugoslav states to gather.

The Split Pride of 2011 marked the first time pride was planned in any Croatian city other than Zagreb. The idea was prompted by the visit of the American women's rights activist Charlotte Bunch, for which the Split feminist and rights organization Domine organized a small conference on Discrimination of Lesbians in Public and Political Life. According to the head of Domine, Mirjana Kučer, the idea for a conference was suggested by the Serbian anti-war, feminist, and lesbian activist Lepa Mladjenović. The conference, sponsored by the City of Split in May 2010 to mark the International Day against Homophobia, was attended by Mladjenović from Belgrade as well as Sanja Juras, of the organization Kontra, from Zagreb (interview Mirjana Kučer, March 2012). One result of the conference was the opening of a gay support group through Domine. Sanja Juras suggested either bringing Zagreb Pride to Split or holding a separate pride in Split, which was supported as well by Edo Bulić of Iskorak/Zagreb and announced in January 2011 – for June 11.

The reaction from those opposed to the parade was swift. Mayor Željko Kerum, a member of the conservative HDZ (Croatian Democratic Union) party with political support of the Catholic Church, first said that it would be hard for him to comment on Split Pride, but then clarified, "All human rights and freedoms must be respected, but it's obvious that the citizens of Split don't want it. How can one then satisfy one side and the other?" (Pejković-Kaćanski 2011). The same article demonstrated Split priorities, that is, that football and football clubs come first, by opening with a quote from the secretary of Torcida, Split's powerful football club, the oldest club in Europe, which also celebrated the centenary of the founding of their team Hajduk in 2011: "We are definitely opposed to any kind of gay parades in our city. No matter how that sounds to anyone. Our position is loud and clear. We hope that the parade will not take place." While the article did quote Mirjana Kučer of Domine that "there is a community of young people in Split who need it," the author breathlessly paraphrases her claim that "they expect no problems and Split simply yearns for such an event!" Meanwhile the sub-headings in the article paint a different picture: "Already the announcement of Gay Pride has stirred up passions in Dalmatia," "Let them pay for the space," "Excesses are possible," "It's not normal for men to bear children, these individuals are sick." The last headed up the sound bites from two conservative politicians, with which the article closed. At least the article was prophetic, since the combination of football fans, conservative politics, and indifference on the part of the city government set the stage for the events of 11 June 2011.

As is often the case, there was some objection to the location of the parade. Authorities in Belgrade in 2009 attempted to move Pride from the center of the city to the outskirts. The organizers refused, considering that the state had effectively banned the event (Johnson 2012: 6). Similarly, Darja Davydova (2012: 41) describes how authorities refused to allow Baltic Pride 2010 to march in the streets of old Vilnius, instead moving the march to an undeveloped area across the river that was "void of national and cultural significance." Hadley Renkin (2009) considers that it was precisely the queering of national space by Hungarian Pride marchers that led to the backlash from anti-gay nationalists. Initially the organizers of Split Pride wanted to march from the Djardin Park around the old city to the Riva (waterfront promenade) and conclude with a program at the Peristyle (the formal entrance to Diocletian's Palace), which they considered decorating in pink or rainbow flags. City authorities wanted to move the concluding program to the Prokurative, a less symbolically significant U-shaped space built in the 19th century, ostensibly because it would be easier to protect. Eventually both sides agreed that the program would take place in the middle of the Riva, a very public and prominent open promenade between the Palace and the sea.

While the modified route was agreed to in May, Deputy Mayor Jure Šundov denied the request of the pride organizers to raise the rainbow flag on the city flagpole and said city officials declined to participate in the parade: "We politely declined, since this city government does not politically support such gatherings" (Lulić 2011). Dean Vuletič (2013) has documented the Croatian Democratic Union's long-standing opposition to expanding gay rights. Though their views may have softened with the benchmarks for EU membership, Kerum's and his administration's reluctance to support the parade was symptomatic of their previous position, and their lukewarm support of the parade may have given cover to more violent homophobic opposition.

Before the parade, graffiti and small posters appeared around the city with texts such as "My Split is against it, and you? 11.06 Parade of Shame," "Parade of Illness," "Death to Fags," "Fags not wanted," and most commonly "Stop the Gay Parade" (Ladišić 2011). Social media sites such as Facebook also sprouted anti-parade groups with titles such as "Ljubitelji kita odjebite od Splita" [Lovers of cock, fuck off from Split], for which the profile photo included an Ustasha symbol with the text "Fags to the camps." Another Facebook group was titled "Ulicama Splita krv će liti, gay parade neće biti" [Blood will flow in the streets of Split, there will be no gay parade]. Both groups were of course shut down, and the Croatian ombudswoman for gender equality Gordana Lukač Koritnik pointed them out to authorities before the march and suggested they be investigated for inciting hatred toward homosexuals (Lukač Koritnik 2011).

On 10 June, Croatia was green-lighted by the European Commission for entrance into the EU on 1 July 2013. Split's first Pride took place the next day. Some 200 marchers gathered in Djardin, and the day began with a festive atmosphere. The theme of the march was "Different Families, Equal Rights," and marchers carried signs that read, "My dad loves my dad!" "My partner is my family" and "Same taxes, same rights." Among the marchers were activists not only from Zagreb (Sanja Juras of Kontra, Edo Bulić of Iskorak, Mima Simić) but also from elsewhere in the region: Lazar Pavlović from Serbia's Gay Straight Alliance, Lepa Mladjenović from Belgrade, and Tatjana Greif from the Slovene organization ŠKUC LL (Student Cultural-Art Center – Lesbian Lilith). Europe was represented by Marije Cornelissen, a European Parliament member and member of the Committee on Women's Rights and Gender Equality, and by Linda Freimane, co-chair of ILGA Europe. As they marched down kralja Tomislava and turned onto Marmontova, they met only a handful of opposition and many locals and tourists waved and smiled. The marchers were accompanied by some 400 police in riot gear. Participants did not realize that several thousand anti-gay protesters (estimates range from 4000 to 10,000) had gathered on the Riva to greet them as they came out onto the promenade.

Police had cordoned off part of the Riva, but many protesters were close enough to throw things at the marchers: rocks, tomatoes, eggs, ashtrays, firecrackers, bottles, and anything that came to hand, even some potted oleander plants. The opponents were mostly young men, and they held their arms out in a fascist salute while chanting "Kill, kill, kill the gays!"– the same chant that had been used at Belgrade Pride in 2001. At first some of the organizers decided to cancel the parade, because the police had underestimated the crowd and could not guarantee the safety of the marchers. After a while, the police pushed the anti-gay demonstrators back far enough so the marchers could gather in front of the stage on the Riva for the program. Cornelissen claimed that a state must be prepared to defend everyone's rights and that "with the entry into the European Union the rights of the gay community will have to be protected in Croatia" (Nacional 2011). At least part of the program went on as planned, but it was shortened, and the participants were eventually evacuated by the police to the Domine headquarters in the old town.

The event resulted in 137 arrests, and eight people were hospitalized, including a TV cameraman who was hit with a rock. Video footage of the parade immediately went viral on the internet, prompting support for the marchers and criticism of the police and counter-protestors from various gay groups. Response from the Croatian government, poised as it was to enter the EU, was swift: President Ivo Josipović said the violence showed "that there are still some non-European parts of our society," and insisted that this was "not Croatia's real face," while Prime Minister Jadranka Kosor warned that violence and hatred were "something that cannot be tolerated in Croatia" (RFERL 2011).

Within Croatia, then, both at the march and at the level of the state government, the idea of European values was deployed in defense of the LGBT community against the violence. The EU Parliament also reacted, specifically tying Croatia's path to accession to the right-wing extremists who attacked Split Pride. Ulrike Lunacek, Member of European Parliament for the Greens/European Free Alliance and Co-President of the Intergroup on LGBT Rights, stated: "Yesterday's outbreak of homophobic hatred and violence shows that European values – including freedom of assembly and the protection of all minorities – are not yet fully at home in a country two years away from joining the EU" (LGBT-EP 2011a). A few days later the co-chairs of the intergroup filed priority questions to the European Commission and the European Council specifically, linking Croatia's accession to addressing Split Pride (LGBT-EP 2011b).

Zagreb Pride was scheduled for a week later, and the events at Split, coupled with criticism of the violence from European leaders, inspired many to turn out and show Croatia's "real face." Kristina Olujić (2011), for example, wrote in the interim that Split was the best advertisement for Zagreb Pride: boosted by the many voices of European leaders, even the lukewarm reaction of Croatian leaders when they realize they have to stand before the European court is better than no comment at all. Activists printed stickers for Zagreb Pride combining the Split Pride logo with a flying oleander plant, one of the iconic images of the homophobic attacks and the word "Survivor" in the font from the American TV series of the same name (Figure 10.1). They thus deftly combined local, specific, European, and global into one short package.

Most indicative, though, was the front page of a Zagreb newspaper immediately after the successful Zagreb Pride: "Split like Belgrade, Zagreb like Vienna." The sliding scale of the nesting Balkans was used, with the old Hapsburg capital of Vienna standing in at the European end (the goal of a Croatia entering the EU), while Split was compared to the opposite

Figure 10.1 Stickers used at Zagreb Pride 2011 by those who had been at Split Pride the week before

Source: Splitpride Tumblr 2011a.

pole, Belgrade, emblematic of the Balkans. A caption read "Gay Prides throughout Europe: violence only in the Balkans." A further heading asked, "Where do you belong?" The montage showed color photos of rainbow balloons and hands held for Zagreb and Vienna contrasted to black and white images of riot police and a bloody man on the ground for Split and Belgrade.

Further images showed Budapest (including some riot police and neo-Nazis), Sofia, and Toulouse. In case the implications were not clear, a short text clarified:

> While last week's Split Gay Pride showed Croatia to the world as an intolerant, primitive, and homophobic environment, Zagreb Pride showed that a different Croatia nevertheless exists – one that accepts differences and whose citizens can be measured with the citizens of Western Europe. Split's Gay Pride unfortunately many compared with Belgrade's, while Zagreb's we can proudly compare to exemplary ones held today in Vienna or Toulouse. (Index.hr 2011)

After commenting on the numbers and security in all these cities (fewer participants, greater security in Budapest and Sofia), the article concluded "Let's hope that in future Split looks for an example to Barcelona, rather than Belgrade, because Split deserves that" (Index.hr 2011).

The motivation of the opponents of the Split parade received little analysis in the press. It was assumed that they were connected with

Torcida, which was confirmed when some of those charged turned out to be members of the fan club. In this, they were not unlike the opponents in Belgrade, who were also largely football fans (Trost and Kovacevic 2013). On the Riva they appeared to be equal-opportunity haters: occasionally they varied the chant "Kill, kill, kill the fag!" with "Kill, kill, kill the gypsy!" or "Kill, kill, kill the Serb!" (This paralleled the graffiti, where "Death to fags" was sometimes varied with "Death to Serbs.") A TV cameraman from RTL was hit by a rock and called a "Jew" (Domi 2011). The counter-protesters claimed Croatian nationalism and sang patriotic songs as well. They presented themselves as local and Croatian nationalists, not Europeans. As Croatian patriots, they interestingly borrowed their chant from Serbian anti-gay, right-wing extremists. They also received support in Facebook groups and YouTube comments from Serbs and other right-wing homophobes from the region. That the idea of Europe included LGBT rights was the only thing both protesters and counter-protesters agreed on.

Queering the local and queer interventions

As in Hungary, the organizers in Split were good at tying gay rights to local Croatian ideas as well as the European, the international, and even the cosmic. The logo chosen for Split Pride appealed simultaneously to local and European symbolism: it was a rainbow-colored laurel wreath, modeled after one found on an old flagpole base that once stood in the central square of Split, the Pjaca (the very flagpole from which Kerum refused to fly the rainbow flag) (Figure 10.2). According to the website, the original sculpture dated from the Venetian period in the 15th or 16th centuries and is currently in the Split City Museum. The choice was brilliant, since it connected Split Pride with Split history – both Venetian and Roman. Today's Split centers on the former palace of the Roman Emperor Diocletian, who retired to Dalmatia in AD 305. The nod to the Roman Empire clearly appeals to Split's European roots.

The parade inspired further queering of national/local symbols. Meštrović's statue of Grgur of Nin had his toenails painted in the colors of a rainbow flag, or so Dalmacijanews (2011b) reported (the colors are not quite right). Grgur was a 10th-century Croatian bishop associated with Croatian nationalism (he supported the use of Croatian in services, defying the Pope), and his statue, the most prominent in Split, is near the Djardin Park, where the Split Pride route began.

During the parade, participants found other ways to queer local culture. One of the signs carried read "Mare i Kate vole se, da znate!"

Figure 10.2   Split Pride 2011 logo
Source: Splitpride Tumblr 2011b.

["Mare and Kate (women's names) love each other, just so you know!"].
"Mare i Kate" is a song created by a former football star and coach, Igor
Štimac, who once played for Hajduk, but had a brief pop career with
this song (Bohem and Igor Štimac 1998). The original text, which is
in local Split dialect, is rather macho, with the singer lamenting that
he doesn't understand women, whom he used to have in abundance,
while now they have all been bought by thugs. "Mare and Kate, where
are they, come back! My pretty little Ane, whom did you sleep with last
night?" The hero is "still the same old one," and "a real man moves on
and doesn't get spoiled." So the sign not only queers a popular Croatian
heteronormative song, but even pokes fun at a football hero. Remember
that Torcida, the football fan club for Hajduk, was one of the main opponents of the parade. Marchers also carried cardboard cutouts of Kerum,
the mayor who had declined to attend, Thompson, a right-wing nationalist Croatian singer, and Severina, a pop star.

As in Belgrade, Split activists responded to anti-gay posters and graffiti with their own. On the eve of the parade the center of town was

decorated with posters of Banksy's famous drawing of two cops kissing – a queer and European appeal to the police, perhaps, and Tomislav Ladišić, who went on to make a documentary film about the events, put signs on trash cans around town that said "You can leave your homophobic commentaries here," that is, in the trash (Ladišić 2011, and interview with the author, March 2012, Dalmacijanews 2011a). Afterward, activists queered graffiti that had not been cleaned from the walls a month after the parade. "Stop gay parade" was changed to "Start gay parade" or "Everyone to gay parade." "Parade of shame" was changed to "Parade of Pride." "It is my right to say no" became "It is my right to say no to homophobia" (H-Alter 2011). Similar queering of the homophobes' messages took place in the middle of the confrontation as well, when the chant of "Ubi, ubi, ubi pedera!" [Kill, kill, kill the fag!] was defiantly changed by Mirjana Kučer, who stood to face the hooligans as they threw whatever came to hand, to "Ljubi, ljubi, ljubi pedera!" [Kiss, kiss, kiss the fag!/Love, love, love the fag!]

Split Pride 2012 and 2013

There is little doubt that, troubling as it was at the time, the Split Pride of 2011 ultimately led to some success in making space for queer Split citizens to be more comfortable in their own city. As Gordan Duhaček (2011) wrote the day after the parade, "even a Split Pride like this has expanded the boundaries of freedom." Because of the violence of the preceding year, Split Pride 2012 was attended by several national politicians, including some ministers. They were there in significant enough numbers that right-wing and clerical officials were disgruntled: after a mass to celebrate Croatian Statehood Day, unofficial complaints from Kaptol (the religious center of the country) reported that there had been more government ministers at Gay Pride than in St. Mark's for the national holiday (Index.hr 2012). Security at Split Pride in 2012 was, if anything, too efficient: marchers were secured, but the perimeter of the police protection line was so wide that nonparticipants were so far away that they likely could not hear the speeches. Still, this time around some Split residents had come out, and by the 2013 Pride there was a new group founded in Split for LGBT people, Rišpet, whose leader Ljubomir Mateljan made many public statements in the press. On the eve of the 2013 Split Pride a new mayor was elected, Ivo Baldasar, who not only allowed Split Pride to fly the rainbow flag from the city flagpole, but also marched at the head of the parade.

Gay rights were very much the focus of public discourse in 2013 in Croatia, though this time the debate was not initiated by the LGBT community. Instead, an anti-gay, church-backed "civil initiative" group, In the Name of the Family, collected signatures for a popular referendum to insert the definition of marriage as a man and a woman in the Croatian constitution. In this case the idea of Europe was deployed on both sides. The pro-European government set off the debate by vowing to deliver on promised civil partnership legislation for gay couples. Yet the anti-gay forces also couched their campaign in appeals to democratic values to "let the people vote." The campaign pointed to France, where the anti-marriage movement mobilized citizens to protest on the street, to show that Croatians who wanted to "protect marriage" were not alone in Europe. Youth activists presented Pope Francis with a T-shirt for the campaign in Rome, and the movement's leader Željka Markić finagled an invitation to speak at the European Parliament (through conservative Slovak delegates). In the Name of the Family eagerly pointed out that European bodies, such as the European Court of Human Rights, had never established a right to marriage for same-sex couples. If anything, the new debate revealed a new homophobic European coalition – after the referendum passed 65%–35%, anti-gay forces in France looked to Croatia as a model and began collecting signatures for a referendum there to repeal marriage equality. Yet the referendum results also showed that the more European (and less Balkan) parts of Croatia were indeed more tolerant: the major cities and counties that voted against the ban were all in the North and West of the country, close to Slovenia. In spite of the constitutional ban on marriage, Croatia is on track to have some of the most sweeping partnership rights in the region, better even than in neighboring Slovenia.

Activists at Split Pride 2012 and 2013 foreshadowed these events by expanding their messaging, queering even more local culture. The queering of the song "Mare i Kate" was joined by a direct quotation from a very well-known local folk song about two guys from the neighboring island: "Neka cijela Riva zna za Bračanina dva" ["Let the whole Riva know about the two boys from Brač!"] (Komarčević 2012). This queering was doubly appropriate because in this case they did not even have to change the words, and it mentioned the Riva, which is where the parade ended. Oddly, though, the quotation was in standard Croatian, not local dialect. That oversight was fixed in the 2013 iteration of the parade, at which a sign read "Nek cili svit zna za Hvaranina dva!" ["Let the whole world know about the two boys from Hvar"] substituting an island further out, a queer expansion of Dalmatian territory, but in the appropriate local ikavski like the original "Mare i Kate" song. This time around the original reappeared with a further emendation: "Mare

Split Europe: Homonationalism and Homophobia in Croatia 229

i Kate žene se, da znate!" ["Mare and Kate are getting married, just so you know"] (Blic 2013). While marriage equality was not yet legally attained in Croatia in 2013, the slogan shows that Croatian LGBT Pride participants were not so different from their sisters and brothers in Europe and the West.

References

Bakić-Hayden, Milica and Robert M. Hayden. 1992. "Orientalist Variations on the Theme 'Balkans': Symbolic Geography in Recent Yugoslav Cultural Politics." Slavic Review 51(1): 1–15.
Binnie, Jon. 2004. The Globalization of Sexuality. London: Sage.
Blagojević, Marina. 2000. "Patriotizam i mizoginija: Mit o srpskoj muškosti." In Mapiranje mizoginije u srbiji: diskursi i prakse, ed. Marina Blagojević. Belgrade: Asocijacija za žensku inicijativu, 281–310.
Blic. 2013. "Održan prajd u Splitu, gradonačelnik na čelu povorke." Blic Online. http://www.blic.rs/Vesti/Svet/386992/Odrzan-prajd-u-Splitu-Neka-cili-svit-znada-se-vole-Hvaranina-dva (accessed 11 July 2013).
Štimac, Bohem and Igor Štimac. 1998. "Mare i Kate." http://www.youtube.com/watch?v=O2WavTjVp54 (accessed 5 July 2013).
Butler, Judith. 2008. "Sexual Politics, Torture, and Secular Time." British Journal of Sociology 59(1): 1–23.
Butterfield, Nicole. 2013. "Sexual Rights as a Tool for Mapping Europe: Discourses of Human Rights and European Identity in Activists' Struggles in Croatia." In Queer Visibility in Postsocialist Cultures, eds. Andrea Balogh and Nárcisz Fejes. Farnham: Intellect, 11–34.
Dačić, Ivica. 2012. "Dačić: Izem ti takvu Uniju u koju je gay parada ulaznica!" Novosti 15 Sept. 2012. http://www.novosti.rs/vesti/naslovna/aktuelno.290.html:397083-Dacic-Izem-ti-takvu-Uniju-u-koju-je-gej-parada-ulaznica (accessed 9 July 2013).
Dalmacijanews. 2011a. "Akcija gay-gerile: Split osvanuo grafikama policajaca koji se ljube." http://www.dalmacijanews.com/Hrvatska/View/tabid/77/ID/58264/Akcija-gay-gerile-Split-osvanuo-grafikama-policajaca-koji-se-ljube-FOTO.aspx (accessed 5 May 2013).
——. 2011b. "Grguru Ninskom lakirali nokte bojama gay zastave." http://dalmacijanews.com/Hrvatska/View/tabid/77/ID/58966/Split-Grguru-Ninskom-lakirali-nokte-bojama-gay-zastave.aspx (accessed 5 May 2013).
Davydova, Darja. 2012. "Baltic Pride 2010: Articulating Sexual Difference and Heteronormative Nationalism in Contemporary Lithuania." Sextures 2(2): 32–46.
Domi, Tanya. 2011. "Croatia President, Prime Minister Condemn Violence at Gay Pride Parade." The New Civil Rights Movement. http://thenewcivilrightsmovement.com/croatia-president-prime-minister-condemn-violence-at-gay-pride-parade/politics/2011/06/12/21908 (accessed 11 July 2013).
Duhaček, Gordan. 2011. "I ovakav Split Pride je pomakao granice slobode." Vijesti http://www.tportal.hr/vijesti/hrvatska/133106/Split-Pride-mora-ici-dalje.html (accessed 5 July 2013).

Graff, Agnieszka. 2006. "We Are (Not All) Homophobes: A Report from Poland."
    Feminist Studies 32(2): 434–449.
———. 2008. "The Land of Real Men and Real Women: Gender and E.U. Accession
    in Three Polish Weeklies." In *Global Empowerment of Women: Responses to
    Globalization, Politicized Religions and Gender Violence*, ed. Carolyn Elliott.
    London: Routledge, 191–212.
———. 2010. "Looking at Pictures of Gay Men: Political Uses of Homophobia in
    Contemporary Poland." *Public Culture* 22(3): 583–604.
Gruszczynska, Anna, ed. 2012. "Parades of Pride or Shame: Documenting LGBTQ
    Visibility in Central and Eastern Europe." *Sextures Special Issue* 2(2): 1–6.
H-Alter. 2011. "Ulična akcija protiv govora mržnje." http://www.h-alter.org/
    vijesti/hrvatska/ulicna-akcija-protiv-govora-mrznje (accessed 5 July 2013).
Index.hr 2011. "Split kao Belgrade, Zagreb kao Beč." *Index.hr.* http://www.index.
    hr/vijesti/clanak/split-kao-belgrade-zagreb-kao-bec/557330.aspx (accessed 7
    March 2013).
———2012. "Na Gay Prideu je bilo više ministara nego na misi za domovinu." *Index.
    hr.* http://www.index.hr/vijesti/clanak/kaptol-na-gay-prideu-je-bilo-vise-min-
    istara-nego-na-misi-za-domovinu-ministri-to-je-stvar-osobne-prirode/622335.
    aspx (accessed 27 January 2014).
Johnson, Dana N. 2012. "We Are Waiting for You: The Discursive (De)construc-
    tion of Belgrade Pride 2009." *Sextures* 2(2): 6–31.
Komarčević, Dušan. 2012. "Nek cila Riva zna za Bracanina dva." e-novine. http://
    www.e-novine.com/drustvo/66168-Nek-cila-Riva-zna-Bracanina-dva.html
    (accessed 11 July 2013).
Kuhar, Roman. 2013. "In the Name of Hate: Homophobia as a Value." *Southeastern
    Europe* 37(1): 1–16.
Kuhar, Roman and Alenka Švab. 2013. "The Interplay between Hatred and
    Political Correctness: Privatization of Homosexuality in Slovenia." *Southeastern
    Europe* 37(1): 17–35.
Kulpa, Robert. 2011. "Nations and Sexualities – 'West' and 'East.'" In Kulpa, Robert
    and Joanna Mizielinska, *De-Centring Western Sexualities: Central and Eastern
    European Perspectives*. Farnham: Ashgate, 43–62.
Kulpa, Robert. 2013. "Western Leveraged Pedagogy of Central and Eastern Europe:
    Discourses of Homophobia, Tolerance, and Nationhood." *Gender, Place, &
    Culture: A Journal of Feminist Geography* 21(4): 431–448.
Kulpa, Robert and Joanna Mizielinska. 2011. *De-Centring Western Sexualities:
    Central and Eastern European Perspectives*. Farnham: Ashgate.
Ladišić, Tomislav. 2011. *11. Lipnja – Prvi splitski Pride*. UMAS, Film i video.
    Documentary film.
LGBT-EP. 2011a. "Unsafe Pride Event in Croatia Casts Shadow Over Accession
    Prospects" European Parliament Intergroup on LGBT Rights. http://www.
    lgbt-ep.eu/press-releases/unsafe-pride-event-in-croatia-casts-shadow-over-ac-
    cession-prospects/ (accessed 3 October 2013).
———. 2011b. "Priority question to the Commission and Council: Hate violence
    at Split Pride in Croatia" *European Parliament Intergroup on LGBT Rights*. http://
    www.lgbt-ep.eu/parliamentary-work/priority-question-to-the-commission-
    and-council-hate-violence-at-split-pride-in-croatia/ (accessed 3 July 2013).
Lukač Koritnik, Gordana. 2011. "Pravobraniteljica o nasilju na Gay Prideu: Imam
    dokaze kako policija provodi dvostruka mjerila." *Index.hr,* http://www.index.

hr/sport/clanak/pravobraniteljica-o-nasilju-na-gay-prideu-imam-dokaze-kako-policija-provodi-dvostruka-mjerila-/556477.aspx (accessed 2 July 2013).

Lulić, Nikolina. 2011. "Kulturno smo odbili da budemo u povorci gay pridea." *Slobodna Dalmacija*, http://slobodnadalmacija.hr/Mozaik/tabid/80/articleType/ArticleView/articleId/138108/Default.aspx (accessed 2 July 2013).

Massad, Joseph. 2002. "Re-Orienting Desire: The Gay International and the Arab World." *Public Culture* 14(2): 361–385.

———. 2007. *Desiring Arabs*. Chicago: University of Chicago Press.

Moss, Kevin. 1995. "The Underground Closet: Political and Sexual Dissidence in Eastern Europe." *Genders22: Postcommunism and the Body Politic*, ed. Ellen E. Berry. New York: NYU Press, 229–251.

———. 2006. "Who's Renting These Boys? Wiktor Grodecki's Czech Hustler Documentaries." *InterAlia: An Online Journal of Queer Studies* 1. http://www.interalia.org.pl/en/artykuly/homepage/05_whos_renting_these_boys.htm (accessed 12 February 2014).

Mosse, George. 1985. *Nationalism and Sexuality: Middle Class Morality and Sexual Norms in Modern Europe*. Madison: University of Wisconsin Press.

Nacional. 2011. "Gayevi kontra fašizma na splitskim ulicama: Državne institucije su opet zakazale." *Nacional.hr*, http://www.nacional.hr/clanak/110043/gayevi-kontra-fasizma-drzavne-institucije-su-opet-zakazale (accessed 3 July 2013).

Olujić, Kristina. 2011. "Split – najbolja reklama za Zagreb." *Libela*. http://www.libela.org/prozor-u-svijet/2097-split-najbolja-reklama-za-zagreb/ (accessed 3 July 2013).

Pejković-Kaćanski, Maja. 2011. "Kerum: Splićani ne žele paradu homoseksualaca." *Večernji list*, http://www.vecernji.hr/vijesti/kerum-splicani-ne-zele-paradu-homoseksualaca-clanak-238767 (accessed 1 June 2013).

Puar, Jasbir. 2007. *Terrorist Assemblages: Homonationalism in Queer Times*. Durham: Duke University Press.

Queeria. 2002. http://www.queeria.org.yu/queeria/komentari.htm (accessed 12 June 2002).

Rédai, Dorottya. 2012. "Un/Queering the Nation? Gender, Sexuality, Nationality and Homophobia in the Media Discourse on the Violence against the 2008 Gay Pride in Budapest." *Sextures* 2(2): 47–64.

Renkin, Hadley Z. 2009. "Homophobia and Queer Belonging in Hungary." *Focaal – European Journal of Anthropology* 53(1): 20–37.

RFERL. 2011. "Croatian Leader Slams 'Shameful' Gay Pride Parade Violence." Radio Free Europe Radio Liberty, http://www.rferl.org/content/croatia_leader_slams_shameful_gay_pride_parade_violence/24232632.html (accessed 3 July 2013).

Splitpride Tumblr. 2011a. http://splitpride.tumblr.com/post/6588915002/split-pride-survivors-d (accessed 5 July 2013).

———. 2011b. http://splitpride.tumblr.com/post/4215741128/stari-standarac-in-spirirao-vizual-split-pride-a (accessed 5 July 2013).

Štulhofer, Aleksander and Ivan, Rimac. 2009. "Determinants of Homonegativity in Europe." *Journal of Sex Research* 46(1): 24–32.

Takács, J. and I. Szalma. 2011. "Homophobia and Same-Sex Partnership Legislation in Europe." *Equality, Diversity and Inclusion: An International Journal* 30(5): 356–378.

Todorova, Maria. 1994. "The Balkans, from Discovery to Invention." *Slavic Review* 53(2): 453–482.

——. 1997. *Imagining the Balkans.* Oxford: Oxford University Press.

Trost, Tamara Pavasovic and Nikola Kovacevic. 2013. "Football, Hooliganism and Nationalism: The Reaction to Serbia's Gay Parade in Reader Commentary Online." *Sport in Society: Cultures, Commerce, Media, Politics* 16(8): 1054–1076.

Vuletic, Dean. 2013. "Out of the Homeland: The Croatian Right and Gay Rights." *Southeastern Europe* 37(1): 36–59.

Zagreb Pride. 2013. "Zagreb Pride za LGBT jednakopravnost." http://www.zagreb-pride.net/web/index.php?option=com_content&view=article&id=145&Itemid=105&lang=hr (accessed 1 July 2013).

11
Conclusion

Phillip M. Ayoub and David Paternotte

The authors of this volume have argued that European LGBT movements exist in relation to a specific idea of Europe. Claims by LGBT movements have a long history of referring to a vision of Europe, and an understanding of Europe that contains a human rights mandate inclusive of LGBT people is increasingly common in contemporary discourses. From the beginning, LGBT activists had a clear vision of what Europe should represent, and how this imagination could contribute to the advancement of LGBT rights in various domestic arenas. This association has been strengthened by the endorsement of European institutions and a growing number of national governments across the continent. By linking LGBT rights so closely to Europe in their work, activists contribute to the project of building Europe from the ground up, by further constructing an imagined idea in which Europe is inextricably linked to LGBT rights. This becomes apparent by looking not only at the claims of LGBT movements, but also at those of their opponents. Over the years, an "idea of Europe" has shaped LGBT activism, just as LGBT activism has come to shape what "Europe" means. This relationship has transformed Europe into a privileged space for LGBT rights and a club whose members must, at the very least, address the fundamental rights of LGBT people.

The ten preceding chapters in this book have comprehensively and critically charted the development of this phenomenon by investigating the link between LGBT rights and Europe across time and space. Our goals were twofold. First, by looking at the place of Europe in LGBTQ activism, we aimed to unpack the specific relationship between Europe and LGBT rights. Second, we assessed the role of LGBT activism in promoting a specific understanding of Europe, one that has contributed to making Europe from below. Theoretically, the chapters have addressed sexuality studies as they are related to both the political sociology of Europe and the study of social movements, with special attention given to processes of meaning-making, practice, and identity formation. The authors, on the one hand, have raised questions about the allegedly unique character of the European polity toward LGBT issues. On the other hand, they have investigated the links between activism and the construction of sexual, political, and regional identities.

Meanings of Europe

After setting the theoretical and analytical framework for the book in the introductory chapter, we turned our attention to the early roots of the movement with Leila Rupp's (Chapter 2) study of homophile activism in the 1950s. The homophile movement, she argues, was deeply entangled with the European space in three ways. First, the homophile movement was transnationally oriented and European groups played the predominant role, with the node of activism shifting from Germany in the early twentieth century to the Netherlands in the 1950s. Second, the fostering of a homosexual cosmopolitanism and the debate surrounding the eroticization of male youth in homophile publications took a specifically European character. Third, the different approach of European homophile activism, and the criticism of its US counterparts, illustrates the existence of the "idea of Europe" in such activism. Throughout the analysis, she finds evidence for the often-problematic presence of the "idea of Europe" and the meanings it has shaped in the transnational homophile activism of the 1950s – meanings that still serve as a historical lens with which to understand the contemporary LGBT movement.

Cai Wilkinson's chapter (Chapter 3) brought us to the European neighborhood of Central Asia to explore the broad reach that the meaning of "Europe" takes in LGBT activism beyond the traditional conceptualizations of its borders. She explored the development of local LGBT advocacy organizations that emerged at the turn of the century in Kyrgyzstan. Though lacking formal institutional support from the EU, she recognizes an impact that organizational ties to European LGBT advocacy groups have had in a context with minimal LGBT visibility. In making her argument, Wilkinson traces the specific meanings that the idea of a "rainbow Europe" takes on in the discourses of Kyrgyz LGBT activists, including as an identity referent, a donor of practical support, and a source of human rights norms. The dissemination of expertise, as well as the personal and professional support of these networks, has created a role for "Europe" in LGBT activism in Central Asia, serving as an imagined benchmark for the rights that LGBT activists aspire to.

Gianmaria Colpani and Adriano José Habed (Chapter 4) shifted the focus to the contemporary politics of the southern periphery of Europe. They problematize the meaning that Europe comes to take in the Italian context, and highlight the ways through which, by using Europe as a rhetorical strategy against conservative sexual politics, Italian LGBT movements contribute to ideas of European sexual exceptionalism and Italian "backwardness." This approach allows the authors to conceptualize the distinctly European elements of homonationalism and to study its deployment in Southern Europe, at the margins of "enlightened Europe." By asking what is European (rather than merely national) about homonationalism, the authors make theoretical progress in tracking the ways in which "Europe" is produced and reproduced as a site of sexual exceptionalism, and its impact on the production of new forms of exclusion.

Such an understanding of Europe, as an imagined community, allowed this first set of authors to explain several elements of the "special relationship" that unites issues of sexuality and Europe. They also contributed to illuminating the connections between sexuality and (Euro-) nationalism, a topic that is being reviewed because of the recent debates on "homonationalism." While the stories charted can be viewed in part as a social movement success, their chapters highlight the critical open questions that remain. Given that there is a distinction between who reflects "the idea of Europe" and who stands outside of it – historically, geographically, and culturally –, these chapters have foregrounded important future research areas in this first part of our analysis.

Practicing Europe in LGBTQ activism

In the second part of the book, we shifted the analytical lens from meanings to practices, and we looked at the various ways in which Europe was used and experienced by LGBT activists across the region. In her chapter, Kelly Kollman (Chapter 5) compared domestic debates on same-sex unions in the Netherlands, Germany, and the United Kingdom. While she highlights manifold references to the "idea of Europe" in these three countries, she also emphasizes the distinctive ways in which national activists strategically deployed Europe to advance their claims. In the Netherlands and in Germany, Europe was used as a benchmark for national policies; the Dutch also insisted on the specific role their country plays in a "progressive" European project. Conversely, British activists have avoided direct references to Europe in recent years, opting instead to reference successful LGBT policies in other key European states such as Denmark. Relying on the literature on norm diffusion, Kollman discusses the multiple national facets of the European project, and the domestic reception of an emerging European norm against sexual orientation discrimination and for state recognition of same-sex couples. She shows that transnational LGBT rights activists have helped make Europe a force to be reckoned with, but also that national SSU supporters have had to construct a discursive imperative for relationship recognition by drawing on different strands of the polity and European identity.

Anna van der Vleuten (Chapter 6) examines the interaction between LGBT activists and European courts, elucidating the various ways in which the courts empower the former while contributing to the building of Europe. She shows that both judges and activists rely on the idea of Europe as linked to specific values, which have come to include the defense of LGBT rights. After describing the composition of the legal network in favor of LGBT rights in Europe, she highlights the interactive relationship between activists and judges. On the one hand, van der Vleuten argues that the European Court of Justice and the European Court of Human Rights have been empowered by the early campaigns of LGBTI activists. On the other hand, she shows that LGBTI activists have been empowered by access to the European courts (vis-à-vis their governments) when the national political arena was blocked. Importantly, throughout the chapter, she identifies three strategies through which a European legal norm of protecting LBGT rights is constructed: a search for consensus, norm-stretching, and interaction between the two European courts.

Rounding out the part on practices, Konstantinos Eleftheriadis (Chapter 7) drew our attention to non-institutionalized forms of activism by focusing on transnational queer activism across Europe. His analysis of queer festivals in Amsterdam, Berlin, Copenhagen, Oslo, and Rome revealed that activists, although they do not make explicit references to Europe and are often reluctant to be identified with this project, unconsciously practice Europe and contribute to its construction from below. His chapter emphasizes the informal, yet dense, regional networks of communication and interaction among activists, including on the Internet, alongside their specifically European forms of organizing. These often intersect with the European global justice movement, and tend, for instance, to balance out the use of English as a lingua franca with a defense of linguistic diversity. In sum, activists at queer festivals practice Europe outside of institutional frameworks, and their collective action highlights distinct forms of transnational practices as well as the construction of multiple European civil societies.

These three authors not only emphasize the importance of Europe as a frame or a project, but also highlight the various ways in which it is embodied in activists' practices. Europe, they have shown, is not only imagined by activists but also experienced in the everyday activity of the movement. Activists give it a specific meaning by referring to "Europe" in national debates, presenting it as a crucial reference both in courts and in parliaments, and they create uniquely European modes of organizing. These findings then invited us to look beyond discourse to explore and understand better the scope of the special relationship uniting Europe to LGBT rights.

Becoming European: transnational identities

Carsten Balzer and Jan Simon Hutta (Chapter 8) studied the transnationalization of the trans movement in Europe and the establishment of a specific European umbrella group, Transgender Europe. They studied the process of institutionalization undergone by trans groups across the region, arguing that these groups retained their early focus on community politics and grassroots networking despite novel involvement in policy initiatives at a European level. As shown by Eleftheriadis's chapter (Chapter 7), this stands in contrast to gay and lesbian groups across the region, especially at a transnational level, and questions the consequences of the Europeanization and professionalization of social movements in the region. The authors also emphasized the constitutive role of the heterogeneity of Europe in the development of European trans activisms. Furthermore, Balzer and Hutta highlighted the processes through which new identities are established as they become less bounded by national borders.

Jon Binnie and Christian Klesse's chapter (Chapter 9) explored transnational solidarities around LGBTQ activism in Poland in the mid-2000s. Against the backdrop of a homophobic political and public discourse around that time, activist alliances between domestic groups and those from other EU member states were formed, particularly during Pride marches. The chapter paid attention to these transnational linkages, investigating whether they sustain relations of solidarity. Offering a critical review of the literature on solidarity, Binnie and Klesse examine the extent to which transnational activism around Polish LGBT politics both reproduces and contests hegemonic political meanings of Europe, and strengthens the East/West binary. Relatedly to Colpani and Habed

(Chapter 4), European sexual exceptionalism can also appear as a source of exclusion at the margins of the region.

Finally, Kevin Moss's chapter (Chapter 10) illustrated what is divided about Europe in his case study of Croatia's accession to the EU in 2013 – accession being considered by many observers to be truly symbolic of the road to "becoming European". In Croatia tolerance toward homosexuality was consistently framed as a European or Western value, one opposed by local nationalists who portray homosexuality as a Western perversion that has no place locally. Based on a detailed account of deployment of the "idea of Europe" during the Split Pride in Croatia in 2011, Moss showed that Europe and the inclusion of LGBT citizens in Croatian society are linked in the discourses of both LGBT activists and their opposition. In making his argument, he takes a critical stance in debates about European homonationalism. In contrast to literature that strongly denounces the imposition of sexual values by the West, he also highlights the willingness of local activists to frame their struggle as part of the European project to oppose strong heterosexual variants of nationalism.

Where there is no mass consensus around a European value-based identity in the public sphere, these chapters recognize a link between LGBT rights and European values. In this sense, Europe appears both as a set of values and normative commitments (shared and felt by European institutions and LGBT activists), and a strategic means by which to gain rights in various domestic realms. By discussing the contours of "Europe" that social actors imagine, we have shown that these beliefs – and more importantly the various ways in which they are embodied – further contribute to building Europe by making national identities less pertinent in some respects, an insight that is crucial for the future of European integration.

A rainbow Europe?

Taken together, we have argued that the "idea of Europe" is linked to LGBT activism, both at a transnational level and on the ground across the region and in the neighborhood, through its role as a set of values and as a tool by which to claim rights. In the imagination of activists and sympathetic elites, LGBT rights are not to be disentangled from the meaning of Europe, even if physical realities for LGBT people are vastly diverse within and across states. The fact that transnational activists so often call for the mobilization of support and the recognition of LGBT peoples in a language of European values and responsibilities suggests that they contribute to building Europe in a certain image from below. Going back to the introductory chapter, the work of LGBT activists shows that "Europe" runs in both directions. While LGBT issues are linked to Europe's normative structures from above, by using "Europe" as an argument for demanding LGBT recognition from their states and societies, the activists on the ground subsequently, and indirectly, recreate the idea that Europe is united around the LGBT issue. In turn, the link between being European and accepting LGBT people is established, and an understanding of LGBT rights as a European value is further cemented. This imagined idea has been intensified in modern European politics, as official EU and CoE institutions increasingly echo the movement's rainbow "idea of Europe," a process that has both served as a successful movement strategy and reinforced problematic binary divisions within the continent and at its margins.

This process of constructing a rainbow Europe has indeed created a durable association between LGBT rights and a certain idea of Europe, advancing the visibility of LGBT across the region and beyond (as shown by Cai Wilkinson's chapter (Chapter 3)). LGBT activists have practiced Europe by crossing borders to create new forms of solidarity and by establishing European umbrella groups to organize at new levels and articulate new claims. They have been able to use "Europe" as a powerful frame within domestic settings and with which to approach European institutions for political support. All this has led to a reinforcement of European LGBT identities, which cannot be understood only as national variations of a common transnational project but also as complex forms of multilevel identity arrangements. The ten chapters have also problematized and exposed the darker sides of this relationship. With a rainbow Europe come new forms of exclusion, forms that can emerge as a consequence of using a European frame or as a revival of older divisions that have marked the continent in times past. Even opponents increasingly use the LGBT rights frame as an evocative symbol of Europe and the West more broadly, with which to advocate discrimination and fuel backlash.

In sum, our analysis of LGBT movements and Europe, as an imagined and an experienced community through time, has important implications for research on the sociology of Europe, on the relationship between Europe and social movements, and on the study of sexualities. While other publications have looked at the development of LGBT rights in the European polity, none has examined the intersections between the concomitant development of LGBT rights, activism, and European identities across the continent. By bringing the fields of Europe, social movements, and sexualities together, we hope to have made a unique contribution to academic debates through the lens of an intriguing and understudied topical area: rainbow Europe.

Index

CPI Antony Rowe
Chippenham, UK
2017-05-26 09:59